PENGUIN BOOKS
THE BIG BOOKSHELF

Sunil Sethi (b. 1954), journalist, columnist and television presenter, has hosted the weekly literary show *Just Books* on NDTV since early 2005. He was one of the founding editorial team of *India Today*, has worked for the *Hindustan Times* and been a columnist for the *Times of India* and the *Indian Express*. His journalism has appeared in *The Economist*, the *Boston Globe* and several international publications; he has scripted and presented documentaries for the BBC and Channel 4. A recipient of the Nieman Fellowship at Harvard University and the Japan Foundation fellowship, he is married to the textile designer Shalini. They have one daughter and live in New Delhi.

THE BIG *Bookshelf*

SUNIL SETHI

IN CONVERSATION

WITH 30

Famous

• WRITERS •

PENGUIN BOOKS

PENGUIN BOOKS
Published by the Penguin Group
Penguin Books India Pvt Ltd, 11 Community Centre, Panchsheel Park, New Delhi 110 017, India
Penguin Group (USA) Inc., 375 Hudson Street, New York, New York 10014, USA
Penguin Group (Canada), 90 Eglinton Avenue East, Suite 700, Toronto, Ontario, M4P 2Y3, Canada (a division of Pearson Penguin Canada Inc.)
Penguin Books Ltd, 80 Strand, London WC2R 0RL, England
Penguin Ireland, 25 St Stephen's Green, Dublin 2, Ireland (a division of Penguin Books Ltd)
Penguin Group (Australia), 707 Collins Street, Melbourne, Victoria 3008, Australia (a division of Pearson Australia Group Pty Ltd)
Penguin Group (NZ), 67 Apollo Drive, Rosedale, Auckland 0632, New Zealand (a division of Pearson New Zealand Ltd)
Penguin Group (South Africa) (Pty) Ltd, 24 Sturdee Avenue, Rosebank, Johannesburg 2196, South Africa

Penguin Books Ltd, Registered Offices: 80 Strand, London WC2R 0RL, England

First published by Penguin Books India in association with NDTV 2011
This edition published 2012

10 9 8 7 6 5 4 3 2 1

ISBN 9780143419273

Typeset in Bembo Roman by SÜRYA, New Delhi
Printed at Chaman Offset Printers, Delhi

ALWAYS LEARNING PEARSON

To all those who regard books as enduring companions in life

Contents

Introduction

In late 2004, Radhika and Prannoy Roy of NDTV held a series of meetings to decide on programming for the network's new business channel, NDTV Profit. A considerable amount of business channels' daily news is devoted to analysing stock market behaviour. But since markets close on Friday afternoon and reopen on Monday morning, a range of strong television features would be required to cover the weekend.

That afternoon, smart ideas were being tossed around like market indices. I had come out of presenting a weekly arts and entertainment omnibus for some years. Should it be revived or tweaked in a new avatar? Radhika Roy, an avid reader and book buyer, interrupted to ask why there was no quality literary programme to be seen anywhere, but no one in the room seemed enthused. I was bemused by the idea. Books are difficult to put across week after week on what is, after all, a visual medium—no film clips, no performances, no colourful art. Besides, I pointed out that writers, or the few I had interviewed, were cagey and not very forthcoming about their art. Who would watch, I wondered, unless it was Salman Rushdie revisiting the fatwa? Would conversations end up with long pauses, like an Atal Bihari Vajpayee speech?

But Radhika was convinced it was worth a shot. 'No, I think the show should only be about books. We shouldn't mix it up. It should be just books. In fact, there you are—let's call it "Just Books". Sunil, I think you should give it a shot.'

Mainly as a way of organizing my own sparse thoughts, I began tapping out a few ideas on what the segments of the show might focus on—'Book Pills' for short takes on literary happenings of the week; 'My Bedside Book' in which well-known people talk about their favourite books; the week's best-seller list; and 'My Pick', a list of new titles in bookshops. The last segment, I thought, should be the show's main strength—an interview with a writer on a book that was just out. But where were the authors? I had to bank a few interviews before the show was due to go on air in a few weeks.

Just Books went on air on 5 February 2005. But the murmurs of approval were not enough to quell my apprehensions about being able to sustain the show. I discovered that I needed to do a couple of things to move ahead. The first was to net a few exclusives with big international names for the show to be noticed. 'The trouble with opportunities is not that they don't come,' the English writer E.M. Forster once observed. 'It is that they are not punctual.' Persistence, however, can beat the waywardness of opportunity. The first star author I managed to corner was the Italian novelist Umberto Eco, author of *The Name of the Rose*, between a lecture and dinner at the Italian embassy, brazenly bundling him into the ambassador's study, where the cameras and lights were set up. He turned out to be a figure so captivating in his ideas, wit and expansive personality that we decided to run the full half-hour with him. But persistence, too, needs a little help from friends—for instance, when all attempts to reach the South African Nobel laureate Nadine Gordimer failed, I found a resourceful hotel manager to smuggle in a fervent handwritten plea.

The challenge was, and remains, for the show to reach out to new viewers, to break away from the notion of being an exclusive literary club and include those who are not necessarily professional writers. There are many among the great and the good who write and are published, even if it is just the one book, because they have something original to say about their lives or their subjects. It is a fact of our times that many people in the public orbit become hyphenates. You have the actor-memoirist, the civil-servant-novelist, the politican-poet and the corporate-honcho-turned-soothsayer on India's future. These began to alternate with Booker Prize winners and first-timers, thriller writers and unstoppable best-sellers, historians, journalists, jurists and crusaders—if they had a book that was talked about, then they had a booked space, though rights of admission are reserved. Eventually, I came to think of *Just Books* as a kind of literary *adda*, a place where writers, of whatever persuasion, open up about their work, their lives, their causes. But I also recognized the limitations of certain categories of writers. Lofty punditry and God-like voices (spiritual, business and self-help gurus) are best avoided. Some titles spell their own exclusion: 'Bharatanatyam Mudras Explained and Illustrated', or '101 Positions—The Story of Ecstasy'. And there are writers so plainly derivative that I could set up a pavement stall of campus capers, chick-lit dramas and a farrago of look-alike thrillers.

Readers buy books because they want to be gripped by a story, engaged by an author's ideas or be better informed about the world they inhabit. But they also want to know more about the books they read, and in the process, about the lives of those who write, their motivations, and the labours of the writer's craft. How is a writer made and what is the nature of the writing impulse? Are writers born with a burning creative drive or do they steadily hone their art? How do they shape their characters and stories in fiction, or develop their subjects and themes in non-fiction? The advent of *Just Books* also coincided with—and gained from—the progress of the writer-celebrity. Writers like Shobhaa Dé and Chetan Bhagat have become pop-culture icons, with a vast fan following and staggering book sales.

Just Books has soldiered on for 300 interviews over six years. But TV shows don't easily lend themselves to the kind of documentation and instant access we are used to in our web-driven age. Many of the writers I interviewed had so much of value to say on life, letters and the human condition in general that they deserved the more permanent home that a book provides, rather than the ephemeral TV screen. The thirty interviews reproduced here, about one in every ten recorded, are a representative but not random selection. Many of the questions recur time and again. But the answers are diverse, complex and often surprising.

Several of the writers featured in this book did not set out to be writers or poets at all; they found their vocations by accident. The Nobel Prize-winning Turkish novelist Orhan Pamuk wanted to be an artist and studied architecture. The poet and novelist Vikram Seth wrote 'incredibly unskilful poetry' as an undergraduate at Oxford and his first book, an account of an overland journey from China to India, was produced while researching his PhD in Chinese demography. It was written at the behest of his father who suggested that he put down his adventures in a book. Khushwant Singh trained as a lawyer and worked as a diplomat before starting to write fiction, and he was forty-one before his first novel was published. 'I flopped at everything I did in my early years. I threw up job after job. I became a writer because my generous and remarkable father stood by me. I lived off his bounty for years,' he admits candidly. The immensely popular film lyricist Javed Akhtar took to writing poetry 'at an age, thirty-two or thirty-three, when people generally stop writing poetry'. He was so busy pursuing a successful career as a screenwriter that he had to be coerced by the movie mogul Yash Chopra to write his first songs for the film *Silsila* in 1981.

Others were writing from an early age, privately filling up notebooks. The novelist Anita Desai, nominated three times for the Booker Prize, wrote from as far back as she could remember but came to think of writing as a 'secret activity'. As a wife and mother raising four children, she would write in hiding. 'My children always remark that they never saw me writing. And the book would one day appear, as though it just happened; it came from somewhere else.' In contrast, her daughter Kiran Desai, the Booker Prize-winning novelist, although inspired by her mother's example, was propelled by no such early desire: 'I was twenty years old when I started writing. My mother fought for her art and she fought to be able to write. I didn't have to fight that fight.'

Early or late, single-minded or circuitous, every writer's journey begins with the pursuit of a particular idea or subject. This was more apparent in the case of writers of non-fiction. A person, a place or even a line embedded in a poem could trigger off the creative process and ineluctably change the course of their lives. The Bengali writer and social activist Mahasweta Devi felt the urgency to explore the oral legends surrounding the life of the Rani of Jhansi for her first book, a biography of the warrior-queen, with such intensity that 'I borrowed money from relatives, got into a train, left behind a small baby with his father and went to Jhansi.' Similarly, the British biographer Patrick French's lodestar led him to follow in the footsteps of Sir Francis Younghusband, the nineteenth-century Victorian explorer whose expeditionary invasion of Tibet in 1903–04 led to one of the worst colonial massacres in the subcontinent. The result was a compelling historical narrative shot through with the bizarre truths of a strange and secret life. Often, the need to investigate such stories was bolstered by a writer's need to break from the mould of convention or the narrow confines of an ordered life. For the historian Ramachandra Guha, trained for an academic career, to write his biography of the anthropologist Verrier Elwin was a 'difficult transition because the study of an individual and singular life is disparaged in the academy. Because of the great influence of Marxism we are supposed to deal with aggregates: with classes, peasants and workers, or with the State and the nation as a whole. I came to it with some diffidence and some recklessness.' At the age of twenty-two, William Dalrymple took an ambitious step that forever marked his life. As a Cambridge graduate he set off to look for the 'stately pleasure dome' in legendary Xanadu, decreed by Kubla Khan in the opening lines of Samuel Taylor Coleridge's famous poem. Out of that journey, from Jerusalem to modern-day Shangdu in northern China, came *In Xanadu*, a first book that brought him early recognition.

The writer's outward journey was often inspired by wide reading and a love of letters. Whatever the motivation or their chosen route to writing, most authors professed an abiding passion for books from childhood. Reaching across to tap my knee, the novelist Nadine Gordimer, whose early education was patchy, admonished: 'Reading, my dear, is the only training for a writer from a young age. You only become a writer by being a compulsive reader.' Asked what his advice to a young writer would be, the American travel writer and novelist Paul Theroux offered a tip: 'Go away. Yes. Leave home, leave your parents and leave all the comforting things that hold you back . . . because if you stay . . . people will always ask you what you are doing—what you are writing, what you are publishing. They ask you questions that you can't answer.'

Paradoxically, despite the quest to break bounds and defy a circumscribed life, a writer's job is revealed in these conversations as a hardship post, an act of self-willed and often punishing discipline. Many follow an implacably enforced regimen. Here is the best-selling thriller writer Jeffrey Archer's regime that he briskly rapped out: 'I write up to seventeen drafts. I get away for two months and I wake up at 5.30 in the morning. I write from six to eight and take a two-hour break, I write from ten until twelve and take a two-hour break, I again write from two until four, followed by another two-hour break, then I write from six until eight, light supper, go to bed at 9.30 or 10.00 and begin again at 5.30 the next day. Fifty days of that in a row.' Khushwant Singh rises at 4 a.m. every day, hasn't missed a newspaper deadline in sixty years, and is ruthless in dismissing visitors. 'People don't drop in. I don't see them without an appointment and when I invite them it's strictly between 7 p.m. and 8 p.m. I can be very rude to anyone who stays even a minute after eight.'

Younger writers are equally fierce about guarding their writing time and space. The novelist Upamanyu Chatterjee, who leads a double life as a senior civil servant, sets himself a certain number of words a day, or how to resolve an idea or a problem in the plot, as a daily target. He writes every morning before leaving for office. Returning home in the evening, 'I sit down and peg away. Sometimes I achieve that target just before I go to bed.' Chatterjee takes about five years to complete a novel but there are others who take longer. It took Kiran Desai nearly seven years of a sequestered life to finish *The Inheritance of Loss*. A more extreme example is that of the British-Pakistani fiction writer Nadeem Aslam who took more than eleven years to complete his prize-winning novel, *Maps for Lost Lovers*. Aslam grew up in a small town in Pakistan, attending an Urdu-medium school till the age of fourteen, when his family was forced to migrate to Britain to escape political persecution. 'When I arrived in England my English was, "This is a cat," . . . My life was broken in half.' Instead of going to college, for many years he eked out a meagre living, working on building sites and in bars so that he could read in libraries. He would retreat into a private world to be able to write. 'There were times when I draped the windows with black cloth. There was no phone, no TV, no radio, no newspapers and I just filled up the freezer with food and didn't leave the house for two and a half months.'

Migration, moving away and leaving home—voluntary or involuntary forms of exile—were a recurring leitmotif in the lives of many writers featured in this book. It was a subject or metaphor to which they were repeatedly drawn—as a way of excavating the past, relating to the present, examining notions of homeland and identity or locating their axis in the world. The idea of a globalized world may have swept aside some of these concerns, but the question of why some of the best Indian writers in English live abroad persisted. The answers, I found, were part of a much older and layered narrative.

In the interviews collected here, the earliest example of going away is captured in the haunting image of a father putting his four-year-old boy, who has lost his eyesight due to an attack of cerebrospinal meningitis, on a train from Lahore to Bombay in 1938. The father was Amolak Ram Mehta, an exemplary doctor, and his son became the writer Ved Mehta. Realizing that future prospects for his son were bleak, he took the bold step of sending him 1300 miles away to the Dadar School for the Blind. In 1949 Ved Mehta left India to enrol in a college in the United States, and later took degrees from Oxford and Harvard. His chief literary achievement is a sequence of twelve books, explorations of family history, collectively known as *Continents of Exile.* They contain stories of the upheaval of Partition, his own uprooting, and reflections on the human spirit to build, and rebuild, new lives. Sitting in a bookstore in Delhi in 2009, the writer spoke movingly of migration and disability: 'Originally the series began as an attempt to explain to myself my own origins . . . Blindness has been a continuing thing. Perhaps that is why I wrote these books at all, because blindness has traditionally been associated with profound loneliness and solitude, and one way of dealing with it, if not overcoming it, is to reach out and explore the world that you can't see and that you can't accept. So the books, in a way, are my attempt to reach out, to explore and to accept.'

Anita Desai, who left India nearly half a century later in the 1980s, to find a parallel career as a teacher of creative writing in America, perceived migration as a continuum of history. 'I grew up with a sense of history because of my parents, my father having come from what was East Bengal, now Bangladesh. It was taken away from him and he never returned to it. Or my mother coming from Germany and never returning to it either. So there was always a sense of the past in our home . . . I knew about it, they talked about it, but it was gone.' The sweeping whirlwind of history shapes the protagonists of her novels *Baumgartner's Bombay* and *In Custody*. 'It was a view of history not being something you could participate in, but something that could overwhelm you and trample on you like a juggernaut. In both cases, it is history that destroys these people's lives. It doesn't make them, it destroys them.'

Writers like Salman Rushdie and Suketu Mehta (who are present-day New Yorkers) originally left home because their families migrated but were unable to sever their umbilical cord from the city of their childhood and adolescence; Bombay was an influence so powerful in their emotional lives that it came to be memorialized in their best-known works. Asked to explain where he actually comes from, or belongs, Rushdie's answer is: 'I am from Bombay—that is where I am from. I have always been a Bombay guy and I have always thought of myself as that. I see Bombay in other places. One of the reasons why I like it here in New York is because I see Bombay in it; I see all kinds of echoes and similarities.' And though the characters in his novels keep saying goodbye to India forever, the trouble, he confessed, is that 'the author never succeeds in doing it'.

The idea of India, of a place real, imagined, evoked, reclaimed and adopted, was often inescapable. Writers as disparate as Amartya Sen, Vikram Seth, Amitav Ghosh and Kiran Desai left India early for studies abroad; some were students of outstanding merit. Home, however, was India. Asked if he thought of America as home after many years of living there, Ghosh categorically replied: 'It's not home. It's a place where I live. I don't really think of it as home.' He compared himself to the characters in *Sea of Poppies*, the first part of his trilogy about nineteenth-century immigrants leaving Indian shores. 'I think of myself as a *girmitiya*. It was the word used for the indentured labourers who left in the nineteenth century because they signed agreements, which they called *girmits*, and so, they became the diaspora of Mauritius, Fiji and so on. I think of myself like that; you sign that agreement for five years or ten years and you are away for a while. But that essential connection to India doesn't evaporate . . . and for me it certainly hasn't evaporated . . . My inner life and my imaginative life is completely fuelled by India, but it's not fuelled by localized India; it's fuelled by that aspect of the Indian experience which is a global experience.'

Like Ghosh, who has now returned to live part of the year in Goa, the economist, social philosopher and Nobel laureate Amartya Sen also unfailingly returns to India to spend his winter vacation at his home in Santiniketan. I interviewed him after the release of his latest book, *The Idea of Justice*. It is my practice to spend a little time with authors before the recording starts, to run through questions, reconfirm facts and seek clarifications; it's an exercise that helps clearer communication, improves comfort levels and moves the proceedings along smoothly. I generally inquire if there is any question I have left out that the author might like me to ask. Was Professor Sen sure that I had not missed out a subject that he would like to address? 'Yes, one,' he replied with a wry smile. 'Please ask me about the current state of politics in Bengal. It is a place that matters to me greatly but I'm afraid its politics baffle not only the Bengali mind but many others too.'

The critical concern and continual engagement with India, however, was not the exclusive province of Indian writers. Almost every foreign writer included in this book is, or desires to be, part of the Indian experience; to partake of or participate in its unfolding story. As book sales stagnate in the west, chart toppers like Jeffrey Archer and Ken Follett have discovered a burgeoning and vigorous Indian market. Archer was upfront about it: 'When the *Wall Street Journal* said, "Jeffrey, you're better off in India than you would be in America", I believed them. That's why I am here. It's all right to be the number one on the *New York Times* best-seller list, it's all right to be number one on the *Sunday Times* in London, but to sell at traffic lights in India is different.' His compatriot Alexander McCall Smith, creator of unforgettable female sleuths like Precious Ramotswe of Botswana and Isabel Dalhousie of Edinburgh, writes four to five novels a year, has sold more than forty million copies in forty-six languages and is a brand that involves fifty publishers round the world. Until recently, he was also a distinguished professor of medical law. I interviewed him not in his beloved Edinburgh but in the depths of rural Haryana in an ersatz Lutyens bungalow called 'Tikli Bottom'. McCall Smith turned out to be an ardent fan of R.K. Narayan. 'I think he was one of the greatest writers of the twentieth century and I think it's a great pity that he did not get the Nobel Prize for literature because I believe he rightfully deserved it. I am currently writing introductions to new editions of a number of the Narayan novels which are going to be published in New York.' People fall in love with India for many reasons, he added, but he came back because he enjoyed conversations with Indians. 'I think people still take pleasure in conversations in this country and I like that very much.'

Paul Theroux, familiar with India from the days of his 1970s best-seller, *The Great Railway Bazaar*, returns because the parallel running tracks of India changing and India unchanged are a riddle and a snare. 'I love coming back . . . because I notice these differences but [they are] not the same differences that you notice in China. China has obliterated its history. India has preserved it.' It is unsurprising that Theroux's two most recent novels are set in India.

~

But India is an older two-way crossing and there are writers who have made it their adopted home, the centre of their life's work. The best-known story in this book is probably that of the broadcaster and author Mark Tully; as his interview reveals, his personal search in India was to seek nourishment for the spirit and soul. Born in Calcutta in the twilight years of the Raj, he was sent away to school and college in England, restless years when he seriously considered becoming a priest. In 1965 he returned to India in a junior position in the BBC's Delhi bureau. He evocatively describes that moment of return but it was, in fact, a ninety-two-page book, *The Hindu View of Life*, by the scholar-statesman Sarvepalli Radhakrishnan, that transformed his inner life. He stayed on in India to become a revered figure. Foreign correspondents affirm that they are still frequently accosted in the far-flung parts of the country with the words, 'BBC? Tully sahib?' But he regards the tumultuous decades of being at the front line of wars, political assassinations, famines and other events, great and small, in the subcontinent as the sum of a deeper learning: 'India has taught me that there are many ways to God; but it is more than that. It has taught me that we are always on a journey, not a pilgrimage because a pilgrimage comes to a stop when you reach the destination. It is a sense of the transcendental, occasionally glimpsed in your search . . . such a sense makes us humble.'

Twenty years after Mark Tully, nineteen-year-old William Dalrymple, taking a year off between school and university, arrived like thousands of young overseas backpackers. 'I had never travelled before and had hardly been to Europe. I came from a very sheltered background in Scotland. India had a very dramatic, almost devastating effect on me . . . It was like a lightning strike in my life. Everything before the 26th of January 1984 is one life. The rest is really in India.'

The reverberation of Dalrymple's 'lightning strike' is to be felt elsewhere in the subcontinent. A variety of gifted young writers have returned to remake their countries in their words and tell stories that capture the core of their contemporary reality. Two Pakistani novelists featured here are good examples. Mohsin Hamid and Daniyal Mueenuddin, products of western education including superior law schools, both authors of widely applauded books, have returned to live in their country. Hamid's latest novel, *The Reluctant Fundamentalist*, is being made into a film by Mira Nair. At the Karachi Literature Festival in 2010, after an onstage interaction I conducted with the author, a reader in the audience rose to denounce him as a corrupt and degenerate influence for creating characters such as the young hero of *Moth Smoke* who falls into drug addiction and other bad habits in decadent Lahore. When the diatribe was over, the writer quickly regained his composure. 'Sir,' he said, 'you're entitled to your opinion. It is said that nightingales only sing to nightingales. But does that mean that nightingales shouldn't sing at all?'

Not all writers are as vivid in their expression or as articulate in speech. Some, like Jhumpa Lahiri, Aravind Adiga or Zadie Smith, are uncomfortable with the medium of television and routinely decline requests; when they do agree, which is but rarely, they prefer to answer questions by email or perhaps talk to someone with an unobtrusive notebook. When he won the Booker Prize for his first novel, *The White Tiger*, in 2008, Adiga sent a polite email saying that he was unused to television and apologized for begging off.

~

Unfortunately the television journalist cannot arrive with only a notebook. But my assumption that writers are generally a shy and retiring breed turned out to be largely unfounded—there wouldn't be a weekly show running for six years if they were. Several of the authors featured here, for example, Amartya Sen, Umberto Eco, Ramachandra Guha and Alexander McCall Smith, are distinguished professors with illustrious teaching careers. Accustomed to delivering lectures, addressing students and large audiences, they have the masterly assurance to present a corpus of facts, concepts and arguments with lucidity and vigour. Like the best of teachers, they carry their erudition lightly; they regard it their duty to put their interlocutor at ease rather than the other way round.

Others, like Nadine Gordimer and Mahasweta Devi, whose vast output of fiction is interwoven with their passionate crusades for political and social justice, can bring a scene dramatically to life in a few sentences. Gordimer's account of being mugged by three young men in her home and Mahashweta Devi's memory of villagers singing folk songs eulogizing the Rani of Jhansi around a fire on a cold night in Bundelkhand were so affecting that I fell silent for a few seconds and stumbled for words to phrase my next question.

Writers like Salman Rushdie, Vikram Seth and Javed Akhtar have a natural talent for conversation. Once they have agreed to the interview, their talk, laced with quicksilver insights, literary allusions and witty asides, can never pall. Explaining how he 'sponged off' his parents for years while finishing his long opus, *A Suitable Boy*, Seth quipped: 'They acted as my patrons, or patron and matron, you could say.' The interviewer can come away wishing that the cameras could have rolled on and on. And writers like Mark Tully, William Dalrymple, Shobhaa Dé and Paul Theroux, as professional journalists, are unfazed by any kind of question. They also have their timing pat: wired to an internal clock they know exactly when the half-hour is up.

Just occasionally, there may be a writer who is genuinely diffident or, distracted by television's paraphernalia of cameras and cables, finds it difficult to describe the creative well-springs from which words, characters and stories emerge. As a heartfelt compliment to Anita Desai, Salman Rushdie once described her as 'the great student of solitude'. My efforts to interview this quietly reflective writer got nowhere until, one day, she had a sudden change of heart in the city of Turin where she was being honoured by a major award. Sensing that a seated face-to-face recording might be inappropriate for such a writer, my cameraperson colleague came up with an excellent solution. On his morning walk he had passed through a public garden and he suggested that we should take a leisurely stroll while chatting. In that relaxed setting on a fine autumn morning, she came through with intense clarity as she evoked the finer nuances of life and her art.

A writer's life is often solitary and, emerging from that cloistered world, it can sometimes be unnerving to condense and explain the creative process under the glare of lights. But a literary interview is not an inquisition: a few words of encouragement and careful listening will generally thaw a guest who freezes mid-sentence; a cup of tea will restore lost cues and frayed nerves. I haven't actually had a writer walk away in six years.

After a show, I often receive a flurry of YouTube clips, Twitter updates and website links—not an unsurprising occurrence in the increasingly competitive world of books and authorship. Though comprehensive data on Indian publishing is not available, it is estimated that the English language market in non-academic books is growing at a rate of 15 to 18 per cent a year, as opposed to a 2 to 3 per cent annual increase globally, mainly due to saturated western markets. A rise in disposable incomes, major corporate houses entering the publishing and book retail business, Indian authors walking away with top international prizes, and a proliferation of literary festivals attest to its robust health. There are more book launches in a city like Delhi every week than there are film openings; I can confirm this from the number of review copies I receive. They could fill a small library every few months.

In the 1970s, I read a remarkable set of novels by the English writer Anthony Powell. His twelve-volume sequence, produced over thirty years, is collectively known as *A Dance to the Music of Time*. Each book has an individual title, but like a jigsaw, some are obscure while others are alluringly enigmatic. The one that book lovers and viewers of *Just Books* will find irresistible is called *Books Do Furnish a Room*. Of course they do; they also furnish our thoughts, our lives and our world.

SUNIL SETHI
December 2010

Javed Akhtar

Among his many gifts, Urdu poet, and screenplay and lyrics writer Javed Akhtar (b. 1945) has a matchless talent for conversation. Whether at a small gathering, in a one-on-one dialogue or at any public platform, his flow of scintillating anecdote and wit, literary and musical insight, social and political commentary—often laced with Urdu shairi—pours forth in a sparkling stream.

In January 2010 the Jaipur Literature Festival organized a special tribute to the legendary Urdu poet Faiz Ahmed Faiz; the poet's daughter Salima Hashmi presented an audio-visual memoir, the young Pakistani novelist Ali Sethi sang two famous ghazals and Shabana Azmi recited verse by him. But it was only when Akhtar took the stage to recall his encounters with Faiz that the audience felt they had got their money's worth. Akhtar's account ranged from the comic and self-mocking (as an impoverished young man in Mumbai he had dogged the great poet's footsteps and ended up, none the worse for wear, in Faiz's hotel bedroom) to the deeply reflective (in explaining the universal and unifying truths of poetry). When he finished, there was hardly a dry eye in the audience and he received a rousing ovation from a more than a thousand people in the open-air garden setting.

Born in Madhya Pradesh, the son of the left-wing poet Jan Nisar Akhtar, he was named 'Jadoo' from a verse of his father's that carried a hint of prophecy: '*Lamba, lamba kisi jadoo ka fasana hoga*' (Long will be told that tale of magic). He was educated in Lucknow and Aligarh but his wide learning was acquired, almost by osmosis, from a strong family tradition in poetry and literary critique; both his grandfather Muzter Khairabadi and his maternal uncle Majaz were Urdu poets of influence.

Like thousands of aspirants in search of a future, he arrived penniless in Mumbai in 1964. He movingly describes that early period of hardship in the introduction to his best-selling volume of verse *Tarkash* (2004). Working as a piece-dialogue writer for Hindi films, he gradually rose to prominence in a partnership with Salim Khan to produce screenplays for all-time film hits in the 1970s like *Zanjeer*, *Deewar* and *Sholay*. The duo's efforts in creating a new cinematic language—path-breaking for their narrative structure, linguistic style and character development—helped forge the image of stars like Amitabh Bachchan as the anti-hero superstar.

But Javed Akhtar wore his mantle of star screenwriter lightly. He came to writing poetry and film songs later in life—as he describes in this interview—but they became his abiding interest, winning him an audience far and above his film writing. His deep culture, instinctive understanding of the power of words and charismatic personality have turned him into a celebrated public intellectual in promoting India's secular and syncretic tradition.

I first met Javed Akhtar by chance in 1983 when, as staff correspondent on *India Today*, I was commissioned to write a cover story on Shabana Azmi, then an emerging and forceful presence on screen. She invited the photographer Raghu Rai and me to spend a few days with Javed and her at a hill station near Bombay. She had not assumed the role of social activist and they had yet to cement their partnership in marriage. That early acquaintance has led to a friendship, enriched over the years by the range and refinement of his inquiring mind.

Among many honours, Javed Akhtar was awarded the Padma Bhushan in 2007 and nominated to the Rajya Sabha in 2010. This interview was recorded in his Mumbai home after the publication of the book *Talking Songs: Javed Akhtar in Conversation with Nasreen Munni Kabir.*

~

Shabana Azmi has written a telling introduction to the new book in which she speaks about your extraordinary ability to be able to write a song anywhere–in a moving car, in the middle of a dinner party, or on your way up and down in a lift. Does it really come as naturally and easily?

As a professional writer, what matters ultimately is the deadline. It does not matter where you are—in a car, aircraft, train or at a party; when you have to deliver you just have to.

But finding the right words, to weigh each word and locate the metre, is surely something that takes time and thought?

It takes time to learn the process. What happens is that sometimes people start doing something for which they have been preparing themselves for years. I was interested in poetry and film music from the age of ten. By the time I was twelve or thirteen, I remembered hundreds of couplets, and when I was about fifteen or sixteen, I remembered hundreds of film songs. In a way, I was getting prepared for the work but I was not aware of it then.

Poetry was in your blood as Jan Nisar Akhtar's son, Muzter Khairabadi's grandson and Majaz's nephew—all great Urdu poets—so would you ascribe some of your talent to a collective gene pool?

You must ask that of a scientist who is working on genes. Only he could tell you how much talent travels through genes. But I suppose that one's environment and upbringing contributes a lot. Luckily for me, I was born in a family filled with the atmosphere of poetry all around me so I imbibed and learned poetry, metre and choice of words quite early. And I learned it without any attempt to learn it.

Did you always write poetry?

No, I did not. In fact, I started writing poetry at an age when people generally stop writing poetry. I was interested in poetry and remember thousands of couplets even today. I can recite other people's poetry for eight to nine hours without stopping for a second. But I started writing poetry in 1978 or 1979 when I was thirty-two or thirty-three years old. I never wrote poetry as a teenager or when I was in my twenties. So it was a rather late beginning as far as my literary poetry is concerned, and there is very little romantic poetry; that was left unwritten. Perhaps film songs became my outlet for that kind of poetry.

Before you took to writing film songs you had a flourishing career as a screenplay writer. Film lyrics came almost accidentally in 1981 when Yash Chopra asked you to write the songs for his film *Silsila* in which the hero is a poet.

Yash Chopra asked me and I resisted. I said no, I will not. He said, why not? I said I am not interested. I am writing film scripts, and am quite happy, because I write poetry for myself and I don't even get it published. Yash Chopra was one of the few people who had heard my poetry at that time. I don't know why he was so convinced that I would be a good songwriter or of any use. I gave him impossible conditions but he kept insisting. He saw to it that I wrote the songs. It was fortunate for me that I started my career as a song writer for him and with a film like *Silsila* because he is one of those few directors who have an ear for poetry, who respect words and who demand a literary flavour in lyrics. I had scope for writing songs which are not the usual film songs.

In what way were the *Silsila* songs unconventional?

If you take a song like '*Yeh kahan aa gaye hum*', there is a lot of poetry recited by Amitabh Bachchan in the movie which you don't generally get in film songs. The very diction and metaphor of the song was two rungs higher than the usual film song. It was more poetry than song, it was very effective and people appreciated it.

You point out in this book that Hindi film songs are governed by certain parameters and conventions. How difficult is it to break away from them?

I have never felt any pressure; as a matter of fact when I have felt any, or if someone has tried to pressurize me, I have left that director and project. I work with a clear conscience—I do things according to my sense of aesthetics and decency. You have to understand that you are communicating with a very large segment of society where many people may not be trained to understand poetry and many may perhaps have never read it. So many vulgar, obscene and meaningless songs are written, some of them gibberish, that pander to the lowest common denominator.

A film song requires your expression to be accessible and communicative. The language, metaphor and the structure of the lines should be simple so that they are within everybody's reach, but not at the cost of emotion or literary value. Look at the work of poets and lyric writers like Shailendra, Sahir Ludhianvi, Majrooh Sultanpuri, Shakeel Badayuni and Anand Bakshi. It is not an easy accomplishment.

Is simplicity of language the key?

Yes, to a great extent, but along with honesty and honest feeling.

Give us an example from what you consider a classic film song, say, from Majrooh Sultanpuri's repertoire, that you admire.

Majrooh has written many wonderful songs but take this song: *Aaj main upar, aasman neeche / Aaj main aagey, zamana hai peechhe.* It is in the simplest possible language but he perfectly captures the exuberance of a young girl. I think its lighthearted quality is remarkable. And the same Majrooh, when he wants to plumb emotional depths, also wrote *Chupa lo yun dil mein ye pyaar mera / Ke jaisey mandir mein lau diye ki*—what an elegant and nuanced juxtaposing of images and metaphors.

So a range of idiom and linguistic style is at the heart of a successful film lyric?

Yes. To be a successful film lyricist you need not be a great poet but you need to have tremendous versatility.

Still, several other things matter when you are writing a film song. The writer is bound by the setting, the situation and the character . . .

Not only that; more often you are bound by a tune too. Generally, the tune is given to us. I have a situation and I have to write the lyrics for this particular situation to this tune because the tune is predetermined.

When it comes to assessing a situation, for example, in a rural film like *Lagaan*, quite distinct from the urban and youthfully heady *Dil Chahta Hai*, how do you switch into the personalities and cadence of the characters?

I think a film writer, whether writing scripts or lyrics, is a kind of a latent actor. You have to place yourself in that character and think from the character's point of view. That is how you write dialogue. When you are writing dialogue for Gabbar Singh you think from the point of view of a ruthless, sadistic outlaw.

How fast and sure-handed must a songwriter be? I am thinking, say, of a song like *'Radha kaisey na jale'* in *Lagaan*. How quick-witted do you need to be to switch from that to a song like *'Ek ladki ko dekha'* in *1942—A Love Story*?

When you are writing such things, whatever you have learned, heard and read comes to your aid. I come from Lucknow, and Avadh is known for the reverence that the region traditionally had, and still has, for Krishna. Right from the time of Wajid Ali Shah, Janmashtami has been a major happening in that part of India. They celebrate Janmashtami everywhere but in central Uttar Pradesh, which was once called Avadh, there is a special reverence for Krishna. I was brought up in an atmosphere where I saw Krishna leelas and heard those folk songs and lyrics. I once had to write a Krishna aarti but the music directors Laxmikant–Pyarelal were slightly apprehensive that a man with the name of Javed Akhtar could do it. They did not say so in as many words, but I could feel their sense of insecurity. I asked them to give me twenty-four hours; I said I would try. When I went back to them, they were pleasantly surprised because aartis have a crescendo, each aarti ends in one. I wrote the crescendo with the many names of Krishna. It went like this:

Krishna kanhaiya murlidhar, manmohan kaan murari hai,
Gopal manohar dukhbhanjan, ghanshyam atul banwari hai,
Wo kansvinashak maharathi, sudarshan charkadhari hai,
Bankunj phiraiya sawariya, nandlala ka murari hai,
Sab roop niraale hain uske, har leela uski nyaari hai,
Wo gopinath madanmohan, wo shyam pitambar aayega,
Aayega yugandhar, aayega
Aayega yugandhar, aayega . . .

[This lyric is an invocation to Lord Krishna in his many appellations.]

From Krishna's raas leela you go on to write cool songs for *Dil Chahta Hai* or fast-paced songs like *'Ek do teen'* in *Tezaab*. Where do these varying insights come from?

'*Ek do teen*' is an accusation. I often have to face the question, '*Wo "Ek do teen" aapne kyon likha*?' [Why did you write '*Ek do teen*'?] The situation was that the girl who works in a nautanki is singing a song on stage and obviously you could not give her a ghazal or a song with a traditional literary flavour. I wrote a song that would be as simple as a folk song. In folk music there is something known as *baarah maasa*—a description of the passing seasons. So this is a song where a *birhan*, a woman pining for her lover, describes how time has passed and she counts each day before his return—this happened on the fourteenth day and this happened on the sixteenth, and so on. Basically, that is the structure, a take on a very traditional musical and literary structure. It is difficult to describe it like this but you have to have enough simple words at your disposal. Your vocabulary must feel comfortable.

You give an example, a good one, that the three commonest words for love in Hindustani are *pyaar, ishq* and *mohabbat*. But they are used quite differently by disparate characters in particular types of songs and settings . . .

Obviously, if you show a villager singing, then use of the word *mohabbat* is inappropriate. *Mohabbat* is an urban and sophisticated expression. *Pyaar* or *prem* perhaps would be more appropriate in a rural setting. *Ishq* carries a certain obsessive quality. *Mohabbat* is gentler. If you say, '*Mujhe tumse mohabbat hai*' it somehow has social sanction because *mohabbat* can exist between mother and child, siblings and friends. *Ishq* has a certain rebellious quality. It speaks of passion, passion that is generally disapproved of by conventional norms because *ishq* challenges the rules.

I don't at the moment remember if I have used *ishq* and, if I have, then how? But the poet Sahir Ludhianvi has written a kind of lyrical thesis on *ishq*. He wrote a *qawwali*—it is fifteen minutes long!—in *Barsaat ki Raat*. The way he described *ishq* and its different aspects is the last word in a film song. *Pyaar* is more colloquial—you'll find it often in traditional poetry. In Hindi poetry you will have *prem*, in Urdu you will have *mohabbat* or *ishq* but *pyaar*—poor thing—is the common man's word to describe love.

While you accept that the 1950s and 1960s were the golden age of film music and songs, you express disappointment at the vulgarity and coarseness that has crept into the language of film songs today. You seem particularly upset at how a song like *'Choli ke peechhe'* could become such hit . . .

As a matter of fact, let's not say it *has* become a hit. I can say with some satisfaction that it *had* once become a hit. Because I think the worst is behind us. There was a time from the mid-1980s to mid-1990s when, I think, aesthetics took a dip. This was the worst time for Hindi film music or, in fact, for Hindi films. Films or songs are not created in a vacuum; they are a part and parcel of society. It was a time when our society was going through a moral or aesthetic low. Our politics were the worst independent India has seen. Somehow it became clear to producers of Indian music that audiences don't approve of obscene and vulgar songs. I don't see many vulgar songs in the pipeline any more. It is part of the past.

The songs which we remember the most are the songs that are wel written and have emotional appeal. So in the 1950s and 1960s the tunes were conducive to writing, their tempos were at peace, and there was enough time to register words. The stories were more meaningful and had more emotional depth. There was room, or time, for introspection. Good poetry is written and delivered when there is time to reflect.

You were an enormously successful screenplay writer but once you took to songwriting, the screenplays went out of the window. You haven't written a screenplay for nearly eleven years. What has caused this change, and as a writer, what is the essential difference between the two modes of writing?

The difference between screenplay writing and songwriting is the difference between a marathon race and a hundred-yard race. Neither is easy but they are two different disciplines. In a marathon, the runner has to decide that, all right, up to this point I will have this tempo and I'll gradually increase it; and in the last two laps, I'll make the final thrust. You have to completely chart out that thirty-two-mile race. But in a hundred-yard race you hear the gunshot and you go. And you have to be perfect because every step matters. A song has ten–twelve lines generally but you have to create an impact within those ten–twelve lines. You have to be precise and perfect. Both these requirements are different and difficult. The kind of work I was doing lately as a scriptwriter was not giving me any happiness and, I am afraid, it wasn't giving much happiness to others either. On the other hand, my songs were being appreciated and I immensely enjoyed writing them. I thought one should do things one enjoys doing and feels passionate about. I was also tired; I had been writing scripts for twenty-five years so I gave up.

But you won't give up writing songs, will you, because you've written them for a quarter of a century?

You're right. But now I have decided that I will write at least one script a year alongside my lyrics.

May 2005

John Swannell

Jeffrey Archer

If life can imitate the plot of a thriller, then Jeffrey Archer's has been a dramatic roller coaster ride. The combined book sales of the former British politician and best-selling author total more than 135 million copies, and *Kane and Abel* (1980), his tale of two siblings at war, continues to sell at the rate of a thousand copies a day. Archer (b. 1940) set his sights on a political career after Oxford and was elected MP, sitting in the House of Commons from 1969 to 1974. A confidant of Margaret Thatcher, he was made deputy chairman of the Conservative Party (1985–86) and a life peer in 1992. Officially styled as Baron Archer of Weston-super-Mare, controversy has long been Lord Archer's middle name.

Libel suits, links with prostitutes, bankruptcy claims, dodgy accounting practices and allegations of insider dealing have tainted his career; it has even been said that he was never a full undergraduate at Oxford. In 1986, Archer was forced to resign as deputy chairman of the party because he paid a prostitute £2000 to go abroad; as a fall-out of a libel case in 2000 he was charged with perjury and perverting the course of justice, expelled from the party for five years, and served a two-year jail term; and in 2001 it was alleged that millions of pounds had disappeared from Archer's charity for Kurds. The satirical magazine *Private Eye*'s nickname for him is 'Lord Archole'.

But he bounces back with resilience, often in unexpected ways. In jail he produced three volumes of prison diaries and was let out to star in a production of his courtroom drama, *The Accused*.

This conversation with Archer followed a glittering lunch given in his honour by a sports impresario and was attended by the capital's political, bureaucratic and cricketing elite. As befits a former athlete, Archer has the reputation of behaving like a feisty pugilist with the media; he is a master at the politician's skills of subtle evasion, over-simplification and rhetorical exaggeration. In this interview, however, he was frank, freewheeling and often quite funny.

One best-selling thriller after another and, indeed, sometimes your own life reads like one. Fame, fortune, political dramas, scandals and the infamy of serving a two-year jail term—how much of it goes into your books?

I think any author is prone to use his own experiences. When young people come to me and say, 'Jeffrey, I want to write a book, what should I do?', I say that you must not think like that. You shouldn't do a ghost book or a spy story or a war story because they are fashionable. You must write about what you know. I always quote Jane Austen who only wrote five books in her life, arguably five of the greatest novels ever written. She lived in a small town in England. She wrote about a mother who was trying to get rid of four daughters, a mother trying to get rid of three daughters, a mother trying to get rid of two daughters and a daughter trying to get rid of herself. You write about what you know, what you understand, and if you are any good at it, and you can make readers turn the page, they will turn the page.

You spent two years in jail on charges of perjury and you turned the prison term into a page-turner: you produced three volumes of *Prison Diaries* and also a play with you appearing on stage. So you turned a period of adversity, in one of the harshest prisons in Britain, into a publishing success. How tough was that?

Well, you are right, because the three prison diaries ran into a million words. That was my output in one year. Normally I write 150,000 words in a year. I wrote *Prison Diary* I, II and III all within a year. When people come to me and ask how to finish a book, I say that you must get away from what you are doing. You must get away. You must have at least three months away from everyone. So I was sitting in a cell with a pad and pen, with three meals a day, and no one bothering me. This was exactly what I needed, but it was also very noisy.

What is it about your personality that you have managed to turn every disadvantage, in fact serial disasters, from public litigation to scandals, into an advantage? You just picked yourself up from the bootstraps, in crisis after crisis, to produce best-sellers which have sold about 135 million copies in all.

Yes, there have been some disasters but you have got to get yourself up and get on with it. You can always find excuses, you can always say it was someone else's fault, it wasn't really fair, but that's rubbish. It is always your fault. So get on with life and start again.

When you came down from Oxford, writing wasn't really on your horizon. It was a political career that you were after, wasn't it?

Correct. That was what I wanted to do. I entered the House of Commons by the age of twenty-nine in the days when Harold Wilson was prime minister. But writing came strangely because I made a very foolish investment in a company and I lost everything I had earned, and more, because I was stupid enough to invest more than I had. It was then that I sat down and wrote my first book called *Not a Penny More Not a Penny Less*, the story of four men who between them lose a fortune and, one of them, an American, brings them together. Nowadays I read regularly in the press that this was an instant best-seller but, in fact, it wasn't. It sold 3000 copies and it took a whole year to sell those 3000 copies before it began to sell well. My writing life really didn't take off until *Kane and Abel*. Even today it's selling a thousand copies a day. It changed my entire life.

What is at the core of writing thrillers? Is it actually the craft of writing, creating characters, inventing situations or do you first get down and figure out a cracking good plot?

You have to have the plot. You have got to have a story that has a beginning, a middle and an end and you have got to make people turn the page. I write up to seventeen drafts. I get away for two months and I wake up at 5.30 in the morning. I write from six to eight and take a two-hour break, I write from ten until twelve and take a two-hour break, I again write from two until four, followed by another two-hour break, then I write from six until eight, light supper, go to bed at 9.30 or 10.00 and begin again at 5.30 the next day. Fifty days of that in a row.

If anyone thinks that it can be done in a weekend, it can't be. I was in a restaurant the other day and saw a man of my age with a young lady, who certainly wasn't his daughter, and as I was passing his table I heard him say to her, 'Oh, look, that's Jeffrey Archer . . . does he knock off another book this weekend?' They have no idea that it's hour upon hour of craftsmanship to hone it sharper and finer.

Apart from the rigorous discipline of sitting at your desk and writing, correcting draft after draft, the key to thrillers is the twist in the tale, to borrow a title from one of your books. Where do the slick, often outlandish, twists come from?

Often the young will come and ask that question. I say to them, 'Do you play the violin?' They say, 'No, Jeffrey, I don't play the violin.' I say, 'Do you paint a picture?' They say, 'No, I am not an artist.' I say, 'I tell a story. It's a God given gift.' I can tell a story any day of the week; words never stop coming out, they are there all the time.
But in the end it's the readership, people out there, who make the decision. Ironically, with all one's experience and professionalism, it isn't the prose that makes the decision, it's the public. You've got to give them a story they will love. They won't come back to you if they don't. One of the joys of India is that many people come up to me and say, 'I have read them all, Jeffrey!'

Despite your success as a thriller writer you never set out to be a writer. Was it an accidental vocation?

Totally. I fall in with the Proustian theory that we all end up doing the thing we are second best at. I wanted to be a politician. But I couldn't get a job when I was out of politics and facing bankruptcy. I sat down and wrote my first book. Then someone said, 'You ought to write a second one, Jeffrey.' I did, instead of listening to my wife who said, 'Go out and look for a *real* job.'

That's the 'radiant, fragrant Mary Archer' as described by a judge in one of the court actions you faced. What is it about your life that lands you in real trouble as opposed to many of your heroes who also land into trouble but manage to get out unhurt?

I think I trust a person too much and there's a naivety about me. I often say that if I had to make a decision between being a tough cynic and a naive enthusiast, thanks very much, I will be a naive enthusiast. You only get one life. So what if I have made mistakes, who hasn't? I am not talking about individual things that happened to me. Most people have disasters in their lives. Most people have had tragedies or things gone wrong from which they had to fight back. Very few people sailed smoothly through life. If you have, 'Well done, sir.'

It's your first long tour of India and you're going to several cities. What does the country mean to you apart from a big readership and your old love of cricket?

A love of cricket goes way back. I had the honour today at lunch to meet up again with the Nawab of Pataudi who was captain of cricket at Oxford when I was president of athletics. But he captained India before he met with the tragic accident, from which he recovered and played just as well. Indians are among the greatest players of cricket in the last fifty years. Watching Virender Sehwag the other day get his triple hundred and watching Sachin Tendulkar and Rahul Dravid score those amazing runs! It's also a personal thrill for me because they read my books. A book tour of India is very thrilling because it's the nation everyone is looking up to at the moment. In Britain we are very conscious that India is striding to the fore and people talk about the next two decades belonging to India. When the *Wall Street Journal* said that Jeffrey you're better off in India than you would be in America, I believed them. That's why I am here. It's all right to be the number one on the *New York Times* best-seller list, it's all right to be number one on the *Sunday Times*, but to sell at traffic lights in India is different.

What is it about the British political establishment that produces best-selling writers, the British propensity to combine fiction writing with public life? There's Ken Follet, a champion of the Labour Party, whose wife is a minister, and who's your competition as a thriller writer. There are others too. Top-selling crime novelists P.D. James and Ruth Rendell are both members of the House of Lords.

Disraeli wrote novels during the holidays when he was prime minister and so did Winston Churchill. John Buchan gave us *The Thirty-nine Steps* when he was the high commissioner in Canada. Douglas Hurd as foreign secretary was still writing novels. I think that one of the things about politics is that you meet fascinating people and you face problems every day that are unbelievable.

Big political changes have occurred in British politics during your long political career, with the move from Conservative to Labour rule. But how have public attitudes to politics and politicians changed?

When I entered politics forty years ago there was a clear left and a clear right and people were not fighting for the centre ground. Nowadays everybody stands on the centre ground. Tony Blair as prime minister was, frankly, a couple of points right of centre. Everyone is fighting for the centre ground, that's the big difference. The strategic difference is what Margaret Thatcher always pointed out. I had to accept her judgement when she said, 'Jeffrey, you know, what happens these days, they put an idea in the air, and they get an opinion poll, and if the opinion poll says that's what the people want, they go ahead with it.' She said that that was not conviction politics. Conviction politics is a belief in something.

The era in which I was brought up was under Harold Wilson, a highly intelligent and sophisticated man, who knew that he couldn't move without the backing of the trade union movement and he couldn't run a parliament without their support. That's no longer true. But, in the end, people get bored with the person who is in power. After Margaret Thatcher had ten years, they wanted her out for no other reason than she had done ten years. After Tony Blair had done ten years, they wanted him out. The truth of the matter is that, after a certain period of time, your sell-by date comes up, and they take whoever is the leader of the other party.

You're a rich man. Your books have made you a millionaire many times over. What do you spend your money on?

Art mainly—I love collecting art. So if a large cheque comes because of a book, I go out to buy some art.

You have an impressive collection of Impressionist art, haven't you?

I love the Impressionist period and I have been collecting for twenty years but I will let you into a secret: I can't afford my own pictures now and I will tell you why. The world has gone mad. You could once buy a Picasso for a certain sum, but now, the Russians and the Chinese have knocked the markets silly. I can't afford to buy those paintings any longer. I have come down to lower levels.

So what are you buying nowadays?

I have just seen and am fascinated by Australian artists. They're much underrated. I have also been buying Fernando Botero, the great Colombian artist who now lives in Italy. I am always looking for the next young artist who I think will make it good. But in my own country, if you take someone like Damien Hirst, he is now five or six million dollars for a picture. The world has gone mad.

Perhaps you're in the right country, after all, because the Indian contemporary art market is undergoing a boom. And it was recently reported that you met M.F. Husain, one of our great artists, in London.

I had the great honour of meeting him. But if I may say so, the difference between him and many other modern artists is that you give Husain a pencil and he knows what it's for and that he can actually draw. I went to an exhibition the other day where they put two egg boxes together and framed it and were charging £72,000 for it. I say the best way to find out if someone can draw is to give him a pencil.

Do you think India will feature one day in a Jeffrey Archer novel?

You've got to be careful about that and I will tell you why. This nation has produced some of the greatest writers on earth, some legendary names, and it would be very foolish to go and tread on their territory, just as I wouldn't expect them to write a book about a man who escapes from Belmarsh prison and seeks revenge on four people, which is all very English. Indians have a worldwide reputation in literature and I am not going anywhere near that.

May 2008

Nadeem Aslam

If you present a books show, publishers, book editors and writers will inevitably be in touch to acquaint you with what is in the pipeline; but it is also likely that some of your good friends and colleagues happen to be discerning readers and will recommend books that have stirred their hearts and minds. It was one such friend who gave me *Maps for Lost Lovers* by the British-Pakistani novelist Nadeem Aslam (b. 1966) and made me promise that should he ever appear on *Just Books*, I would have her meet him.

Maps for Lost Lovers (2004) is an astonishing, award-winning novel that took Aslam eleven years to complete. Set in a nameless English town that its immigrant community calls Dasht-i-Tanhaii, the Desert of Solitude, it opens with the mysterious vanishing of Jugnu and his lover Chanda. The shock and disgrace of the couple's relationship and disappearance is exacerbated by the arrest of Chanda's brothers for murder, and the events of a year observed through the eyes of their close-knit families and neighbours. The alienation of each character, entrapped in individual notions of morality, honour and piety, is heightened by limpid descriptions of the passing English seasons in crystalline prose.

'To read Aslam's physical descriptions is to be reminded of the ability of language to make us re-see the world through analogy and metaphor,' wrote the novelist Kamila Shamsie in a review. 'So, a woman's gold bracelet is composed of a series of semi-colons; dead tulips lean out of a bin like the necks of drunk swans; a falling icicle is a radiant dagger.'

Impressed by its sense of loss and by the luminosity of his writing—innate features of Urdu poetry that he had somehow immutably made his own in English—I quickly devoured Aslam's first novel, *Season of the Rainbirds* (1993), set in a small town in Pakistan, that presages the stylistic construction of *Maps for Lost Lovers*.

And as luck would have it, the writer himself arrived in town soon after. I invited him to lunch at home with my friend Suparna Singh who had introduced me to his work; to this day we talk of the impression this young man made on us. His careless good looks and ease in answering questions—in a mixture of Urdu and English—had a beguiling, childlike transparency because the unusual circumstances of his life and writing hold no easy answers.

Nadeem Aslam was born in Gujranwala, a small town in Punjab, and attended an Urdu-medium school till the age of fourteen, when his father, a communist poet, was forced to flee General Zia-ul-Haq's regime and seek political asylum in Britain. Admitted to a local school in Yorkshire, he knew only kindergarten English, and was advised to stick to science subjects for his high-school exams because of his imperfect command of the language.

His learning and mastery of English prose came from extended periods of hardship and self-imposed withdrawal from the world outside. For years he eked out a living by working on building sites and in bars so that he could read in libraries all day. 'There were times when I draped the windows with black cloth,' he told an interviewer of the time he was writing *Maps for Lost Lovers*. 'There was no phone, no TV, no radio, no newspapers and I just filled up the freezer with food and didn't leave the house for two and a half months.'

Aslam's most recent novel, *The Wasted Vigil* (2008) is set in Afghanistan. It is a story of cruelty and bigotry; but for all its brutality it is like a medieval Mughal painting in its evocation of the country's landscape and fragile beauty. This interview is an edited version of a conversation conducted in the lawns of the India International Centre in 2008.

The Wasted Vigil is set in a time frame that spans the turbulent history of Afghanistan from the Soviet occupation in the 1980s to its Talibanization and disintegration in the early twenty-first century. What made you choose war-torn Afghanistan as a setting?

I wanted to write about Afghanistan because I thought Afghanistan had been forgotten. That sounds a strange statement because Afghanistan is in the news every day; how can it have been forgotten? But it is in the news every day for what it is doing to the rest of the world and what the world did to Afghanistan over the past thirty years. For example, when 9/11 happened, the reaction in America was: Who are these people, why do they hate us? It was as if that moment was an aberration. But that moment came out of the history of America's involvement with Afghanistan, which began in 1979 when the Soviet Union went in and America, the west and Saudi Arabia decided that they would go in through Pakistan and pour billions of dollars worth of weapons into Afghanistan to defeat the Soviets. And once that goal was achieved, when the Soviet Union left in 1989, the world withdrew its gaze. And the civil war—in which hundreds of thousands of people were dying every year—was not at the forefront of anyone's mind. The Afghans were just people on the other side of the world, people who are always fighting each other in the dust and among the stones. Who cared? But suddenly after 9/11, everyone cared. I wanted to write a novel which went back thirty years and explained how we arrived at the current political and moral chaos that we see every time we pick up the newspaper.

Yet the main cast of characters in *The Wasted Vigil* are mainly westerners: Marcus the English poet who lives in a painted house with a perfume factory; Lara, the Russian girl in search of her lost brother; and David, the ex-CIA operative-turned-jewel trader . . .

Marcus, I think, would disagree with you. Though he is a white man, he has lived in Afghanistan for most of his adult life. He married an Afghan woman and raised half-Afghan daughters. Let me say that first of all I am not an Afghan: I wanted to write a novel in which I could explain how Afghanistan ended up at the confluence of various ideologies and cultural movements. I wanted to see if I could go in as an outsider and see what happens . . .

And when you go in, you find a war-torn country but also a place with a civilizational past, at the cultural crossroads of history. This comes through in the lyricism of your prose and yet, like intensely felt poetic language, the imagery is haunted and doomed. That is particularly evident in the opening chapters. Was that intentional?

Afghanistan has been through some horrible things in the past thirty years and I thought I would be doing a disservice to the Afghans—disservice is actually not the word—I think it would be a crime if I tried to soften it. The book is quite brutal in places and I wanted to bring the cruelty of what happened to the surface, and present it to the world, as it were. Afghanistan is a beautiful country but it is a beautiful country that has been torn to pieces.

At the beginning of *The Wasted Vigil* is a haveli with five main painted rooms and each of those five rooms is dedicated to one of the senses. I wanted the house to stand for the human body, now shattered because of the war that surrounds it. And next to the body is the soul which, in my novel, is the perfume factory, because the sense of smell is closest to human memory. So I wanted that location to be the soul, as it were, or the repository of human memory, Afghanistan's memory. And in the factory there is the head of a giant Buddha which is Afghanistan's past. This is my way of saying that Buddhism is a kinder religion than Islam. It is Afghanistan's past, yet the Taliban said only one book is allowed to exist: the Quran. So the Ramayana, Nizami's *Shahnama* or Homer's *Odyssey* were not allowed. I don't want to live in a world where there is only one book.

An extraordinary aspect of your life is the range and depth of expression that you acquired in English. Was it something that was painstakingly reached late in life? You were brought up in a small town outside Lahore and went to an Urdu-medium school and you had no English . . .

No, I did not. When I arrived in England, when I was fourteen, my English was, 'This is a cat.' But I was young enough. English was just a language, you picked it up. I keep saying that there are other writers who also learned English late, but then I realize that I am thinking of geniuses. Nabokov learned it, Conrad learned it. And these days we have the Bosnian writer Aleksandar Hemon. They are all brilliant minds. I am nothing like them. But it is a language, you pick it up.

It must have been a difficult apprenticeship. I remember you telling me that when you took your high school exams, your command of the English language was imperfect and your teachers persuaded you to take higher studies in the sciences because, they said, you would not be able to complete an essay in English . . .

Absolutely. The things I was interested in—history, sociology, literature, politics—were closed to me. I had been in Pakistan until I was fourteen;

my life was broken in half. Had I stayed in Pakistan I would have studied those subjects in Urdu and I would have become an Urdu writer. But we had to leave, and the subjects that I excelled in at school were the sciences, because for sciences your English needn't be that good. All you need is to study formulae and be able to do maths. So I went to university to read biochemistry, but by the third year, I realized that my English was now good enough and I wasn't interested in pursuing a career in biochemistry. So I dropped out and began to write a novel which took me eleven years to write. It was called *Season of the Rainbirds*.

You asked how I learned English. Some weeks ago I came across a notebook of mine from when I was seventeen. By then I had been in England for three years. It is a 200-page notebook and it is filled with words. I began trying to work out why I had written those words down. Was I trying to learn their spelling? What was it? And then I realized, about a week later, that I had then said to myself that I will never learn the meaning of a certain word because I don't like the way it sounds. My first novel was written on a typewriter but I have the computer files for my later novels, *Maps for Lost Lovers* and *The Wasted Vigil*. So I thought, just as a bit of experiment, I had that old notebook and those computer files. I opened both to see if any of those words in the notebook appeared in these two novels. And they don't! They actually don't because those words are the most distant from the sounds of Urdu. That is how deeply I am connected to Urdu. I actually don't like anything, any word, that veers too far from it.

When you wrote your first novel, *Season of the Rainbirds*, set in a small town in Pakistan, were you thinking in Urdu and translating it, as it were, into English?

No, by that time I had been in England for ten years and—consciously perhaps—I was telling myself, 'Don't think in Urdu, because you need to learn this new language.' But subconsciously, it must have happened.

You were lucky that your first novel was almost immediately accepted for publication. But it took eleven years to complete *Maps for Lost Lovers*. I remember you saying that you became so consumed in getting that book right that it was a period of hardship—you worked in bars and as a manual labourer on building sites . . .

Yes, I did. I had dropped out of university and had no qualification and no money. I couldn't work in an office. For about three months every year I would do two jobs at the same time but I would not write, I would just read and make notes. And I would save as much of that money as I could. Then for the next three months I would not work and live on that money. It was quite a difficult time. I was alone and had to break myself away from my friends because you can't go out with friends and expect them to buy you a meal. You can do it once, you can do it a hundred times, you can do it a thousand times, but there comes that thousand and first time when he or she might think, 'Dude, what is going on? If you want to do this, do it on your own.' I have spoken to them since then, and they say, 'Oh my God, we would have bought you a meal for that thousand and first time as well.' But I was afraid to be a burden on anyone. And that, I think, goes into the novel because every character in the novel is lonely.

It was a time of self-exile and everyone in *Maps for Lost Lovers* is also exiled . . .

Absolutely. The town that they live in . . . I did not want to name it specifically because I wanted the reader to share the confusion that my characters feel. They are mostly uneducated people, who left their villages in India and Pakistan for the first time to arrive in this alien land which is painfully different from what they have left behind; they are lonely and apprehensive. The 1950s and the 1960s were a tough time to be an immigrant in England; it was quite a racist society at that time. These people were actually afraid to go beyond their immediate neighbourhood, they did not know what lay beyond certain roads because they were too afraid to venture there. So I wanted the reader to share that confusion and think: 'What is this place, where am I, where in England exactly is this place?' So I did not name the town. For a long time I did not know how to go about doing it. But then I thought, why don't the immigrants, when they arrive in England in this town, this intense loneliness that they feel, say that this town is *Dasht-e-Tanhaii*—Desert of Solitude? So they actually name the town Dasht-e-Tanhaii and they pass it on to the next generation. Even the next generation, the children who were born in England and who know life beyond that street, actually refer to the town as Dasht-e-Tanhaii because the loneliness is passed down.

In Urdu poetry *Dasht-e-Tanhaii* is a metaphor that also implies inner desolation. In *Maps for Lost Lovers*, the ghettoized community of immigrants in that English town are Muslim and Sikh, but their intricate relationships refer to the fissures that move the plot with inexorable sadness. Would you say that the lyrical beauty of the writing intensifies the sadness?

There is sadness in the novel but, I promise you, there are compensations with enough beauty. But I am wary of falsification. There is a utopian impulse behind everything a writer does but one mustn't lie. If something is wrong, you have to look at it straight on.

The brilliant American writer Cormac McCarthy gave an interview last year to *Rolling Stone* magazine, in which at one point he said the world was worse than it used to be fifty years ago, for who would have thought fifty years ago that we would see beheadings on TV? Every writer must disagree with his heroes and I don't agree with McCarthy. Fifty years ago we had the beheadings but we just didn't have them on TV. If something terrible is happening in the world, I wish to know about it so that I can become angry, upset or become galvanized by that news and try to put an end to it. What is the alternative? Not knowing about it and going about thinking that I live in a wonderful world? It's not something I am prepared to do.

One of your main creative wellsprings is Urdu poetry and at the core of so much of that poetry is a sense of irretrievable loss. Your characters are haunted by death; a current of violence runs through their lives, of disappearances, abductions and murder . . .

It links up with Islamic mysticism, the quest for the beloved, the search for the soul and the need for the soul to connect with something other than what is tangible. Hence the image of the flame and the moth, *shama* and *parwana*, and the cypress and dove; these images are linked with the spiritual life of the culture that I come from. But it also has to do with the country I come from.

History has been kinder to you in India than it has been to Pakistan. Within my consciousness, though, I remain an optimistic person. Let me quote the poet Faiz Ahmed Faiz: '*Lambi hai gham ki raat magar raat hi toh hai* (Long is the sorrowful night, but a night is all it is).'

***The Wasted Vigil* evokes the brutality in Afghanistan against a landscape of its history and natural beauty. And in a larger scheme of**

things your characters are doomed because of oppression and tyranny outside their control. Do you believe that writers, say, in the case of India and Pakistan, can help alter the tide of history?

What can writers do? Pakistani writing is now at the forefront of people's minds but it is not because Pakistani writers are explaining our country's problems to the world. Actually we are doing it for ourselves; we are trying to understand the country for ourselves.

There is no end to the ingenuity of hate. The idea of Pakistani writers and performers coming here and Indian writers going to Pakistan is a great thing. I am also aware that there may be a small bit of India's population who say, 'Pakistani artistes come here to earn money and to swindle us.' Anything beautiful can be twisted and made ugly. While we celebrate cultural exchange, we must not romanticize it. The fact is that although there has been exchange in previous decades, there have also been wars. Certainly in Pakistan our rulers—military leaders, intelligence agencies and politicians—have never cared anything about what we feel. So for us in Pakistan to say 'We love Indians, please don't go to war,' doesn't mean anything if our rulers decide that they want war. They need reminding again and again that they cannot do the thing which people don't approve of.

Let me quote something from the great Polish Nobel Prize-winning poet Czeslaw Milosz. I actually have this poem written on my wall over my writing desk. This is an English translation of Milosz, who says to a ruler:

You who wronged a simple man
Bursting into laughter at the crime,
And kept a pack of fools around you
To mix good and evil, to blur the line,

Though everyone bowed down before you,
Saying virtue and wisdom lit your way,
Striking gold medals in your honour,
Glad to have survived another day,

Do not feel safe. The poet remembers.
You can kill one, but another is born.
The words are written down, the deed, the date.

I don't know whether writers can change anything. But my job is to write down the words, the deed and the date, a kind of log of injustice and a log of cruelty that you think you have escaped, that you are powerful enough to have escaped, but you haven't escaped in the pages of my book. There you are held accountable.

January 2008

Chetan Bhagat

Like him or loathe him, you can't ignore Chetan Bhagat. The IIT and IIM graduate (b. 1974) grew up in Delhi, chose investment banking as a career, but became an instant best-seller with his first novel *Five Point Someone: What not to do at IIT* (2004) about the pressures and let-downs of life at a premier educational establishment. Three more rapidly followed: *One Night @ the Call Center* (2005), *The 3 Mistakes of My Life* (2008) and *2 States: The Story of My Marriage* (2009). Bhagat built upon his initial success by becoming, quite simply, a publishing phenomenon. The *New York Times* called him 'the biggest selling English language novelist in India's history' and, in 2010, *Time* magazine listed him among a hundred of 'the world's most influential people'.

With their simple plot lines, easily identifiable characters and situations and inexpensive pricing, his books target an aspiration-driven youth market. Bhagat himself—in casual T-shirts, jeans and stubble—has the air of the unaffected boy next door. Middle-class fathers hope their sons will grow up to become like him and middle-class mothers wish their daughters might marry someone like him. Imitation being the best form of flattery, his success has spawned a host of IIT and IIM graduates taking to fiction-writing. Having sold three of his novels to the movies, Bhagat quit his job in 2009 and set himself up as a full-time writer and public speaker.

You have written four books in five years and been described by the *New York Times* as the biggest selling Indian writer in the subcontinent. What does it feel like to become a kind of one-man fiction industry in so short a period?

I feel great, of course, and there's no reason to feel otherwise. The way you describe it, it seems like I have been working as hard at writing fiction as I did as an investment banker. I am used to those fourteen-hour days that banking demands—and maybe I have been too prolific.

You have certainly turned fiction writing into something more profitable than banking. Are you laughing all the way to the bank?

I feel a tremendous sense of power that whatever I write is read by millions of people of the younger generation and that has empowered me to become bolder in my fiction writing. I have started writing columns in English and Hindi newspapers which, of course, aren't fiction. I take up topical issues and the response is also empowering. It feels like the power of the pen is back.

Your first book, *Five Point Someone*, was about your experiences at IIT—what to do at IIT or, rather, what not to do there. It was fairly autobiographical and took you several years to write. Was its success a fluke?

I can't say if it was a fluke, but yes, it was definitely random. There were so many publishers that rejected the book; and even when it came out, people said it's nice, but no one had a clue that we would be talking about it in 2009, six years after its release, what with *3 Idiots* [the film based on the book] coming out. You could call it fluke or divine intervention.

Certainly *Five Point Someone* touched a chord. Why was that? Was it a formula, a particular style of writing, or did it have an honesty that made your first novel a cult?

I think it was fresh. I feel that the literary industry, ever since we started chasing prizes like the Booker, became very pretentious. Imagine if the Indian film industry only produced films for international film festivals. Where would Bollywood end up if it only did that? My readers say that they *find* themselves, an insight into themselves, in my books. It is things they can associate with, for example, the depression of getting low grades. They feel that they are not alone.

You were exceptional in terms of your education. You not only made it to IIT Delhi but also to IIM Ahmedabad, the premier management institute. In that sense you are an achiever. Do you think many of your readers aspire to such standards of educational success?

If my books were not so successful and I was a failure, readers would certainly not identify with me as much. It's human nature to chase success. I agree I am the poster boy of Indian middle-class success. I went to these colleges, became recognized for my work, so in a sense I am an 'achievable' aspiration. When you see Hrithik Roshan or Shahrukh Khan on screen, you feel, 'Oh, they're so great but in no way I can be them.' But when they see me they think, 'Oh well, he kind of looks like me. Maybe one day I could get there if I work as hard.'

Your subjects moved from the campus to call centres. And your third novel, *3 Mistakes*—about three chaps in Ahmedabad who set up a cricket shop, against the backdrop of your IIM life—cashes in on the Indian craze for cricket. And now, your new novel, *2 States*, draws upon an inter-regional marriage, just like yours: a Punjabi boy marrying a Tamil girl. It's the classic Indian conflict, of love versus arranged marriage. In real life you also married a Tamil classmate at IIM. So whole chunks of your life go into your books?

I shamelessly borrow from my life. However, I do fictionalize and dramatize it to make interesting stories. I feel my story of an inter-regional marriage, with growing migrations in India, would appeal to younger people who leave home to study or find jobs. They are likely to meet Indians of the opposite sex, not necessarily from their region. They may face resistance when they go back to their parents and say that they would like to spend the rest of their lives with this person. And I feel that until this resistance and prejudice ends, India cannot be one country. We say we are very secular but when it comes to marrying your child in another community, then your true prejudices come out. I feel what I did, marrying a woman from another community, was a good thing for India. In a broader sense, if everyone was to do the same, we would overcome regional divisions. We would become pure Indians. And if we become a pure Indian race then we deserve to be a superpower and will be one.

But it's still the boy-meets-girl formula, with many Bollywood or Hollywood clichés . . .

You know I was very worried about that because every second movie in India is a boy-meets-girl story and every second novel is the same. So I worked on a theme arising from a very basic observation—that in India a love story never exists in isolation. You cannot have a boy in love with a girl or a girl loving a boy and them getting married. Two families and communities, even clans, have to fall in love with one another. Everyone has to fall in love with everyone. And by the time you make that happen, there is almost no love left between the boy and the girl. So 75 per cent of my book is about convincing the family.

How do you work? Do you produce drafts and write with regular discipline every day?

Earlier I would write in fits and starts because I was working in a bank; it was very stressful to find time. Having left my job to become a full-time writer, I'm more disciplined. Typically I write when my kids go to school. I drop them to school, come back and write; but when they get back home, I can't concentrate. I do lots of drafts. My editors also make points like, 'Chetan, for your readership the word "cognizable" may not work.' I know my critics think I'm a lowbrow hack but . . .

Lowbrow formula writer, commercial-minded and playing to the gallery. Does such criticism hurt?

Call it what you will but if I were writing to please critics it would mean that many readers in the country would not be able to read my books. I would think that selfish. Think of the thrill when a young Indian kid from a Hindi-medium school reads an English book, and enjoys it; his self-confidence is changed forever. He will put it on his resumé, 'I read in English.' That is a very big thing for me. A writer wants impact. Some writers want aesthetics and want to be appreciated for it. I am more about impact.

Your outreach with four novels has in fact been so massive that you have actually given up a very well-paid career in banking to become a full-time writer. Any regrets?

I don't think there are any regrets. I'm a happier person. Of course I make less money than what I would have with two jobs. But writing for me, compared to a well-paid banking career, is an incredible experience. What is money really? Someone once said that whatever money you keep in the bank the day you die is the extra work you have done. It's money you shouldn't have. There's no point.

But you're still doing double duty, as writer and house husband, while your wife, as a professional banker, is the regular breadwinner. Is that tough?

Yes, it's very hard. Now my wife comes home and says, why hasn't this bill been paid and why is there no gobi in the house? I have to give an answer. I need to keep the dhobi account. I just paid the milkman's bill before I took the flight to come here. But it's fun and I'm very lucky. Sometimes I feel that in my whole IIM batch I'm the only guy who is in the park with his children on a Tuesday afternoon. They are working in a bank, making rich people richer. I am trying to make some kids read. I think that's kind of cool.

Three of your four novels have been turned into screenplays. Do you see books-into-films as the bigger opportunity?

If I want to reach out to the public, knowing that Indians love films, the answer is yes. It's a good avenue to earn more and it's a challenge for me. Now I am more involved in the film adaptations of my books because I've left my job. And I also want to learn to write scripts. At the time of *3 Idiots* I couldn't. I wasn't even in India. Now I want to master scripts. In fact for two years I will only do screenplays.

As a professional screenplay writer will you write original stories or do you hope to write to order for film-makers?

That's a very good question because no matter how commercial I may seem, I have written my stories in my own way. Someone may say that a superstar wants a script, can you write it and, I would say no, I can't. I have not sold my soul. Broadly, Chetan Bhagat is going to use Bollywood, and Bollywood is not going to use Chetan Bhagat.

September 2009

Upamanyu Chatterjee

Upamanyu Chatterjee (b. 1959) is a prime example of a group sometimes lumped together as the 'St Stephen's and civil service' school of writers. But given their disparate backgrounds and forms of writing, it isn't quite as clubby a group. Born in Patna, Chatterjee grew up in Delhi, the son of an official, and joined the Indian Administrative Service in 1983 as a member of the Maharashtra cadre.

His first novel, *English, August: An Indian Story* (1988), later made into a successful art house feature film, became an instant cult classic. A study in boredom and torpor in that decade of drift, it follows a year in the life of Agastya Sen—nicknamed August by his friends—a novice administrator posted in Madna, 'the hottest town in India'. Displaced and disconnected, August passes his days smoking pot, masturbating and observing the petty bureaucracies of a distant outpost in a jaundiced haze.

Chatterjee has steadily built upon that early success in four more novels and a growing fan following. His subject matter and narrative structures have grown dense as he applies his mordant wit to dysfunctional families in a decaying urban landscape. In *The Last Burden* (1994), he introduces the eccentric brothers Jamun and Burfi, their parents and a network of relatives and retainers, who personify decrepitude, loss, unrealized ambitions and furtive, often unfulfilled sexual longings. The family reappears in his most recent novel, *Way to Go* (2010).

Chatterjee's voice is consistently and darkly comic; and as might be expected of such a writer he is, in person, a difficult interview—at once sombre and reflective, disarmingly funny and flippant. His dedication to his craft however remains unassailable, not an easy double role as he adroitly manages a career as a senior bureaucrat.

These two interviews, combined as one, were both recorded in his Delhi home after the publication of his two most recent novels, *Weight Loss* and *Way to Go*.

In a way, all your books in the twenty years up to *Weight Loss* are about the same character or type of character. They are rites-of-passage novels about young men coming to terms in a dysfunctional world . . .

Yes and no. The character is the same in *English, August* and *The Last Burden* and in *Weight Loss* too, but in *The Mammaries of the Welfare State* the central character wasn't essential. He was marginal to the concerns of the book which were comic, more than anything else. For the other three, yes, it's the central character that is my main concern.

***Weight Loss* is about a young boy straining to be slim. On the other hand, it could have been called 'Weight Loss and Sex Search' because a lot of it is about adolescent and adult sex. Bhola is a tragicomic figure, which is also true of your other protagonists. They are picaresque characters but do they think of themselves as funny, or are they observed as comic?**

Weight Loss is meant in all its senses—as metaphor for a kind of fear of emotional commitment. He is unable to take on baggage that he feels he can't handle—weight both physical and mental, I guess.

I think my central characters are self-observant and, at the same time, very self-conscious. It is not as though they are being funny, but they are conscious of feeling ridiculous.

They come from the same milieu. Some like Agastya Sen in *English, August* are civil servants like you. Many of your books are set among the urban English-speaking middle class. To what extent is the material autobiographical?

A lot actually. Some clever guy said that people who write fiction need not write autobiographies. It is not like turning something that happened to you into fiction but you are looking for incidents that will reflect something that you have been thinking about. That is true for all writers of fiction.

The reason the characters are English-speaking is because it's as though I need English as the extra filter through which one can sift the world portrayed in the books. In *Weight Loss*, for example, much is made of the fact that the people Bhola falls in love with don't speak English, but he does and so one language is being set off against another.

The social context is similar in my books because it is the world that I know and the world that interests me. It doesn't mean you cover each and every inch of your life but you return in each book to the ideas that interest you. Even when you cover them in one book, those ideas don't exhaust their interest for you, so you go back to them again and again.

Since 1988 you have regularly produced one novel, on average, every five years. Is that the way your creative life is carved up because you have a professional career as an IAS officer?

I always intend to publish a book to coincide with each Olympics, slow and steady, but if I look back I am three or four years behind schedule.

Death, disappearance and disintegration—everyone in your latest novel, *Way to Go*, a sequel to *The Last Burden*, is falling apart—from the dying father Shyamanand who disappears, to his two sons Jamun and Burfi, to the characters in the decaying middle-class neighbourhood corroded by the sea air. The tone is often mordantly comic. Is it a black comedy of corrupt, collapsing and grasping new India?

The characters are just human beings. At one point in the book, early on, I say that 'life was simple but dreadful'. The book is a kind of an elaboration of that theme but I don't see it as black, at least not as black as its predecessor was. *The Last Burden* is I think the blackest of the tribe after *Weight Loss*. This I find is a graceful song, a nice way to say goodbye to the characters.

I see the decay all around me; it's a way of looking at the world and it's there in all my books. Most people identify me with *English, August* because it is by far the most accessible but possibly also the funniest. So in some ways readers are disappointed that the later novels are not as funny but decay is funny, too, isn't it? We are all struggling against something which is not worth struggling against. And to me, that is funny.

Apart from old protagonists, *Way to Go* introduces a new cast, some of them typical of new urban India—Monga the land-shark hovering like a vulture to take over the old houses, and the TV producer Kasturi making a serial called *Cheers Zindagi*. Are these satiric inventions?

Satire is not primarily the intention of the book. It is a book that is played out in the head. It is not a book about India going to the dogs, no, not at all and, therefore, not a book about decay. I see characters like Monga and Kasturi as part of urban life anywhere in India; they are dreadful even when you encounter them in your daily lives. But they are not the book's target. It is just that you need them for the atmosphere. *Way to Go* is not even ironic. If you die, if you leave behind this emptiness that your sons try to fill up, that is the way to go. It is Shyamanand's way of saying goodbye. In *Way to Go* the two brothers finally find each other. It is one of the reasons why I thought *The Last Burden* was incomplete. Even though I shouldn't be saying it, I like the way the two brothers, at the end of the book, finally reconcile to both the loss of their father and to finding an added value to their relationship.

Do you revise and rewrite a lot to find your balance between the dark, decrepit world you create with its picaresque observations?

I am always terrified by the heavy passages. I need to get them down because finally those are what the book is about, but I keep thinking, 'Oh my God, no one's going to read this,' and then I think that this has to be made funny so that people can turn the page. If you have a dirty mind, then what you think of as funny is more often, to your surprise, just disgusting. It takes a long time to decide whether it is funny or disgusting. Comedy is a great page-turner, more than a thriller.

Is J.D. Salinger one of your literary heroes? Many of your characters are as dysfunctional as *Franny and Zooey* and members of the Glass family . . .

I loved *The Catcher in the Rye* when I first read it and then I made the mistake of reading it again. There are certain books that one should never reread. *English, August* was compared to it. They said it wasn't really Indian. That seemed a bit off the mark but *English, August* is about feeling out of place in your own country, which is very disturbing.

You joined the IAS in 1983 and belong to that club labelled the St Stephen's and civil service group of after-hours writers. You are a consistent writer and have produced five novels in twenty years. How does the double life of being an after-hours writer work for you?

Well, before hours actually. I have a habit of getting up early in the morning, working for a bit before I leave the house, and if a have a bright idea—which is very rare—then I try and come back and finish before I get to bed. I am comfortable now with a double life. I actually set myself a certain number of words a day, or how to resolve an idea or a problem in the plot, as a kind of target. Then I sit down and peg away. Sometimes I achieve that target just before I go to bed.

Is one life an escape from the other?

No, because it has been twenty years of doing my quota of words every day; it is almost as automatic as shaving. One life doesn't intrude on the other. You close the shutters down when you move from one to another, quite akin to people who jog five kilometres a day before going to work. It's difficult not to work at it if you're on vacation because, just like going back to jogging after a gap, you have to start from scratch. That's why I try and work every day.

January 2006 and March 2010

William Dalrymple

In 1984 at the age of twenty-two, William Dalrymple took an ambitious, even audacious step that forever marked his life. Just out of Cambridge as an undergraduate, he set off to look for the 'stately pleasure dome' in Xanadu decreed by Kubla Khan in the opening lines of Samuel Taylor Coleridge's famous poem. Out of that journey, from Jerusalem to modern-day Shangdu in northern China, came *In Xanadu*, a first book that interleaved Dalrymple's high-spirited exuberance and irreverent observation with the hardship and endurance of the best of well-paced travellers' tales.

It was an auspicious and widely applauded beginning, but Dalrymple is not one to rest on laurels for long. He had briefly passed through India and Pakistan on the Xanadu journey, but memories of India lingered from an earlier trip he had made in 1984 as a student-backpacker. In 1989 he decided to move to Delhi as a journalist, inviting Olivia Fraser, the talented water-colourist and his future wife, to join him, and wrote *City of Djinns* (1993): it was an invigorating exploration of Delhi, ancient and modern capital, uncovering its layered past and presenting it in an unconventional, inventive way. Dalrymple kept up his prolific output, producing *The Age of Kali* (1998), a collection of essays on India, and venturing into documentaries with *Stones of the Raj*, a six-part television series. Returning to Britain, he undertook another major journey: *From the Holy Mountain: A Journey in the Shadow of Byzantium* (1997) traces the links between Islam and Christianity in the Middle East, and many, including myself, consider it the most insightful and rewarding of his travel books.

By unexpected chance, I got to know William Dalrymple from the moment he landed as a young journalist in Delhi in 1989. The late Bruce Chatwin's wife had introduced us the year before and I first met him in a Soho pub in London. He was desperate to find a place in Delhi and, on the spur of the moment, I offered him the use of a ramshackle barsati on top of my family house. My brother who lived there was going away for a while and he could rent it in his absence. 'Willie', as he is affectionately known to friends, immediately said yes.

Even then, he was a demanding and electrifying presence. Thumping the table over an impromptu dinner, he would pose questions like, 'Do you realize the deposits of history that lie unrecorded, here, in Delhi?' or 'Why have the stories of this great magical beast called India that has lain on the globe for millennia not been told as they should be?' Questions hard to answer after a long day's work. What I remember most of those evenings is our three-year-old daughter becoming hysterical with delight at this large, pink person 'banging on' (in one of his favourite phrases). She would dissolve into paroxysms of giggles and refuse to go to bed.

Willie enlarged his oeuvre—and also, as his friends tease, vastly expanded his girth—by his obsession with India, to search deeper into the complexity of the Indo-British colonial encounter. *White Mughals* (2002), when it appeared, was an instant hit with readers in both Britain and India: in a globalized world, it harked back to the affectionate relationship, often romantically intimate, between Indians and foreigners in eighteenth-century India. It brought together his gifts of storytelling and historical narrative and his journalist's ear for conversation into an immensely readable whole. By this time, Dalrymple had moved back to Delhi with his wife and three children, spending the larger part of each year here. His next book, *The Last Mughal: The Fall of a Dynasty, Delhi 1857* (2006), proved his most ambitious enterprise yet: he achieved his aim by enlisting the aid of young scholars such as Mahmood Farooqui (who later produced his own remarkable history, *Besieged: Voices from Delhi 1857*) to translate hundreds of documents by Delhi's citizens in that tumultuous year, written in the *shikasth* Urdu script, that had lain virtually unseen in the National Archives for 150 years.

Lately, he has veered off in other directions: as an explorer of religion in modern India and, more effectively, as a literary and cultural impresario—involved in organizing the hugely successful Jaipur Literature Festival and carting bands of Sufi singers, Kerala dancers and Bengal's Bauls, from Tina Brown's party in Manhattan to the Sydney Opera House.

He has appeared on *Just Books* on several occasions but this, his most recent and complete interview, was recorded in the bar of the Imperial Hotel in Delhi which, fittingly, is called 'Patiala Peg', after the publication of his last book *Nine Lives* (2009).

Nine Lives **takes you in a different direction from your other journeys; it explores the lives of individuals in various parts of India involved in aspects of religion or esoteric religious practice. What made you choose the subject?**

India is transforming itself at the most extraordinary speed, but religion is not separate from society, so my picks were caste, lineage and the pressures of society that affect people in the way they live. I decided to look at nine different individuals, a Buddhist monk, a Sufi saint, a Jain nun and so on, to see how each separate traditional vocation was reacting to change and how each was caught in a different way by modernity.

Caught by modernity yet trapped by old beliefs such as the devadasis in Karnataka, traditionally driven to prostitution at the shrine of the goddess Yellamma. And many nowadays infected by HIV/AIDS. Does the sacred go hand in hand with the profane?

Every single person in this book is affected in some way by modernity, and the devadasis likewise. Devadasis in medieval India often had very high status; they were the great dancers and singers. Bharatanatyam originated with them; Chola princesses would become devadasis. Many devadasis were not simple prostitutes, but had a high status in temples—they looked after the sanctuary and were consorts of the deity which meant looking after the idol. In many ways they were more like nuns than prostitutes. Then legislation—well-meaning initially—in colonial and post-colonial times made the institution illegal but it didn't kill it, though it cut its link with the temples and destroyed the devadasis' high status. Today the devadasis are almost all Dalits and, frankly, their lives are little different from prostitutes working in brothels in Mumbai or in Delhi. Yet in their minds, it is entirely different.

The world of Karnataka's devadasis is oppressive but the lives of theyyam dancers in Kerala, who are also Dalits, are almost schizophrenic. How did you penetrate their double life?

I was attracted to the story because I thought that the dancers looked amazing in tourist literature and books on Kerala. I went there but I was not aware of the extraordinary social change that takes place when these people perform in the two-month theyyam season from December to February. For two months their life changes—people who are normally shunned, like manual labourers, take part in the dance. The hero of my story, Hari Das, is a manual labourer but during the weekend works in the Tellicherry jail which houses RSS convicts. The CPM convicts are held in the rival Kannur jail. The prisoners don't mix; they would be murdered if they ended up in the wrong jail. So the story got more interesting.

Why did you choose the form of profiles for exploring such a complex and touchy subject?

There is a very particular reason for me choosing to write the book this way. When you write about Indian religion as a westerner, I think there is a great danger because there are so many potential minefields you are negotiating. You don't want to sound orientalist or exoticize, to be like Allen Ginsberg and the dharma bums freaking out on the banks of the Ganges in Varanasi. All that has been done to death and yet, it seems to me, the subject of these extraordinary, diverse and very plural ways of reaching God is a legitimate subject. It does affect millions of people in India still and it's not a world removed from modern India. There is one scene, for example, where I am talking to a Tantric skull collector. On the one hand he is an exotic and extreme figure following an extreme religious path. Yet when I talk to him he's sitting there listening to the radio: 'India is 94 for no loss.' This is the way things work. These people are not disconnected.

You've been living on and off in India for many years but do you fear a backlash of misunderstanding when exploring difficult, contentious subjects like esoteric religion or the rebellion of 1857?

Since I turned up here twenty-five years ago in 1984, I have never on a single occasion felt any personal danger. About treading on sensitivities I think, in general, as long as you tread respectfully and honestly and do not wax lyrical about the Raj, people are amazingly forgiving in this country. It's a great measure of India's self-confidence that I am allowed to survive here.

In 1989 when you were twenty-two you made a great overland journey from Jerusalem to Inner Mongolia, described in your first book *In Xanadu*. In what way was that first encounter with India significant, making you return to live in Delhi and write *City of Djinns*?

I first came to India before that in 1984. Like millions of other kids I was on a year off from university. It was then that I fell in love with India. I had never travelled before and had hardly been to Europe. I came from a very sheltered background in Scotland. I think India had a very dramatic, almost devastating effect on me. I worked in Mother Teresa's home in Kolkata and later taught Indian history at a smart Christian Brothers school in Dehradun. I travelled all over, like millions of westerners do, with a backpack. It was like a lightning strike in my life. Everything before the 26th of January 1984 is one life. The rest is really in India.

It was interesting how things developed because when *City of Djinns* came out it didn't get the acclaim initially that *In Xanadu* had got. I was very lucky with my first book. It came out at a time when a travel book was regarded as a special thing, people were very excited about it and it had immediate success. *City of Djinns* did well in Britain but people in India were quite spotty in their reviews. I got them out the other day and there were some good ones. But in general people seemed quite suspicious about this gora turning up and talking to them about their capital city. And now you see the pirated edition at the traffic lights in Delhi. Books are like children, they lead their own lives after you publish them. After their twenty-first birthday, they're off doing their own thing. Sometimes they get up there and sometimes they sink.

Whereas *City of Djinns* was both an exploration and an excavation of Delhi, your foray into Indian history began with *White Mughals*—about the complex, intimate relationship between British colonists and Indians from the late eighteenth century to the mid nineteenth century. How did that develop as a story for you?

It coincided with a big change in my life, which was the birth of my first daughter. I had just come back from a big journey around the Middle East. There is a book of mine, *From the Holy Mountain*, that few people know of, though some think it is my best. After that, having a small kid at home, the sudden urge to set off with a backpack to somewhere like Afghanistan immediately diminished. I suddenly lost interest in long-distance travel because it meant being away from the young one.

So domestic compulsions made you change track?

Domestic aspirations, actually. It was a pleasure to be at home rather than a duty to be there. So I ended up writing a book that involved going to libraries in London rather than travelling the world; that's how *White Mughals* started though it had its roots in *City of Djinns*. There was a character in *City of Djinns*, William Fraser, who very much did the White Mughal thing. He was a scholar of Persian, a friend of Abdul Aziz of the big madrasa in Old Delhi, a major cultural figure of his time, and he intrigued me. It turned out that in every other court—Hyderabad, Lucknow and Pune—there were similar British figures who fell in love with India in the eighteenth century and had none of the attitudes that one associates with colonial figures working through the will of East India Company officers. I found that, statistically, one in three British men in India in the 1780s was leaving all their worldly goods to Indian women. In other words, at least a third of these men were cohabiting openly and legally with Indian wives.

Each of your books is quite distinctive, each different from the other. Is that a recipe for success?

I keep on trying to change, just to keep it fresh. Certainly *White Mughals* was a big change in terms of sales. It got on the British equivalent of the popular Oprah show and sold a quarter of a million copies in a week. It was like a magic touch.

I am lucky enough to be a writer. One can choose one's path and so, in my life, I have been able to be a journalist, do a bit of television and, in the last ten years, I have been writing history books. You don't have to define yourself. You can follow your own instincts and interests.

From *White Mughals* you went on to explore one of the most embattled periods of Indo-British history in *The Last Mughal,* a life of Bahadur Shah Zafar against the backdrop of 1857. What was it like to change gears—from drawing a portrait of relative adjustment in the Indo-British relationship to one of bitter enmity and bloodshed?

It is extraordinary how quickly the relationship changed from the mutual cultural interchange of the 1780s to 1800s to the complete polarization and hatred of 1857. You could see it statistically in the wills; the same wills which show one in three British men cohabitating with Indian women in 1780s is down to one in four in 1800, one in five by 1810 and one in seven by 1820. By 1830 there is virtually no legal cohabitation that you can trace in the records. So you move from a world of extraordinary multiculturalism to an apartheid world in only fifty years. That is a very radical shift; alongside it come attitudes of superiority, straightforward racism and the theories of racial hierarchy that reach their most noxious form in the Holocaust, with the Nazis proclaiming that Aryans are the master race and Jews are sub-humans. The British behaved more like Nazis than any British historian would like to admit. It was straightforward racial hatred unleashed on a hideous scale. Delhi was the scene of a small but awful genocide after the rumour mills got going with entirely false stories about British women being raped. The British, when they finally took Delhi, determined to kill every adult male that they could find within the city's walls.

Historian, travel writer, journalist and documentary filmmaker—to these roles you've added that of becoming a cultural and literary impresario, running the successful literature festival in Jaipur and taking Baul singers and theyyam dancers round the world. How did that happen?

I'm enjoying it. It beats sitting in the National Archives for ten years.

October 2009

Shobhaa Dé

One of the main transitions in Shobhaa Dé's varied and colourful life as successful model, editor, columnist and author is that from creating celebrities she became one, and from writing racy fiction she has, in the popular imagination, assumed some of the attributes of a quasi-fictional character. In real life, Shobhaa Dé (b. 1948) is energetic, feisty, often funny, and glamorous in the manner of a carefully groomed, mature rock star or diva—cascades of glossy hair, outsize shades, bold printed saris and chunky jewellery.

Once at a book fair in Europe, where she was promoting paperback translations of her fiction, piled high behind her in stacks, I began my piece to camera by saying, 'And here they are calling Shobhaa Dé the Jackie Collins of India . . .' She grabbed the mike from my hand, looked directly into the camera lens, and quipped, 'You're quite wrong. It's in LA that they call Jackie Collins the Shobhaa Dé of America . . .'

As a conservative civil servant's daughter, Shobhaa Dé had an old-fashioned upbringing. She broke into Mumbai's modelling world while an undergraduate at St. Xavier's College and became a much sought-after face of advertising campaigns in the 1970s. Switching to journalism, she made a name as editor of magazines such as *Stardust*, *Society* and *Celebrity*, a widely read columnist and, latterly, a blogger. Her foray into fiction began with *Socialite Evenings* (1989) and continued with several steamy best-sellers including *Starry Nights* (1989) and *Sultry Days* (1994) that earned her the sobriquet of 'Sultana of Sleaze'. Twice-married, with six children, she has produced non-fiction as prolifically: a memoir titled *Selective Memory* (1998), a book of letters *Speedpost* (1999), her views on marriage in *Spouse* (2005) and, casting her net wider in *Superstar India* (2008), on changing India as she turned sixty.

These two interviews, conflated as one, took place in Delhi and Mumbai following the publication of *Spouse* and *Superstar India*.

Your last book *Speedpost*, promoted by the Indian post office, were letters to your children about the problems of parents with adolescents. You were a sort of agony aunt, and now with *Spouse*, you have turned marriage counsellor. Why?

It seemed like a natural progression. Marriage has fascinated me for a very long time. We live in a very marriage-obsessed society and it was the right book at the right time for the right audience.

Somehow one doesn't connect Shobhaa Dé with the institution of marriage. After fiction like *Sultry Days* and *Starry Nights*, one may think you were up to everything outside marriage?

Oh dear. I'm so sorry to disappoint all those people getting vicarious thrills fantasizing about my life. But the truth is that fiction is what liberates you from your own conformist, conventional thinking and living, and a lot of people who write fiction perhaps don't venture into non-fiction, which I have, and I enjoy it. Non-fiction is where I put my opinions on the line. Fiction is fantasy.

In *Spouse* you emerge as a sort of neo-con on marriage. You almost advocate arranged marriages over love marriages and you say the joint family system is terrific. So much easier, you say, for someone else to roast baingan for baingan bharta.

I really believe that was the strength of the whole institution of marriages in India. It allowed young couples to discover themselves without the stress and pressure that they seem to be encountering now. They had support systems. It was a comfort zone and there were elders to guide them when they went wrong, who could soften the blows and absorb little things that require adjustments in the early years of marriage. There was someone to take care of the babies. Young people today are not going into marriage because they don't want the responsibility of a child. Where is the time for working couples? They don't have time for sex, forget the babies.

So will the institution of marriage survive?

It's a tough call. Women have driven this change largely, not just in India, but all over the world. Marriage is no longer a meal ticket. They no longer need marriage as a security blanket.

Meal ticket or male ticket?

Meal and male both actually, you are right. They are saying, why marriage? They can have relationships outside marriage that society no longer condemns. They are earning their own money, they don't need a man to support them. Soon, they won't even need a man to make a baby. They can get it off a test tube. Why do they actually need men at all? But you do want someone to cuddle up with at night.

A lot of the early part of *Spouse* has a touchy-feely tone about keeping marriages going, all cuddles and cooing chat. Is that the foundation of a good marriage?

I completely believe it is because there is a four-letter word; it's not the one we are all thinking about but actually it's called 'talk' and most marriages today are collapsing because there isn't enough investment in 'talk'. What I see young couples discussing is exchange of quick information 'Where you going?', 'I am going to be there', 'What time do we catch up?', 'We have to go there tonight', 'We don't have to go there', 'Cancel that', 'Fix that' . . .

I call them the Post-it marriages because a lot of it is non-verbal. It's just little notes stuck on the refrigerator. They know so little about each other's emotional rhythms and physical rhythms. There is no time to connect physically, psychologically and emotionally, so what are they doing with one another?

Love is the bedrock of good marriages, according to you. That's tricky. What about that thin line between love and lust?

Keeping lust on the boil is tricky, I agree. There's a Gujarati saying which, roughly translated, says that the only true image of a marriage is the one provided by the quilt that covers the couple, because the quilt gives you the true picture of any marriage. I think sex is a vital and a key component. If you don't have great sex, chances are that it is just a companionship.

There is a chapter in your book called 'Raat Baki, Baat Baki' which touches upon other subjects such as adultery. How do you suggest handling adultery in modern life?

I have never seen a marriage survive in its wholeness or in its beauty after an adulterous affair. It's not that it's not possible. I see a lot of marriages trundling along twenty to thirty years later with multiple partners for both. I really wouldn't call that a marriage. I would call it an arrangement. Something vital is missing and that is trust.

You're a pretty old-fashioned girl, aren't you?

Yes, raised old-fashioned. Good *ghati* girl with Maharashtrian middle-class values. What is the one test in a good marriage? It is that when you go to bed at night with the person sleeping by your side, you should have the confidence, even in the middle of the night, to wake that person up, that he or she will be there for you for whatever reason. It could be something trivial, or something happy, or a crisis. That's a marriage with meaning, a marriage worth cherishing.

This is your second marriage. You come from one failed marriage, so is it a case of twice married that reaffirms your belief in the institution?

I saw a very stable marriage with my own parents. They were married for close to sixty years before my mother passed away. And it was a very communicative marriage, a lively marriage. I always wanted it for myself. And children, yes. Lots of kids. If a marriage goes wrong I believe every human being deserves that second chance and you should be able to be honest about what went wrong and not play the blame game. You should ask yourself where you failed.

You lay the blame for failed marriages on bad old Bollywood. Surely marriages go wrong for many reasons other than movies?

Bollywood is a most potent and powerful influence in marriages going wrong—whether it be *Devdas*, the old *Devdas*, or something like *Mujhse Shaadi Karogi*—and the representation of marriage in the whole gamut of Bollywood films. I would also pin it down to films like *Hum Aapke Hain Kaun*, with the idea of marriage being the end-all and be-all of anybody's life.

I want to ask you, and your readers do too, why all your books—*Starry Nights, Sultry Days, Socialite Evenings* and *Spouse*—begin with the letter 's'? And, lately, you have added an extra 'a' to your name Shobhaa. Does 's' stand for superstition?

'S' stands for superstition and, yes, Shobhaa begins with 's' but, more than that, it has a nice resonance. I am very visually vulnerable. 'S' has always worked for me whether it was when I began *Stardust*, *Society* and *Savvy*. As far as the additional 'a' goes, it has again more to do with visual imagery. I had six 'Shobhas' in my class. I felt I didn't have an identity to call my own because we were 'Shobha 1', 'Shobha 2', 'Shobha 3' etc. The additional 'a' makes that Shobhaa—a name I really hate and loathe—stand apart from the garden-variety Shobha. That's all.

December 2005

Your fifteenth book, *Superstar India,* in your sixtieth year almost coincides with India turning sixty. India has changed dramatically in these sixty years but how has Shobhaa Dé changed?

I think the most dramatic change is an inward-looking phase of my life. At the same time I want to break the whole stereotype of women at sixty. I want to say that life can begin in your sixth decade and it can easily be the most productive decade of your life, if you will it. I have always broken through familiar moulds, which I find boring, and I hope I remain as unpredictable at sixty, and more so, than ever before. I have always gone with my inner voice, like Sonia Gandhi, and followed my feelings, my gut instinct and done what my heart compels me to do.

There is a story you tell in your autobiography, *Selective Memory,* about a woman online asking you how you preserved yourself. What did you say to her?

In vinegar, of course, that I soak myself in a tub full of vinegar. And she went on to ask, 'Do you also splash it on your face?' and I said, 'Five times a day.' Now that I have turned sixty a lot of women come up and ask me the same thing. Very recently in Goa, there was someone, a fashion designer I might add, who stared at my back and at my neck, and said that Botox fixes the face but what have you done to your back? I am beginning to feel like a bit of a museum piece or a medical miracle and very soon I am going to start charging tickets.

Your public may regard you as a sacred or profane monster at sixty, but your first phase of fame came with the creation of *Stardust* magazine in the 1970s. You were its editor for over ten years. How and why did *Stardust* give film writing and film gossip a new break?

Bollywood was not what it is now and showbiz without masala, without scandal, without gossip, is not showbiz. Showbiz goes hand in hand with all that *Stardust* eventually chronicled. At that time we only had PR journalism, and we have gone back to PR journalism again because of commercial interests. *Stardust* broke all the rules. It was witty and stylish, ahead of its time, and the film industry took its own time to get used to the idea.

After *Stardust* you entered a phase in the 1980s when you were badly down on your luck. You were jobless with little money. *Celebrity* magazine that you started didn't take off, you had to sell it, your marriage broke up and you had to completely reinvent yourself from scratch. People may imagine that Shobhaa Dé had it easy but it wasn't so.

True. Shall I just be very honest and say that those turning points reminded me of my own strengths and there was not a moment, even during the lowest period, when I felt defeated. I was never a martyr and I never saw myself as a victim, which is what I keep telling women today. All of us are entitled to make some mistakes in our lives and we do. But how you cope with them is what defines your character. So I was never down and out and, like Scarlett O' Hara, I said there is always a tomorrow. I lived for that and I worked very hard to get on top of things all over again.

One of the things you chronicle in your current book are the incredible changes in the Indian media. How has it changed in your opinion?

I would say media has lost its teeth, its claws are missing and the fire in the belly is gone. There is no such thing as dissent, no informed opinion, not enough background research and no investigative journalism worth the name. Journalism and journalists have been co-opted into the system, so there's nothing anti-establishment left. There is no anger, no outrage and no angst.

Another issue that concerns you is the new materialism. Your social commentary and books are devoted to the faults of the get-rich-quick and spend-it-quicker generation of the urban young and you contrast it to the way you were brought up. What's the difference between your children's attitudes and yours?

For example, my nineteen-year-old is so brand-obsessed. She says, 'Oh, Mom, please stop it. We are all like that.' And she is probably right and maybe I am missing the point. But does that stop me from nagging? No it doesn't. Waste is something that I feel very strongly about because we were brought up to value water resources, never keep the tap on while brushing our teeth, switch off lights and fans when we left the room and never waste a morsel of food on our plate. Meat and fish were Sunday treats, never taken for granted. All that has gone with the 'me' generation. Now it's all about themselves, their personal goals and personal targets. There is huge social change out there, both good and bad.

I'm a strong proponent of marriage because I believe in the old Indian social structure of kutumb—of the family being not just your nuclear family but extended family and, therefore, also community and country. It is the basis of stability to which every country aspires. Foreigners envy us and say, 'Look at your families and how you have kept it all together.' I think that's breaking down and, for me, it's definitely a worry.

As an official's daughter you grew up in various parts of the country but it is Mumbai where you came of age and Mumbai that made you. But many people think that this great metropolis has lost its cosmopolitan spirit, its politics are bigoted and it's a city in decline. Do you agree?

You sound like a typical Delhiwala passing judgement on Mumbai with such élan. It isn't a city in decline and I do not agree that it's in a deplorable state. There are deplorable people in this city who are intolerant, who want to kick out anybody who is not a *marathi manoos*. Being marathi manoos myself, I can with total confidence say that this is not the average Marathi's feeling. Why should we allow politicians' agendas to give the city a bad name? We still have five hundred families coming to Bombay every day and no one leaves. Yes, the infrastructure of the city really sucks and we have not had the kind of leadership that a city like Mumbai deserves. We have put up with completely inefficient governments who have done nothing for the city. I think the party is about to end because the average marathi manoos is not in a mood to tolerate anyone, whether one of their own, or someone thrust on them via Delhi, who continues to give Mumbai such an awful name.

April 2008

Anita Desai

The novelist Anita Desai (b. 1937) is reluctant to give interviews. She is by nature a retiring person and, like many writers, reticent on the subject of her craft. She has also lived away from India for many years, mainly teaching in America, and returns on private family visits. My efforts to interview her proved abortive until 2006 when she was given the Grinzane Cavour prize, a prestigious Italian literary award, in the city of Turin. It was an event celebrating Indian writers and Desai, who has a wide readership in Italy, spontaneously acceded to my request. To help her comfort level, we decided to shoot in a park near the hotel, and on that fine morning, she opened up beautifully as we strolled in its flower-filled gardens.

Graceful, gentle and grey-haired, she is as quietly observant and as elegantly nuanced in speech as in her writing.

Born Anita Mazumdar to a German mother and Bengali father, she grew up in Old Delhi, took a degree in English literature from Miranda House and, at twenty-one, married Ashvin Desai, a business executive. Although she wrote from an early age, her skills as a novelist were honed as 'a secret activity' from the quotidian concerns of running a household and raising four children.

Characters trapped by, or breaking free from, the confines of family life recur in novels such as *Clear Light of Day* (1980) and *Fasting, Feasting* (1999). The isolation is intensified in protagonists like the Urdu poet Nur in *In Custody* (1984) and the Jewish émigré in *Baumgartner's Bombay* (1988), against the richly evoked backdrop of cities in decay.

In the late 1980s, Anita Desai distinguished herself as teacher of creative writing at colleges abroad and became emeritus professor of humanities at the Massachusetts Institute of Technology. Living in America also changed the trajectory of writing; her most recent novel, *The Zigzag Way* (2004), is set in Mexico. Although nominated for the Booker Prize three times, it was her daughter Kiran Desai who won it in 2006.

The year after the Turin interview, Anita Desai returned to India on the occasion of the republication of her three best-known novels with new introductions by Salman Rushdie, Suketu Mehta and Kamila Shamsie. This time, she generously agreed to a special studio recording that I moderated, with questions from an invited audience of students and teachers of English literature and aspiring writers. A sample is appended at the end to indicate the kind of questions a famous author and teacher is asked.

~

It's ten years since you went to live in America as a teacher of creative writing at well-known colleges such as Smith, Mount Holyoke and MIT. How did the transition from India to America occur and the change from being a full-time writer to a double life of teaching and writing?

I think there came a moment when I broke away. It was first by going to Cambridge, England, and then being offered a position at Smith in the United States. And then, finding myself truly an outsider, I cut adrift completely, even from India.

How did that affect your writing? I recall you once saying that you didn't see yourself as a 'traditional Indian writer' and that your subject, your canvas, could be from anywhere.

I think that it happened gradually. I had never thought I would write about any place other than India. When I first went to the United States, the experience was so overwhelming that I thought India had vanished and I wouldn't be able to write about it again. It was very frightening because I was not at all certain that I could write about the west. And I sat down and started writing and the next book happened to be about India too. It was *Fasting, Feasting.*

I allowed America to step in a little bit there. But I realized while writing it that I wasn't going to lose India. I was carrying it with me. It was on my back like a tortoise shell all the time. At the same time, the world did begin to open up. It grew wider and that is how I stepped into Mexico.

Yes, your fourteenth novel, *The Zigzag Way,* set in Mexico takes you into new territory and weaves in Mexican, American and English

characters and their countries. What took you to Mexico and this new direction?

I was teaching and living in the United States and, quite frankly, wished to escape winters in Boston when I first went to Mexico. But the minute I landed there, I knew this was a country I was going to write about.

And what was the reason for that immediate affinity?

It was a strange combination of what was totally familiar and totally unknown. It was familiar because it was so much like India. Like India, it's an ancient country. Every stone, every bit of earth there, is ancient. There are so many stories to tell. On the other hand, it was new territory for me. And that's why it took me so long to write a very little book. I travelled a lot, I spent long stretches of time, and it took me many years to focus on one subject.

Although set in Mexico, many of the key characters in *The Zigzag Way* are foreigners. It is a short novel but its span of history and geography is large.

Yes, I distilled it down to the very essentials that I wanted to focus on. By then I had myself become an outsider, a marginal character. So my characters tended to be outsiders who happen to be in Mexico and to share different little bits of its history which is very long.

Many of your memorable protagonists are living on the edge, whether Nur the Urdu poet in *In Custody* or the Jewish refugee in *Baumgartner's Bombay*. Are you drawn to 'marginal characters' as you call them?

I suppose I am. Not deliberately, not consciously even, but I have chosen characters who don't quite belong and who are, therefore, searching. And that is the phase that interests me, people who are searching because they belong nowhere.

What has the experience of teaching creative writing taught you?

It has taught me a great deal. Everything I know about the United States has been through my students. To be in touch with young people is what put me in touch with the country. And it was a challenge. I had to teach myself how to teach because I had no idea how to do it. The students were marvellous. They were willing to help me find my way.

And because I taught writing—they were writing students, writing about themselves—I was allowed to look into their lives which I wouldn't have [been able to] otherwise.

Have these years of being away, of becoming the outsider, made you take a detached view of India, a country in rapid transition?

I think it's impossible to feel detached about India, one just can't. I am certainly in touch with the old India, the India I knew. And now when I visit India, I realize that this is not the India I know anything about. It has become almost a foreign country to me; it has changed so much. Political changes have been grave and very violent at times. That's on the top level, but underneath is the enormous change brought about by the new wealth. That is where I am completely lost because I think that is what has really changed life for young Indians, the quality of life in India. It's something I don't know at all. But, yes, Indians are so much more aware now and have a great new confidence. I think that is what is different. India has a tremendous confidence in itself and I think people are ready to take their destinies in their own hands, which never happened before.

Before your first novel *Cry, The Peacock* came out in 1963 you were a young housewife bringing up four children. You refer to writing in that phase of your life as 'a secret activity'. Why was it so difficult?

As you say, in those days, I was a wife and a mother and writing was not what I was supposed to be doing. I had to do it in hiding. I remember I used to scribble away when the children were at school or playing downstairs and quickly put everything away before they came back in.

My children always remark that they never saw me writing. And the book would one day appear, as though it just happened, it came from somewhere else. And, yes, it was a secret I kept to myself. It created a lifelong habit of writing in solitude; of it being a very solitary pursuit. I used to write in private, hidden moments and nobody knew what I was writing.

There was just one person I shared the writing with and that was Ruth Jhabvala who was a neighbour and friend in Old Delhi and had very much the same writing habits as I did. In those days, a writer had no presence in India. That is what has changed so much now. Now I find that it is a public profession which surprises me. It never was that for me.

Salman Rushdie once admiringly said that 'Anita Desai is that great student of solitude' and, indeed, your earlier novels are peopled by seemingly everyday characters whose inner lives and thoughts are subjected to painful scrutiny . . .

Yes. My characters are people leading very ordinary lives. Perhaps they don't make extremely good material for a book but I was always interested in inner lives; lives that could be in turmoil and which no one can suspect.

Critics of your early novels said that Anita Desai doesn't write about the real world—the hurly-burly of the outside world hardly impinges upon the lives of your characters, mostly women. But that changed with the appearance of *In Custody* . . .

I did myself become conscious that I was living and writing in a very small, enclosed world. And there was a time when I realized that I couldn't endlessly go over and over that same, very small piece of ground. I had to open the gate and step out and look at the world outside. I set myself to doing that very consciously and deliberately in *In Custody*. It is really about a male world. A world I didn't know much about. I set myself to write it as a kind of challenge.

I realized that in order to write about the greater world, I needed to have male characters. Men were the ones that went out and lived public lives. After that, I wrote a series of books with male protagonists because they were the ones that could take part in history.

You speak of the material of novels like *In Custody* and *Baumgartner's Bombay* coming from history and dying cultures. But it is an oblique view of history, a sidelong take . . .

It was a view of history not being something you could participate in, but something that could overwhelm you and trample on you like a juggernaut. In both cases, it is history that destroys these people's lives. It doesn't make them, it destroys them.

I grew up with a sense of history because of my parents, my father having come from what was East Bengal, now Bangladesh. It was taken away from him and he never returned to it. Or my mother coming from

Germany and never returning to it either. So there was always a sense of the past in our home, which we couldn't share. I knew about it, they talked about it, but it was gone.

Lost homelands, a sense of lost history, interested me to start studying people's histories. Perhaps my very first attempt of bringing in that sense of the past was in *Clear Light of Day* where I write about Partition, about Old Delhi, the world I knew caught in the throes of history and, in that sense, being drawn into other people's histories as well. It's more obvious in my most recent novel, *The Zigzag Way*. As a novelist, it's my way of approaching history through individuals and past lives.

Is there a certain regimen you observe when writing and researching your novels?

For me, the mornings have always been reserved for my writing. I have never gone out in the morning, never allowed anyone in, never made phone calls. I have just sat at my desk to see if I could write that day. Some days I can, some days I can't. But I always sit at my desk with a pen in the hand, to wait for that moment. When I am writing a book, I tend to read all the material around it, of course, as I did for *The Zigzag Way*; I read a great deal of Mexican history, memoirs and biographies in order to feel my way into that period.

Where do you think your next book will take readers?

I haven't started another book. To tell you the truth, since this book came out, I have been very involved and wrapped up in my daughter's new book [Kiran Desai's *The Inheritance of Loss*], seeing to it that she actually finished it; she had been working on it for six years. It is a very long, important and big book and I was just there as a kind of a support to her. I almost feel as though I wrote it.

What is it like to have a child who has become a professional writer? Is there a particular quality in combining maternal and literary nurturing?

I just stand back utterly amazed. It has been the most exciting and fulfilling experience of recent years, seeing her grow and develop as a writer.

Will you continue to teach in America or spend more time in India and write about it again?

I'm not sure if I can write another book about India, and yet, I am not sure if I can write a book that is not about India. So I am really not certain about the next step.

September 2006

Questions from the audience

Karan (Student): **You teach English creative writing. I wanted to know whether English creative writing can be taught or is it inherent? Can we be taught how to imagine?**

I am asked this question all the time. I have to say that it makes me feel a little apologetic because, really, creative writing can't be taught. All that a teacher, or a course of creative writing, can do is provide the student with time and a structure and a space in which they feel secure and confident, where their work gets some kind of importance. They need to feel that they are doing something worthwhile and it isn't something that they ought not to be doing. Here we are asking them to continue with their work, to show us their work. Although it can't be taught and, of course, any student who comes to class must have some gift for writing, I have found that, at the end of the semester, students feel much better than they did at the beginning. This is because they have spent that time thinking about the craft of writing.

Nidhi (Teacher): **I am in a dilemma while dealing with my students. Should I be telling them about their obligation towards society as a writer or should I let them be free in creatively expressing themselves?**

That is a good question. My inclination would certainly be to let them be free. They are so young, they still need to find their feet as writers before they can find their ideas and build on them. There will be some students who will be writing because they have ideas to express, other students are writing for the love of language. That will be made evident to you. But at that stage I think one wants to nurture the individuality. I think the writing course that reduces students into the same mould of writing is actually a failure. I think a writing course ought to be encouraging each individual talent.

Swati (Student): **As a writer, what do you want us, as readers, to feel inspired about, to learn from it and to carry with us in our lives?**

I really don't think of my readers while I'm writing. I don't think about what they want and what I should give them. I just remember the days and the times when I have been a reader myself—with what passion I read, say, the Russian classics and how they opened up a whole world for me which I didn't know, hadn't known and never expected to get to know. The books made them so real. And I suppose that's all that my readers can hope to have—that the worlds that I have imagined would enter into their imagination and live there. Because that is what these books did for me. They so enlarged my life.

Adil (Aspiring writer): **If there is one thing, or perhaps two, that you would recommend to an aspiring writer of fiction, what would that be?**

If you are serious about writing, then I would ask you not to be in a hurry. Don't think of just one book that you are going to present to the world which would give you a name and fame. Think of it as a very slow process, of going with it at the pace that it requires. I think a book takes a great deal of time. The more time you give it, the richer and deeper it is.

December 2007

Orhan Pamuk

Kiran Desai

In October 2006 Kiran Desai (b. 1971) was promoting her new novel, *The Inheritance of Loss*, shortlisted for the Man Booker Prize, in Germany. I ran into her in the media centre at the Frankfurt Book Fair just before she was due to leave for London to attend the prize-giving dinner. She would be away for a day or two, she said, as she didn't think she stood a chance; bookies rated her chances a low five-to-one, fifth in a shortlist of six. But her lucky strike came and she became the youngest winner, at thirty-five, of the prestigious £50,000 award. The head of the jury, Professor Hermione Lee, called it, 'A magnificent novel of humane breadth and wisdom, comic tenderness and powerful political acuteness. Her mother will be proud of her.'

It was not till a few months later, when she returned to Delhi, that I interviewed her, in a hidden garden with a small, imposing sixteenth-century monument, behind her family home.

Kiran Desai grew up in Delhi and Bombay, but left at the age of ten with her mother, the novelist Anita Desai, to live in England for a year. She later moved to the United States, where she studied creative writing, first at Bennington College, and then at Columbia. Her first novel, *Hullabaloo in the Guava Orchard* (1998), came out to encouraging reviews; she then retreated into a world of almost monastic discipline for seven years to produce her prize-winner.

Disarmingly unaffected, Kiran Desai—with her slim figure, warm smile, casual hairstyle, jeans and hoop earrings—presents the image of the clever charmer next door; she has something of her mother's observant gaze, tempered by a propensity to dissolve into infectious giggles.

A couple of years ago I was at a small dinner for Orhan Pamuk and her. The two were still shy about their relationship which the Turkish writer, nineteen years her senior, later made public. I watched her watching a young publicist at the table, whose swagger, at once self-confident and self-conscious, clearly tickled her. 'Oh, what a *funny* boy he is,' she exclaimed in her schoolgirlish voice on the street outside, and I found myself laughing out loud. Her sense of the absurd can be contagious.

In late 2010 it was reported that she had received an advance of $2.5 million for her next novel, *The Loneliness of Sonia and Sunny*, to be published in 2012.

What is it like to be back on home ground, in Delhi, in particular?

It's good to be home; it always is. In fact, I felt as though I had never been away as soon as I arrived. This is really my home; it is where my family house is.

How has life changed since that day in Frankfurt last October when we met and you were off to London, you said literally for twenty-four hours, because you had to attend the Booker ceremony and you ended up getting the prize?

Life has been very surreal, very odd and totally opposite to the process of my writing life for the past seven years. It has totally transformed. I hope I can go back to writing, but at this point, I think my life requires different skills. For example, it was seven years of keeping absolutely quiet all day. Now I talk all day long.

Did the prize come as a big surprise?

It was a huge surprise and it still feels very strange. It still doesn't really feel a part of my life because writing this book was seven or eight years of work, and that writing life had settled in so deeply. I am worried that this prize is going to make me stupid. Because I don't read, I don't write and I don't think. I'm just running around all day and talking, which could again be harmful if I continue it longer.

It took more than seven years of virtual isolation and intense labour to produce *The Inheritance of Loss*. Was it a conscious decision to withdraw for such a length of time?

No, it just happened. I was working in a very strange way, not even thinking of a book. I was writing. It was a thing I did. It was my existence. The book came about six or seven years into the process when I realized that I needed to publish something and I had to make a living. Then I stopped and cut back the chapters.

The Inheritance of Loss **is a novel with big themes and diverse locations; it moves from the hill station of Kalimpong in Bengal to England in the 1930s to contemporary Manhattan. A range of characters—from the old Cambridge-educated judge to Sai, his young granddaughter in love with her Nepali tutor sucked into the Gorkhaland agitation, to Biju the cook's immigrant son slaving in New York restaurants—present a variety of conflicts, from insurgency to illegal immigration. How did these characters develop and the strands come together?**

One led to the other. I started with my own story, thinking that I am going to write about my own experience. I quickly found that I couldn't hold it to that because it didn't make sense. I don't think you can tell the story of immigration in the way that American publishers want it to be told. That country creates a myth of immigration that a lot of people want to buy into. But it goes both ways. You leave your brave, un-free, cowardly world for the brave and free world. If you say that as an immigrant, you are really welcomed. And yet I feel there's hypocrisy on both sides.

My leaving India was certainly not taking my destiny in my hands and going to a better part of the world. It was far more complex than that. It goes back to a much older story, and I couldn't have written this book without placing it in that context.

Do you mean the context of family history, given that your one grandfather came from what is now Bangladesh, one grandmother from Germany, and your mother has led a peripatetic life as a teacher on two continents?

Certainly it did. I began to realize the emotional result of a lot of travel that had gone on for many generations. Just to think of simple questions like what does it mean to place a western element in a country that is not of the west? What does it mean to take someone from a poor country and place him in a rich one? These are very old questions, but we have struggled with them for many generations.

Many characters are alienated or dislocated in *The Inheritance of Loss*, whether the judge or the Nepali tutor or the cook's son. Yet for all its melancholy, there are set pieces of comedy such as Biju's triumphant arrival at the American embassy's visa counter or Lola and Noni locked in the world of Wodehouse, Naipaul and Christie in a small hill

station. Your references are both to a post-colonial and post-globalized world . . .

That's how characters come together in one place—certain times when the paths of different classes of immigrants cross at an embassy visa counter—it's a funny situation. Then there is this shiny advertising everywhere you look: the shiny version of a globalized world. You keep hearing that the world is flat and the plain field is levelling up. It may be true for some people, but it isn't true for the majority. It just didn't seem right for me to leave that story out.

I wanted to draw a parallel between Gyan, whose family came from Nepal generations ago, to the experience of new immigrants to the United States. In the western world there is this feeling that immigration is a western issue. It isn't at all. Every country deals with it. But I began to think of it because I, myself, was an immigrant. My first taste of what it was like to be an Indian immigrant led me to think that I am from an immigrant family from several generations on.

What does it really mean if you don't have political or economic power? It is something that's talked about in the immigrant communities in the United States all the time. So I went back to that part of my life when I lived in Kalimpong briefly. Every author works with the material they have.

Obviously your mother Anita Desai has been an influence, but looking back now, which are the other literary influences that drew you to writing?

So many. Ours really was a house full of books, and that's why I like to come back because all the books are here. Certainly authors like Naguib Mahfouz who wrote *The Cairo Trilogy*; Chinua Achebe's trilogy, especially the first one, *Things Fall Apart*; as a writer he tried to map the same sort of landscape that I was trying to. He did it in a linear fashion and I tried to splice it together for the sake of the emotional attachments involved. Also Latin American authors like Gabriel Garcia Marquez for his language or Italo Calvino for his playfulness. I love their work. Michael Ondaatje has been a big influence too and V.S. Naipaul, particularly his early books. And Salman Rushdie for his great attitude. I think he really changed the landscape of Indian writing and he is very generous to young authors. I got an email message after the Booker Prize saying 'HOORAY' in big letters.

Your mother said that she was writing from as far back as she could remember, but when she married and became a young mother with four children, she would have to steal time to write. Did you inherit that early singular focus?

I was twenty years old I when I started writing. My mother fought for her art and she fought to be able to write. I didn't have to fight that fight. I got it because of her efforts. I was given that time and space that she fought so hard to get. I was given all of it in such enormous quantity that I feel myself disappearing. It's the opposite of the problem that she faced. But, yes, it is a gift from her.

When you won the Booker Prize, the first thing you said was that this book feels as much as your mother's book as it does yours. She has really been your deepest and abiding influence, hasn't she?

She has. It really is such an enormous influence that I can't express it. She taught me how to think like a writer, how to live a writing life. I had a taste in literature, and I tried to write differently. My first book was indifferent; it came out of writing workshops in the United States. Creative writing classes and writing for a group makes you self-conscious about the process. I wrote in a public way, as if you were writing for other people, but then I went back to a much more old-fashioned way of writing.

You're the only one of four siblings who inherited this gift from your mother. How did the creative–intellectual relationship between Anita Desai and you develop?

I think a lot of it has to do with the fact that we had to leave India together. When I was about twelve years old she started teaching abroad, and it was just the two of us who left; so we went through the entire experience of going to England and then to the United States.

When I was writing this book, she was the only one who could really, deeply understand what I was trying to say because she knew the entire story; she knew exactly what I was going to do. It was very important to have her the second time around. It was important the first time around too, but the second time, much more so.

You originally thought you were going to be a medical student or take up a more public profession. At what point did you choose the isolated life of a fiction writer?

It wasn't exactly conscious; it just happened. The more I wrote, the more it happened. It just became my life so deeply that I couldn't do anything else, and I didn't want to do anything else. It is an isolated life and the loneliness and isolation is hard. But at the same time I also love it because I need it [the isolation] for my work.

In the time that you were writing *The Inheritance of Loss* in New York, America's view of the world changed radically, and attitudes to America changed as dramatically, particularly vis-à-vis immigrants . . .

Yes, the world changed in many ways while I was working on this book. Immigrants in the United States also changed. There was something new in the air. But this book took me back to Indian soil which I hadn't expected. I thought this book was going to be set entirely in the United States, but I soon realized that I couldn't complete any of my arguments without India. I couldn't write this book without returning.

You once said that writing isn't about winning prizes or even being happy. It's really about doubt. Does writing come from a difficult place?

I think it comes from a very difficult place. I don't think it comes from being entirely happy or entirely content. I love happy books; looking at a beautiful face or reading a happy book is always lovely, but it is much more interesting to look at the darker and the more complicated side of things. I think you write out of emotions that are hardest to deal with—one's doubts, shames and humiliations. I think that is where the heart of the story lies.

Nothing could be more flattering than becoming the youngest novelist to win the Booker and for a second novel. But does it also place a burden and raise unfair expectations of how good your next book will be?

That's what worries every author. Is there going to be another story to tell? And where will it come from? For me, it's just really something that will be revealed at my desk. I never know what I am doing in advance. I really think so much of this book was undoing notions that I had of place and home. Work really was my home all these years and home also was my work. So I don't know where my next book will come from.

January 2007

Mahasweta Devi

One of the ironies of a journalist's life is unexpected settings for interviews. Whereas I recorded an interview with the German writer and Nobel laureate Günter Grass against the backdrop of a crumbling nineteenth-century mansion in north Kolkata, this interview with the remarkable Bengali writer and activist Mahasweta Devi (b. 1926) took place at her hotel suite at the Frankfurt Book Fair. Indian literature and writers were being honoured in 2006 and Mahasweta Devi was at the centre of the celebrations. Although I had read some of her work in translation, and was acquainted with the essential facts of her exceptional life, I did not know what kind of person to expect.

Sitting on a dining chair in the living room was a small, bespectacled woman in a crumpled sari. It was the end of what had obviously been a long and tiring day. But her voice was clear and strong; and once the interview began all traces of fatigue vanished. It became vigorous and expressive as she spoke about her life and work with candour, precise recall and emphatic opinion. There were moments—as when she recited the folk lyric about the Rani of Jhansi—when it resonated and filled the large room.

Mahasweta Devi was born in Dhaka into a family with strong intellectual roots. Her father, Manish Ghatak, older brother of filmmaker Ritwik Ghatak, was a well-known poet and novelist; her mother, Dharitri Devi, was a writer and a social worker and sister of Sachin Chaudhury, founder-editor of the *Economic and Political Weekly*, and the sculptor Sankho Chaudhury. She took a degree in English literature from Santiniketan and knew Tagore; much later, after marriage and motherhood, she went on to complete her MA and taught English at a small college in Kolkata. By then her short-lived, turbulent first marriage to playwright–actor Bijon Bhattacharya had ended.

Mahasweta Devi broke from domestic confines to start travelling into the hinterland and produced her first book *Jhansir Rani* (1956), a retelling of the rebellion of Rani Laxmi Bai through oral accounts and regional folklore. Her journeys to the poorest tribal districts of present-day Jharkhand and Chhattisgarh became a leitmotif of her life and vast output: she has produced more than a hundred books of fiction, non-fiction and collections of her fiery, crusading and relentless journalism.

Many of her real or fictionalized accounts of marginalized lives—the landless, dispossessed, uprooted or grief-torn—are widely available in translation. Among the best-known include *Hazaar Chaurasi ki Maa* (No. 1084's Mother, 1975), *Aranyer Adhikar* (The Occupation of the Forest, 1977), *Agnigarbha* (Womb of Fire, 1978), *Choti Munda Evam Tar Tir* (Choti Munda and His Arrow, 1980) and *Bitter Soil: Four Stories* (1998). Her prodigious writing and activism has transformed the narrative of her life into a seamless whole; she has been honoured with the Magsaysay and Jnanpith awards and was given the Padma Vibhushan in 2006.

Asked once what her leisure reading included, she admitted to a weakness for thrillers by John Grisham and Dick Francis, adding, 'Dick Francis can't make the horses talk but he does invest them with some kind of character.'

It must be a good moment for you, with several of your works being presented in German translation and a whole seminar built round your huge body of work. What does it feel like?

Unthinkable.

Why unthinkable?

I wrote because that was the only thing I could do. I couldn't do anything else—cultivate the soil or break stones or other things. Also, writing meant earning, so I am writing and surviving till date. Book fairs and seminars don't touch me any more. I have come here and I am mighty proud because my government has sent me, and it is very good to meet people, to touch their hearts and to talk to them. Yesterday when I spoke, I said that the right to dream is anyone's first fundamental right. We must be allowed to dream. People must have the liberty to dream. As long as we can dream, we will go ahead.

You come from a family steeped in the reading habit. Your mother made you read Chekhov and Dickens and Tolstoy. How big an influence was that early immersion in books?

We grew up with books; from childhood on, all I have seen is books—purchasing books and keeping them, maintaining a library. My mother was a great reader as was my father. My maternal grandmother was also a voracious reader. From my childhood, she would give me many books to read, all serious books.

Other influences were your first husband, playwright Bijon Bhattacharya, who was deeply involved in the Indian People's Theatre Association, IPTA, and your father's younger brother, the noted Bengali filmmaker Ritwik Ghatak. So reading, writing, making films were a family tradition . . .

My first husband was both a great actor and playwright; he was one of the founder members of IPTA. From his famous play a fantastic film was made by Khwaja Ahmad Abbas called *Dharti ke Lal*. Many families were like that. I repeat, that in our time, our view of the world, whatever we knew about the world outside Bengal, was only through books. Also in my childhood, I was in Santiniketan when Tagore was alive. I saw him very closely. In those days Santiniketan was a very different kind of institution. We were encouraged to read books, use the library, study them and write about what we thought of them. It was something in the air of the country.

What were your earliest writings?

When I was a student of Class Eight, there was a famous children's journal and the editor asked me to write a piece on Tagore. That was my first published writing. But after that I did not pursue writing. Time passed, I got married. Slowly I started writing for weekly papers. It was great to get ten rupees or fifty rupees for a piece of writing in those days.

A turning point in your life was when you started travelling, journeys to places like Palamau, now in Jharkhand . . .

Palamau came later. My first book was *Jhansir Rani*, the biography of the Rani of Jhansi. I read all the available historical material but then I had this intense desire to go and see those places. I knew nothing about Jhansi, Bundelkhand and Gwalior. I just borrowed money from relatives, got into a train, left behind a small baby with his father and went to Jhansi. From that moment my second interest, of collecting oral traditions, became vital for me. I honour and cherish our oral tradition greatly. I will never forget sitting by a fire in Jhansi under the December sky. It was very cold. These Bundelkhandi people were singing, '*Patthar mitti se fauj banayi, Kaath se Katwar, Pahad uthakar goley banaye, chalo Gwalior*' (From stones and earth she created an army/And from wood she fashion a sword. She turned mountains into cannonballs/ And led with the cry, 'Onwards to Gwalior.') From then on, the Rani of Jhansi became a real woman for me.

Despite your rigorous chronicling of the oral tradition, you also speak of your method of research as being forensic—that you are obsessed by statistics, gazetteers and collecting facts . . .

Yes. But I am also someone who always comes back to history. To me history means the blank space between two printed lines. Therein is the true history of the people. This song about the Rani of Jhansi is an example of that space because the words '*Patthar mitti se fauj banayi . . .*' would never appear in history books. So whatever I have learnt in my life is from the people. I have gone to them, I respect them, and I return to them.

The great impetus of your writing came from giving voice to the dispossessed and documenting their lives. Was that what triggered off your trips to the tribal districts that later became Jharkhand?

Yes, I went there in the 1960s, and I saw this horrible custom of bonded labour. There was a man who was bonded to a rich farmer. I saw a bullock cart stacked heavy with paddy. The bullock could not pull it and it crashed. So the rich farmer forced the bonded labourer to pull the cart. While attempting to do so, this bonded labourer named Nageshya broke his shoulder. I asked the rich farmer how he could do such a thing. He said to me that his bullock had cost him a lot of money and that if he had to buy another bullock it would cost him 2,000 rupees, but this man here, he is only a bonded labourer. From these experiences emerged the 1980s movement against bonded labour.

Teaching and travelling ceaselessly to tribal districts, to record and collect stories, and also become actively engaged in their struggles—did all this take a toll on your personal life?

My engagement with tribals started with travels to Palamau. I worked extensively there, then Singhbhum and Hazaribagh, which led to my involvement in the movement for Jharkhand. I remain very connected to the forest movements of the tribals; anywhere you go to in India, to the tribal people, mention my name and they will know me.

I wanted to do it. I had set myself free and I did not want to listen to anyone. I did what I wanted to do. Of course, I had left my husband and my son who was quite young. Leaving him was very heartbreaking. I remarried and that marriage also—it led to nothing. But by that time I had become absolutely absorbed in my work and the people I was working for, the books I was reading and writing.

And you produced not only novel after novel but short stories, prolific journalism and reports.

You may be surprised to know that for the past thirty-five to forty years I have been the most indefatigable journalist. I have travelled and walked through the districts, tribal and non-tribal areas, forest areas and hill areas. I came back and wrote for the newspapers. Three columns, say, in a week.

You also recorded the Naxalite movement in your fiction and non-fiction, the most famous example being your novel *Hazaar Chaurasi ki Maa*, later made into a critically acclaimed film, about a mother who rejects her comfortable life after the killing of her younger son . . .

Movements such as the Naxalite outburst of the 1970s made up a mighty decade. Many of our boys were being killed. I think the reason why *Hazaar Chaurasi ki Maa* was an instant success was because of the way, the technique, in which it was told—a mother remembering her son's life. It touched the hearts of many mothers and these killings were happening all over India. But these are things I have to write about and can't stop. I have two books ready in my mind which I have to put down.

Do you believe that the act of writing—given the range and scale of your work and the readership you enjoy—can bring about social change?

One individual cannot change things but can contribute to a movement in every way possible. Even in my state, West Bengal, there are still two or three persecuted tribes whose cause I have espoused. For twenty years I have been publishing a quarterly journal, *Bortika* (The Lamp), in which tribals contribute stories, not middle-class writers.

I used to print questionnaires because I have a vast rural network so that it would reach people in districts. I would ask them important questions like, 'Are you a school teacher? Are you an agricultural labourer? Are you a cycle-rickshaw puller? Write your life story.' It is not possible for me to do everything alone. But, I hope, many people in India have been moved to think and to work in this way.

In the end, do you see yourself as a novelist, a chronicler or a crusader—or all three?

As a writer. If I write novels, reportage, stories, it is all with the pen. No computers, no emails. Only a pen and paper.

October 2006

Umberto Eco

Umberto Eco (b. 1932) is a polymath in the true sense of the word. The Italian novelist, medieval historian and cultural anthropologist is also a leading semiotician, semiotics being 'the study of signs and symbols of communicative behaviour'—of analysing language, gestures and other responses—that make up communication systems. He is a generously proportioned bearded man in the genre of the operatic tenor Luciano Pavarotti, with a booming voice punctuated by deep-throated chuckles and a mind like a laser beam that sweeps over a vast terrain, from fictional imagery to life in the Middle Ages, and from cultural miscommunication to new media technology.

Umberto Eco was hard to pin down for this interview, but once it happened, he was expansive and friendly. Knowing that he was giving a lecture at Jawaharlal Nehru University, I approached professors I knew to request a recording. But the doors of the academy clicked shut; one learned eminence sounded slightly amazed that I should have the temerity to try and get so close to Eco's hallowed presence. I then learnt that he was also speaking at the Italian Cultural Centre and rang the Italian ambassador, Antonio Armellini, himself a man of letters, whom I knew. He was out of town but his charming wife Giovanella took my call. 'Of course, I shall ask the professor. I am sure he will be delighted.' This interview, therefore, took place in the ambassador's elegant, book-lined study between Eco's talk—which was packed to the rafters—and a splendid banquet in his honour.

Eco grew up in the northern Italian province of Piedmont and showed early academic brilliance, writing his thesis on medieval philosophy at the University of Turin and publishing works like *The Development of Medieval Aesthetics* by the age of twenty-seven. He taught at his alma mater and went to work as cultural editor at RAI, the state broadcasting network. But it was not until 1983 that his first novel, *The Name of the Rose*, appeared in an English translation and gripped the public imagination. At one level it is a mystery, with a Franciscan friar arriving in a fourteenth-century monastery shaken by a series of mysterious deaths. But as the plot unfolds, it becomes an intellectual examination of deductive thought, signs and their meanings, literary theory and Biblical analysis. Eco's second novel, *Foucault's Pendulum* (1988), concerns three young editors in a publishing house, bored with manuscripts, who decide to invent their own conspiracy theory to take over the world by a plan derived from the Knights Templar, an order of Catholic soldiers in the Middle Ages. When the symbologist Robert Langdon appeared in Dan Brown's runaway best-seller *The Da Vinci Code* (2003) and readers made a connection with Eco's work, the medieval professor breezily quipped, 'Dan Brown is one of the characters in *Foucault's Pendulum*, which is about people who start believing all this occult stuff.'

Other than producing more fiction, Eco has continued to develop theories of semiotics, co-founding *Versus*, an influential journal on the subject; he is president of the *Scuola Superiore di Studi Umanistici* at the University of Bologna and an honorary fellow of Kellogg College, Oxford. Since 1988 he has run a programme called *Anthropology of the West* from the perspective of non-westerners, at Bologna.

When you began writing *The Name of the Rose* it was with one idea in your mind: you wanted to begin with a monk poisoned in an abbey in medieval times. Did that novel really start off with the simple premise of a mystery?

I am an academic philosopher, a professor, so people believe that I start by making a complete rational plan. No, I start from an image that strikes me; and for *The Name of the Rose* it was an image of the poisoned monk. The image came from a visit I had made, at the age of sixteen, to a Benedictine monastery and in the library there was a big lectern where I found an old book. That image remained in my mind and one day I thought how beautiful it would be to have a monk reading a manuscript and suddenly falling to his death.

The Name of the Rose was my first novel, written between 1948 and 1950, so I was a very young writer. After that, I thought, well I have said practically everything that I had in my mind, so why write a new novel? But once you have started writing novels you feel the excitement and challenge. I said to myself, which image would for me be as powerful as that of the poisoned monk; and suddenly I got the idea of Foucault's ringing pendulum which I had seen thirty years before in Paris but it obsessed my mind. Then there was the image of a young man playing a trumpet in the cemetery which I had seen when I was thirteen years old during the War. I said, okay now that's done—my book will start with Foucault's pendulum and end with the trumpeter in the cemetery. Then I asked myself, what should I put in between, to pass from the pendulum to the trumpet, and it took me eight years to arrive at the conclusion; and the conclusion was *Foucault's Pendulum*.

Its density of plot, detail of medieval life in a fourteenth century monastery and allusions to figures like Jorge Luis Borges and Arthur Conan Doyle is what makes *The Name of the Rose* so original. But the novel's title is also a literary tease—referring to Shakespeare's line 'What's in a name? . . . A rose by any other name would smell as sweet . . .' or Gertrude Stein's 'A rose is a rose is a rose is a rose.' Was the symbolism of the rose in your mind?

Yes, of course. The rose is a name and image so charged with symbolic meaning that it has lost all of them and nobody can misinterpret or hyper-interpret it. My God, everybody spent a lot of time trying to find archaic interpretations; many people found a relationship to Shakespeare's quotation but 'A rose by any other name' means exactly the contrary. Readers looked for references to the rose by the mystics of the Middle Ages and they found references in Luis Borges. So, you see, strange things happen when you try to put a neutral title.

You are a medieval historian and a professor of semiotics. Do your novels mirror the social tensions and cultural misinterpretations of the modern world?

The Middle Ages were certainly a very racist society. But at the intellectual level it was a very multicultural place because the east and west retrieved the Greek philosophers through Arab mediations; the Arabs of Spain were accepting Christians and Jews without persecuting them. So the Middle Ages had a sort of multi-levelled situation. At the high level there was the idea of possible circulation of culture, at the lower level it was a struggle between two villages. Our country, Italy, was a paramount example of cities fighting.

Can I tell you a nice story? When I am in New York I talk with taxi drivers because they are interesting and they change from season to season—sometimes they are all Armenians or Pakistanis or Russians—and recently one of them was from the subcontinent. I don't remember whether he was from India or Pakistan or Bangladesh but he started talking to me, asking me where I came from etc. Then he asked, 'What language do you speak?' I said that I speak Italian and he said, 'You don't speak English?' and I said, no, I don't. Then he suddenly asked me, 'Who are your enemies?' Our enemies? And he said, 'Yes, the people you are always fighting against.' I said that we have no enemies. Centuries ago we fought against Austria but now it's finished. We don't have fixed enemies but he didn't understand this point because he came from a country which has real enemies. Later, reflecting upon his question, I realized that we don't have enemies because the Italians are enemies of all Italians. Our whole story was once a struggle between cities and states but, now, we don't need external enemies because we have so many internal enemies.

You are responsible for starting an original programme at Bologna university in cultural anthropology, and run seminars on transcultural studies. What is transculturism about?

Transculturalism is an organization of mutual understanding between cultures which is part of semiotics. It was invented by the French historian Alain Le Pichon. He had the idea of looking at cultural anthropology in the post-colonial world. Usually it was European and American anthropologists who described non-western societies, so Le Pichon brought to France Africans who had never been to Europe and asked them to describe France. The results were astounding. The one that struck me the most was that one visitor remarked, 'Oh how curious! French people walk their dogs on a leash.' The African was astonished by this fact because in Africa dogs roam freely.

I repeated this story after arriving in India but, immediately afterwards, I made the extraordinary discovery that India is full of brownish dogs roaming the streets and who do not belong to anybody. So I thought that Indian dogs were the same as African dogs but then I saw people with many non-brownish dogs on leashes. So I began to elaborate the theory that dogs have castes in India. Black or white on leashes are more delicate and so they are pets. So, you see, you can understand culture even through dogs, not necessarily through great monuments.

It is only now in the modern world that we have the ability to put cultures in touch to reach a mutual understanding. Mutual understanding doesn't mean that we are always thinking the same thing. An Indian dog is not a European dog, they are different; mutual understanding means to understand the difference. Don't lie to kids and don't tell them that we are all equal. I would happily argue that we are not equal. We are all different. To mutually understand our differences, and to accept them, is to enrich ourselves, but understanding of differences presents the real problem. I won't say we will be able to arrive at a condition of universal peace but, at least, we may have a little less war.

How would you describe the difference between multiculturalism and transculturalism?

Let's take America which is a multicultural society but not a melting pot because, in fact, it is an 'unmelted' pot, with Koreans who live in one quarter, the Chinese in another and the Jews in another. They don't clash except a few times. But can you have a multicultural society with a configuration of ghettos that don't understand each other? Transcultural means that those plural cultures should try to understand each other without losing their identity.

In the 1960s the Canadian philosopher and communication theorist Marshall McLuhan, who coined the phrase 'the global village', raised the mantra of 'the medium is the message' and predicted a future where the visual imagery of television and advertising would overtake the written word. But this hasn't happened with the digital revolution of new media such as the Internet and cellular technology . . .

The Internet's problem is giving too much information. It is marvellous but without any criteria for filtering information. The biggest problem of our time—and of the Internet—is how to teach people to select. But I do not take the apocalyptic view. I mean, when they invented the telegram, we learned to send messages in a few words but it did not change the way of writing literature. The telegram was invented before Proust but Proust didn't write telegrams. So an SMS is like a telegram. If Marshall McLuhan lived today he would have to radically change his views. He said in *The Gutenberg Galaxy* that we were living in a world of images. Today, I use my sophisticated mobile not just as a phone for oral functions but as a computer to write, record and pick up mail. Its functions are alphabetic. The world is much more text oriented than before.

How have the markers between high culture and popular culture been redefined in our times, especially in language?

We have to split the history of the twentieth century into two parts. In the first part it seemed that culture was divided into highbrow, middlebrow and lowbrow, so James Joyce is highbrow and comic books lowbrow. But around the 1960s something absolutely new happened. First Pop Art, then rock 'n' roll and other phenomena by which the differences between the two levels condensed. This doesn't mean that everything became equal to everything, simply that you have trash in popular culture and you have trash in high culture. But language amalgamated more than it was believed in the first half of this century.

What do you make of Dan Brown's blockbuster thriller *The Da Vinci Code*?

I told the story of Dan Brown in *Foucault's Pendulum*. Dan Brown is one of my characters who decided to invent a plot, except that my characters repent for what they did. The real phenomenon is not Dan Brown though he intelligently uses the material to write a real page-turner, but all these people who now go to see Leonardo's Mona Lisa and go to the English chapel because they really believe that Jesus Christ married Mary Magdalene. I always quote a sentence from G.K. Chesterton who said that when people no longer believe in God, it is not that they believe in nothing—they believe in everything.

This is your first long trip to India. You have been to Goa, Pondicherry, Mumbai and Delhi. Are you surprised or flattered by the number of Indians who have flocked to your readings and lectures?

I didn't believe that I would have so many readers in India. This must be a sign of the corruption of our times.

November 2005

Ken Follett

This exchange with the best-selling British thriller and historical fiction writer Ken Follett (b. 1949) took place at the Frankfurt Book Fair on a sunny morning on an outdoor pavement bench. Following a packed day's schedule, Follett was being shunted from interview to interview by a set of automaton-like female minders, in tight skirts and tighter smiles, their eyes fixed on watches and call sheets. What's there not to like about Follett? He's short, chubby and relaxed, and his tousled white hair and bright blue suit, exactly matching the colour of the sky, were in happy contrast to his handlers.

Follett was born into a strict Christian family in Wales that permitted few diversions—television and films were barred. He read philosophy at University College, London, in part to interrogate his doubts about religion, then took a crash course in journalism and went to work for a London evening paper. His first big success as a spy thriller writer, *The Eye of the Needle* (1978), about a counter-intelligence operation during World War II, later said to have inspired Bollywood's Aamir Khan-starrer *Fanaa* (2006), came after mediocre sales of eleven historical novels and thrillers. He knew he had arrived when his agent called him to say, 'They are auctioning the paperback rights of your book today and the price has reached half a million dollars, but the auction is still going on.'

Much of his subsequent fiction was turned into successful films and TV miniseries, but in 1989 he surprised his readers by publishing *The Pillars of the Earth*, a novel about building a cathedral in the Middle Ages, which made him even richer and catapulted him into the big time. Follett is labelled the 'champagne socialist' by the media, because of his weakness for expensive bubbly combined with his ardent support and fundraising for the Labour Party. In contrast to his best-selling rival Jeffrey Archer, a Conservative Party prominence, it was Follett's second wife, Barbara Broer, who took the political seat. She was Labour MP from 1997 to 2010 but did not run in the last election after being caught in the parliamentary expenses scandal.

Fall of Giants, the first part of his 'Century' trilogy, published in 2010, is a generational family saga that follows the lives of five interrelated families through World War I and the Russian Revolution. Follett will publish the remaining two parts in 2012 and 2014.

~

I have been looking up your website, in which, in ten easy steps, you tell the world how to write the perfect thriller. It's not true, is it? It can't be that easy.

Well, you know, when people ask me, I tell them what I do and there are some simple techniques that I use. I don't think everybody who follows those techniques will necessarily write a good thriller. But they are things that have been useful to me so they might be useful to some young, aspiring writers.

It must be a slog to turn a thriller into a best-seller, especially refining its craft—pace, new backgrounds and characters, and very clever plotting. Do many thriller writers fail because they can't get the plot right?

I think certainly in popular fiction the book is story-driven. People reading popular fiction want to know what happens next, and so the story has to be such that you never feel that this is a good moment to put the book down. What I want you to do is to lie on your stomach in the evening, and come to the end of a chapter, and I want you to look at the clock and I want you to think, 'I will just read one more chapter.' Now to get the reader to feel like that you have to construct the plot very carefully so that there is always something new, always something making the reader think, 'I wonder what comes next.'

You once said what's wrong with a lot of thriller writing is the trick ending because it's something that really belongs to the short story.

Yes, that's absolutely true. But when you write a novel you are asking the reader to stay with you for a longer time. So you can't just hold them in suspense about the end. You've got to constantly keep them in suspense. Every chapter in a good thriller is a cliff-hanger.

Suspense and action in a certain sequence can create pace but what about characters. How complex must they get?

You see, one of the lessons I learned very early on as a thriller writer was that action on its own is not interesting. You have to care about the people who are undergoing this action, who are risking their lives or whatever they are doing; if you care about those characters then the action will be thrilling. But if you don't really believe in those characters, if you think they are a bit artificial, a bit wooden, then you can't quite care so much about the action. For example, you can create a marvellous chase and the reader will think, 'Ah! Who cares?' So that's why I say in my kind of story, in popular fiction, plot comes first, but without characters the plot is boring.

You started out as a journalist, first with a provincial paper in Wales and then at London's *Evening News*. But you started writing thrillers after hours. In fact your initial experiments in thriller writing came through an American agent who was trying to sell your would-be book. How did that happen?

I used to go home after work on the paper in the 1970s and spend two or three hours every evening writing my next novel. I had an American agent and I would send him my drafts and he would write to me and say, 'I am not going to be able to sell this book in the American market because . . .' Then I would follow on with questions—not about the American market but, say, about literature. He would say things to me like, 'In your story none of the characters has any background.' And I would think, 'Oh, my God, that's right.' I hadn't thought about where these people were born and what their parents were like and what kind of childhood they had and where they went to school and university and what their early experiences of romance were like. I hadn't ever thought any of that and you have to think of all of that if you have to create a character that the readers will like and believe in.

You had a middle-class, provincial though staunchly religious upbringing. Later you went to University College in London to read philosophy. What's the link between religion, philosophy and fiction writing?

I was brought up in a family of fundamentalist Christians. We belong to a sect called the Primitive Brethren, quite an extreme Protestant sect. I am not religious now. I don't believe in any of the things I was taught as a child, but it was an important part of my childhood. As a young man I was very troubled by questions such as the existence of God, the meaning of the universe and so on, and that's why I studied philosophy at university. The interesting thing about philosophy is that you have to be imaginative to study it because it asks questions like, how do we know that this bench that we are sitting on is real? Now in some ways that is a silly question, isn't it? But if you want to study philosophy you have to take that question seriously. So it requires you to imagine that the world might be different from how it is and, of course, that's what you need to write novels.

Your last book, *Whiteout*, has sold between three and four million copies. It takes you up to three years to finish a new novel. Do you have such a timeframe in mind when you set about starting one?

Normally a book takes me two years. I spend the first year planning. As I was saying before, a story that keeps the reader interested from page to page has to be very carefully planned; you have to get all your ducks in a row, as they say, and that takes a long time. Then I spend six months on the first draft and six months on the rewrite. That's my normal schedule.

You have always been a political activist and very engaged in the fortunes of the Labour Party since your university. And your arch rival in thrillers, Jeffrey Archer, has been an important Conservative Party politician. How has Britain produced two best-selling popular thriller writers who also happen to political party members on opposing sides?

If you are an imaginative person who can make up a story, you are also probably the kind of person who can imagine the world being a much better place if certain changes were made. So I think that's probably what both Jeffrey and I have in common. We imagine the world to be a different and better place. Of course, we disagree violently on how to make the world better but we both think that it can be done. Although we belong to different parties, I see Jeffrey every now and then, of course, at book parties. I am rather fond of him. I think he is the kind of person who makes life more interesting because he is very lively. Some people find him arrogant but I don't mind that. Of course, he's a great storyteller.

October 2006

Justine Stoddart

Patrick French

British historian and biographer Patrick French (b. 1966) had an early and immediate success with his first book, *Younghusband: The Last Great Imperial Adventurer* (1994), a life of the nineteenth-century Victorian explorer whose expeditionary invasion of Tibet in 1903-04 led to one of the worst massacres in the subcontinent. The prize-winning biography was universally applauded for its compelling subject and form. Two journeys and timelines—the biographer and his subject's—are dexterously interwoven, culminating in a dramatic denouement that unlocks Sir Francis Younghusband's strange and secret private life (in his later years Younghusband becomes a mystic and enters into a relationship with a married woman with whom he wants to produce a 'God-Child . . . greater even than Jesus').

Born in Hampshire, and himself the son of a soldier, French studied literature at Edinburgh University before setting off on Younghusband's trail. His growing engagement with India and Tibet led to two more books: *Liberty or Death: India's Journey to Independence and Division* (1997) which drew flak from Indian historians for its warts-and-all portraits of nationalist leaders; and *Tibet, Tibet: A Personal History of a Lost Land* (2003). But his reputation was burnished with the publication of *The World Is What It Is* (2008), the authorized biography of Nobel laureate V.S. Naipaul. Larger in scale and more unsettling than the Younghusband story, it was controversial in its revelations of the tormented personal life of one of the major literary figures of the twentieth century. It won the National Book Critics Circle Award in the United States, and the Hawthornden Prize in the United Kingdom; and French was hailed for inventing the genre of the 'confessional biography'.

For a scholar and traveller who spends much of his life examining lives in mouldy archives with almost forensic exactitude, Patrick French is a genial, approachable and modest person; he is an interviewer's delight with his ability to speak about complex subjects and themes with lucid simplicity.

While writing his Naipaul biography, Patrick French's involvement with India deepened: in 2007 he married an editor with Penguin Books,

Meru Gokhale. His new book, *India: A Portrait*, was published in early 2011.

—

What did it take to produce your definitive biography of V.S. Naipaul, one of the great English writers of the twentieth century?

To start with, it took me to the United States for the first time. I landed in Oklahoma which is a place full of very bad American food and this tiny little archive. Everything about Naipaul had been kept there and monumentalized, from his school reports to his wife's personal diaries to all his letters and manuscripts. I had to go back for five research trips there. I worked through all that and then, interestingly, interviewed probably about a hundred people around the world, in India, America, South America, Africa, everywhere.

Your biography is an extensive piece of research about a remarkable writer who also comes across as a strange, tortured figure. It tells the story of his huge, brilliant output in a long and complex career, yet it also unmasks a man of contradictory and disturbing impulses . . .

Yes, the strange thing about Naipaul is that he is a very composed person and yet there is the element of torment behind that which, probably, in its roots, goes back to the triangulation between three cultures: the fact that his grandparents were indentured labourers, effectively slaves, sent from Uttar Pradesh to the Caribbean to cut cane; and that later he somehow managed to win a colonial scholarship to get away. He was one of three people in that year who were able to leave Trinidad and go to Oxford and, yes, of course he was Indian because he came from an Indian background. But he was not East Indian, he was West Indian and yet he became British. It is almost the most complicated background that you could imagine one person to have.

Of a double exile, as it were?

Yes, a double exile but also a triangulation. One of the things that people in India often don't realize about the early diaspora is that, in somewhere like Trinidad, Indians were the lowest of them all. They were the minority who were meant to cut cane because the slaves had been freed. They were regarded as low, heathen, illiterate and without any future. When you run this through the life of a man who has ended up as Nobel laureate Sir Vidia Naipaul, he has that awareness of where he came from.

And yet Naipaul's irascible temperament, his love–hate relationships, not just with India but with Britain, are unresolved. He's also a man given to wild denunciations of anything and everything—Islam is awful, journalists are monkeys, women are fat and ugly . . .

It's not that unusual in the Caribbean to talk like that: you go to Trinidad and people love that kind of talk, aggressive street talk. They call it picong which comes from the French word *piquant* meaning 'sharp' or 'cutting'. That is where it really emerges from though, because he talks in this very grand manner, there is an impression that it's just brutish arrogance. But I would say it originates from the Caribbean.

More alarming in your biography is the emotional and physical violence V.S. Naipaul inflicts in his relationships, particularly with women, first on his long-suffering wife Pat and later his Anglo-Argentine mistress of twenty-four years whom he hits till his hand hurts. There are also many instances of associations with friends, editors and colleagues whom he routinely befriends and then dumps. The impression created is that he ruthlessly used them all.

This is somebody for whom the act of creation, the act of writing, is always *the* most important thing in his life. Hence, he is willing to sacrifice anybody and anything, if he thinks it is going to push him further to becoming a great writer. So every relationship is subordinated to that, every friendship tends to be cut off and people seem to disappear from his life. If you say the relationship with Margaret, his lover for twenty-four years, is very disturbing, it is probably the most disturbing thing of all I had to face when writing the book.

It is both sexually charged and explicitly violent . . .

Sexually charged and physically violent, but despite that she wants the relationship to continue. One of the most disturbing things is that she has every opportunity to break off the relationship but she comes back all the way from Argentina to England to be with him in order to be mistreated. There is something very unhappy and disturbing about that part.

Naipaul was once asked, 'You were born in Trinidad, weren't you?' And he answered, 'It was a great mistake.' So he is at war with his origins because he genuinely believes that he was born into this world to 'serve literature' . . .

I think that came from his father. His father was somebody who spoke Hindi or Bhojpuri and was from an agricultural background. He was self-taught, then became a journalist, and published a very good book of short stories. And in his young son he inculcated the idea that literature is everything and that one of the greatest things in the world was to be a writer. So young Vidia had the idea that that was what he wanted to do. But his father was somebody who was mentally and emotionally unstable. I think a lot of Naipaul's aggressiveness to succeed comes from his fear of failure and not wanting to go down the same way as his father.

So you attribute his driving, ruthless ambition to become a great figure of literature—to write book after book, to find subject after subject and to continuously hone his craft—to his desperately unhappy childhood?

Absolutely. All of those things alluded to boil down to the fact that he came from this disjointed Indian community in Trinidad and also from the fact that he was very determined from a young age to escape from that and to make himself into a world figure. One of the things that is very interesting to me is that, in 1950s London, he is a Caribbean writer and he thinks himself to be part of a group of Caribbean writers, many of them working for the BBC show *Caribbean Voices*. But when it's clear that West Indian writing is going out of fashion, then he reinvents himself, and he becomes sort of British, or sort of Indian, and he makes himself into a new kind of writer.

At that time, the idea of somebody being a global writer was not something that was really thought about. It was something that now seems quite an understandable idea, where somebody like Salman Rushdie can hop between cultures. But at that time people were very clear about where they emerged from.

He was also conscious of climbing the social ladder in literary London, being cultivated by writers like Antonia Fraser and editors like Francis Wyndham, who could further his career through connections and journalistic commissions . . .

American profile-writers often present V.S. Naipaul as a wannabe English gentleman, but it is as simple as that he was happy to be taken up by these rather grand English literary figures. Actually, he was always an outsider; he was aware that he was outside, to the extent that he was not giving the kind of things back to these people that they were giving to him. So he was quite happy for them to give to him, using the ladder frame to climb up, but then he quickly kicked them away once he got up to the next level.

What were your conditions when you embarked upon this biography? Did Naipaul completely agree for you to have total access to his complete archive concerning every crevice of his life?

What I said to him was that I was only willing to do the book if I could have free access to the archives and complete control over the final text and he, astonishingly enough, was willing to let me do that.
Obviously, a biography, a truthful biography of a living person, is very difficult, but I was clear that I didn't want to write a moralizing biography because that would be boring. Equally, I wasn't going to write the Indian model of biography where you write in praise of the great man and say how wonderful he is. That is essentially hagiography. I wanted to present the facts as they are and I wasn't going to hold anything back but, equally, I wouldn't try and condemn the subject. This is what he agreed to so that the reader can read and judge his life.

And how has your own relationship with V.S. Naipaul changed since the book came out?

He has been able to detach himself from the project in a rather remarkable way. There wasn't a single question that I asked him that he refused to answer. Yet, at the same time, he was detached and I always knew he really wasn't that keen to read the book. But the thing that really surprised me was how helpful he was with the writing. He saw the seriousness of the project, the way I was doing it, and whenever I said, 'Look, I really need to get hold of this cache of letters and I need you to talk about this', even though he did not particularly want to discuss it, he got up and said, 'I will do it.' The impression of V.S. Naipaul as an ogre has gotten hold of the popular imagination. People would be surprised at just how easygoing he was in many ways about the process.

Do you just suspect, or do you know for sure, that he hasn't read the book?

I'm sure he hasn't read the book. He is not a particularly introspective person. He is somebody who is introspective about his favourite subjects, such as his relationship with his father, as a writer. For example, he has never written about his mother nor, probably, about his grandmother.

Another example of the troubled relationships with women in his life . . .

Yes, troubled relationships, but without those two very strong women there is no way that he could have won the scholarship to go to Oxford and then had the subsequent success that he had. It was a matriarchal family: his grandmother was one of the most powerful Indian women in Trinidad. She was a landowner, and she ran this extended family with a rod of iron.

But, later, he became estranged from his mother for a long time?

Exactly, by the end he was estranged from his mother. The relationship he had with Margaret, his lover, made his family turn against him and he turned against them. So by the time of his mother's death it was quite an unhappy relationship between mother and son.

Naipaul's archive is, you point out, possibly the last paper archive of a major writer's working and private life. How will the digital age of communication, email and cellphones change writing biographies in the future?

It will be impossible in the future to write biographies of this sort because retrospective memory or interviews are not a quarter as good as what we write in a diary or letter. Email does give you some idea of communication but the problem in the Naipaul archives, from the 1980s onwards, was faxes which had physically faded and you couldn't read them. And once we start the use of cell phones, all the intimate exchange in letters, for example between Naipaul and Pat, his first wife, disappears. And now, when we are texting, again there is a whole area of communication that disappears. It is almost as if communication, though getting technically better, does not let the result survive.

Which means that the evanescent material of life is vanishing?

Exactly. It is.

You said that many Indian biographies are flawed because they tend to be congratulatory and flattering portraits. Why is the telling of Indian lives so removed from their truths?

There are exceptions to that but there is a tradition that probably arises out of a kind of sycophancy, particularly in Indian politics. It's the idea that if somebody does a remarkable thing, whether it's Nehru, Gandhi or whoever, then he has to be a great man and you have to draw a portrait of him as a great man. So there are not that many great biographies to have come out of India. But I think that will probably change very rapidly over the next ten to fifteen years.

After the Naipaul biography you have acquired a reputation as a major biographer in English but, in fact, your first foray into the genre was the prize-winning biography you wrote at the age of twenty-one, just out of university, of the British explorer and leader of colonial expeditions to Tibet. *Francis Younghusband: The Last Great Imperial Adventurer* is, again, a strange story of a driven Victorian who goes a bit off at the end of a long life, with his mysticism and weird sex life. What leads you to these portraits of larger-than-life figures, portraits as compelling as fiction?

In a way, you can put the Younghusband and the Naipaul biographies alongside each other. They are based on one of the most important events of the twentieth century—colonialism—and the effect it had on people who were part of it.

Someone said that both these books read as if they are novels because, in a way, they do tell a much wider story: What does it do to somebody when he is sent out to the North-West Frontier, and then told that you have to represent the interest of Queen Victoria? What does it do to somebody when his grandparents are shifted to the Caribbean and he is told you have got to be British, even though you go to the Caribbean because England is the motherland? And when you go to England, you are rejected by the people who say you have got to turn British. It is a big subject and it explains what Younghusband was part of, something familiar to millions of people.

You have also written a book about India's road to independence, *Liberty or Death*, which came in for criticism in India because of your portrayal of Gandhi and nationalist leaders . . .

Yes, because I treated Gandhi and Patel and Jinnah as human beings instead of as just political icons.

Another book of yours that created controversy was *Tibet, Tibet: A Personal History of a Lost Land*. How did you become involved in Tibetan politics?

I had a strange experience when I was a schoolboy, aged fifteen, when the Dalai Lama came to my school. I was very struck by him as a personality. So I went to Tibet and became interested in Tibetan history and politics and became involved in the Free Tibet movement.

Did you start practising Buddhism?

No I never practised Buddhism. I was interested in Tibetan Buddhism but I was not practising it. I saw the conversion ceremonies and never wanted to be part of them.

But your opinion about the Dalai Lama and the Free Tibet movement changed. You came to actively reject it and the Dalai Lama's recent policy towards China . . .

The difficulty I had when I went to Tibet and spent three months travelling and researching the book was the realization that all the propaganda that I had been a part of fails to encounter the reality. And that the battle for Tibetan freedom was lost in 1959 when the Dalai Lama fled into exile in India. The idea of what the Dalai Lama, lobbying in the west, was trying to do is completely unrealistic; and since then, China has become increasingly economically powerful. There in no way that the Beijing government is going to allow a free Tibet. If that same energy had been put in trying to reach inside the Chinese government, then there might have been a better result. Quiet back-channel diplomacy would probably have yielded more than having people wait in the streets of Washington DC.

What is your next book about?

The next book that I am writing, *India: A Portrait*, is about the rapid changes that have occurred socially and, to an extent, politically and economically in India in the last ten to fifteen years. Most of it will be told through personal stories of individuals and individual families.

May 2008

Amitav Ghosh

Amitav Ghosh (b. 1956) appeared several times on *Just Books*. In part, this is because he is the most approachable and affable of authors but perhaps also because, of all the writers featured in this book, I have known him the longest. We were near contemporaries at Delhi University; that makes access easy and creates a congenial rapport.

Of his generation of Indians writing in English, with hasty ineptitude dubbed the 'St Stephen's school of fiction-writing', Ghosh is the universally applauded topper and his is the master class in storytelling. His subjects and themes have grown diverse and increasingly complex, from the passion and remorse of an Indo-British family saga in *The Shadow Lines* (1986) to explorations of the India–Burma connection in *The Glass Palace* (2000), the Sunderbans mangroves in *The Hungry Tide* (2005), and the nineteenth-century opium trade and migration of indentured labour in *Sea of Poppies* (2008), the first part of a planned trilogy. Each successive novel is more densely plotted, with a beguiling cast of characters who powerfully drive the narrative. Ghosh has been as prolific in producing non-fiction, including essays and travel writing that include *Dancing in Cambodia and at Large in Burma* (1998), *Countdown* (1999) and *The Imam and the Indian* (2002).

Ghosh was educated at Doon School, St Stephen's College, and at Oxford where he took a D.Phil. in social anthropology. He has been a Fellow at the Centre for Studies in Social Sciences, Calcutta, and taught literature at Queens College, City University of New York, and at Harvard University. He has been honoured with numerous awards at home and abroad; in 2008 *Sea of Poppies* was shortlisted for the Man Booker Prize.

These two interviews, merged here as one, were recorded at the Frankfurt Book Fair after the success of *The Hungry Tide* and in New Delhi before the launch of *Sea of Poppies*. Ghosh looks very much the distinguished campus professor, with his shock of prematurely white hair, and is a man of flowing moods: the concentrated frown swiftly dissolves into ebullient smiles and loud chuckles.

The book that everybody's been talking about since it came out is *The Hungry Tide* which takes readers into the mangroves of the Sunderbans. It's had a very enthusiastic response. Do you think it's because of the book's theme of the survival of threatened ecosystems and endangered river dolphins in conflict with indigent human populations that is very much a raging debate of our times?

The book has had a wonderful reception in India. When people come and talk to me about the book, I can make out that they are really touched and moved by it and that it has given them a place to inhabit imaginatively that simply didn't exist before. Sunderbans is one of the most astonishing ecosystems in the whole world but it is strange that it is absent from the Indian imagination, even from the Bengali imagination. When you ask anyone in Calcutta, 'What does a forest look like?' they only think of the Himalayan forest or a deciduous forest, they never think of the forest that is literally in their backyard.

Did the book come out of your visits to the Sunderbans when you were young?

Yes, absolutely. I had an uncle who lived there as an officer on Sir Daniel Hamilton's estate and I had a close relationship with him. The extremes that one sees in the Sunderbans are shocking and my visits there profoundly influenced the book. One of the first things that local villagers will tell you is, 'Oh, to you we are just tiger food, aren't we?' The suffering there is very moving. The local people don't necessarily see their existence as a choice between the tigers and their livelihood. That's the dichotomy: I think both can live together but what you have to do is to provide some form of income generation or some form of other livelihood which compensates them for the loss of the forests.

What makes *The Hungry Tide* so accessible to readers is also that the conflict between endangered species and local inhabitants is presented through intricate relationships between outsiders and locals; for instance, between Piyali Roy, the Indian-American marine biologist researcher, and Fokir, the young, illiterate fisherman. They have no language in common yet they develop a close association. In such ways you communicate a layered story with many points of view. How did the characters develop?

When one writes it is essentially the characters that are at the centre of the story and I write about characters who are alive for me. One of the things that interested me, and which really compelled the book, is the idea: how do you create some sort of equitable balance between the demands of nature and the demands of people in an incredibly impoverished land? I think that, in some general sense, we cannot protect other species if we are completely indifferent to our own species. The suffering of our own species is certainly no less than the suffering of other species.

Many of your novels including *The Glass Palace*, which is set against the backdrop of the sack of Mandalay by the British and King Thibaw, the last king of Burma's exile to India, move across frontiers and sometimes across big timespans. Generations come face to face at particular moments, whether in Egypt, India or America, linking the past with the present.

What has been a very conscious thing for me since the start of my career, since my very first book, is to write about the realities of lives, of my life or of my lives. And what are our lives? My family is originally from Bangladesh, what was earlier East Pakistan. My great-great-great-grandparents migrated from that part of Bengal to Bihar in 1856.

And you had an uncle who served in Burma . . .

Exactly, it is that reality, the reality of our lives which become dispersed. It's our experience, it's not an experience contained just in Calcutta or just in Delhi. All of us have travelled. We have studied in various places and we have lived in various places. It's not the experience of, say, the nineteenth-century novel where everybody is rooted in a single place. Our dispersal is what I have always sought to write about. When I first started writing about this, the reaction to my books was, 'Why do you write about people who travel here and there?' Now, twenty years later, people see that writers like me are writing about a world which is coming into being—a globalized world.

In the sense that there has always been an Indian diaspora?

There has always been an Indian diaspora but our consciousness of it is that it did not exist. I remember when we were growing up in Delhi we thought of all those Indians who were abroad with a sense of dismissal, as if they were somewhere else, as if they had left the country. But the current state of India is very different—I mean, where did the

IT industry come from? There has always been an important link between India and the diaspora—Gandhiji connected it to South Africa and Netaji's Indian National Army to Burma and Malaysia. These links are old and powerful but we have ignored them for so long.

You are part of the Indian diaspora because for more than twenty years you have lived and taught in New York. How do you keep this intense connection with India alive? You live in America but your subject matter remains India—most of your characters are Indian and your inner and imaginative life is Indian.

I think of myself as a *girmitiya*. It was the word that was used for the indentured labourers who left in the nineteenth century because they signed agreements which they call *girmits*, and so, they became the girmitiyas of Mauritius, Fiji and so on. I think of myself like that; you sign that agreement for five years or ten years and you are away for a while. But that essential connection to India doesn't evaporate and for me it certainly hasn't evaporated. I spend almost half the year in India; now my children are older, and when they leave for college, I really expect to be spending my life in India. As you said my inner life and my imaginative life is completely fuelled by India, but it's not fuelled by localized India; it's fuelled by that aspect of the Indian experience which is a global experience. And that's where I feel very grateful for having had this time outside because it made me realize that to be Indian is not just to be living in Murshidabad or Moradabad. It's much more than just a localized experience. I found myself fascinated when I wrote *The Glass Palace* by these people who had never been outside a small village in Orissa and then found themselves travelling in a ship to Burma or Malaysia. It must have been an extraordinary experience.

Your principal occupation is as a fiction writer but you trained in social anthropology as an academic and you taught for many years. How did these two lives co-exist?

I really stopped teaching as a professor when I left Delhi University in 1988. Since then I have taught occasionally. I have arrangements which allow me to teach one semester and then take one semester off. Teaching has not been the centre of my life for the last eighteen years. Actually, what has been much more central to my life is journalism. I have done a lot of journalism in the last fifteen years or so and that's informed my work very much.

Your long report on India's emergence as a nuclear power for the *New Yorker* was later published as a book called *Countdown*. In that context, what do you make of the Indo-American nuclear deal?

It was interesting for me to write *Countdown* because I have always been anti-nuclear. Maybe I belong to that generation of peaceniks. I certainly believe in non-violence as a central aspect of political strategy. The Indo-US deal is a very technical deal. Some friends of mine who are experts say that it's good for India and some say it's not. I am not technically qualified to judge it but one thing concerns me—I have a close relationship with America, I am married to an American and so America is the country that I regard with the greatest sympathy.

So is America a sort of home?

It's not home. It's a place where I live. I don't really think of it as home. But the one thing that worries me is that America is like any other great power. When it creates any relationship, it is usually in order to manipulate or to use towards its own advantage. I think India has for many centuries experienced these forms of subordinate relationships. The time has come when India must think of its own future and think about its own interests. What we see very much at play in today's world is a manipulation of India into some sort of adversarial relationship with China. I think this is a very dangerous thing because I don't think that such an enmity exists between India and China. In 5,000 years of our history we have fought only one war with China. No other two civilizations have attained that record. We have existed peacefully with each other and there is a deep sense of understanding between the cultures. India and China have a lot in common and the most important thing they have in common is that neither seeks to dominate the world. I think what India and China want in the future is a system of equal and multilateral relations amongst the important nations of the world. I think China should be our ally in achieving this.

Before the eighteenth century, 50 per cent of world trade originated in India and China. Today, here in Frankfurt, so many people come and say that India and China are the big threat. And I say, but what is the threat? What you are seeing here is the restoration of balance. It is the restoration of balance that once existed and it is going to exist again in the future. India and China have more than half the world's population, so obviously we are going to produce at least half the world's goods and services.

Perhaps the long view of history is that it's not linear but cyclical?

It's exactly that and the world will have to adapt to it . . . but I think we should also frankly admit that India has been a very self-centred civilization for a very long time. In general Indians really did not look outside in a very enthusiastic way . . .

Is that because there are so many Indias that Indians, whether at home or abroad, often regard one another as outsiders, 'the other'? Even though well-versed in the idea of nationhood we are beset with divisions of region, religion, caste, class, Indian and overseas Indian?

I think that began to change in about the 1960s. In literary terms I would say V.S. Naipaul as a writer is an aspect of our connecting with the larger world. In Bengali we had some very major writers who began writing about their experiences of the world. I like to think that I represent part of that phenomenon. I represent the generation that comes from a post-Independence India which is reclaiming its place in the world. I think of it as a very important responsibility that rests, in some ways, on our shoulders because never again must India allow itself to be blind to the world. This was the terrible mistake made by earlier generations.

When we look back to the Middle Ages, at the Mughal Empire for instance—a very great empire with enormous resources—it never woke up to notice the powers building around them. They just never noticed. Emperor Babar's wonderful memoir, the *Baburnama*, is so amazing because all his life, even though he was in India, he was always looking back towards Central Asia. He was never looking towards the sea. He was never looking outwards towards the world. This is something which we can never allow to happen in India. We must be aware of the world and we must understand how the world is changing.

***Sea of Poppies* is a work on a large scale. It's also peopled by an enormous range of characters and situations. The two major themes you deal with are the opium trade and the flight of thousands of impoverished Indians forced to cross the ocean as indentured labour. What triggered off this foray into nineteenth-century history?**

I have always been interested in the story of migration and people leaving India, but I really became interested in the early years of migration of indentured labour, especially the movement into Mauritius, which started in the 1830s, and the migrants who were from the major poppy-growing regions in Uttar Pradesh and Bihar.

Among the range of characters that you develop is an upper-caste widow saved at the last minute from her husband's funeral pyre, and low-caste Dalits. So the migration that took place and the relationships that developed cut across caste lines. Is there basis to this, given that the migrants came from a society with deeply entrenched caste prejudice?

It's one of the most interesting things about migration. When you are actually on that ship, people who are forced together on that ship, and are crossing the black water, *kala pani*, in a sense all of them become outcasts because they are crossing the polluting kala pani; and so they create their own communities, you know, they create their own world. They create their own little *sansar*.

So the *jahaj*, ship, on which they travel, the *Ibis*, creates a kind of *bhai-bandi*, a brotherhood and a sisterhood. It becomes a floating island on the ocean.

In fact if you speak to girmitiyas, as they are called, they will tell you that you know his father and mine were *jahaj bhais*, a kind of kinship; they think of themselves as cousins, like you and I might think of ourselves as being from the same village. The migrations may have diluted caste but they didn't do away with caste altogether. Because if you go to Mauritius today, caste is very important, important to their politics and important in many parts of their lives. But it's not like caste in Bihar, it's something else, it has changed and become more malleable.

What's also fascinating in *Sea of Poppies* is your richly detailed and researched portrait of nineteenth-century Calcutta—its high life and low life, from the indebted raja and his *rajabari*, feudal estate, to overnight fortunes being made by European shipowners, to the flood of impoverished humanity from the hinterland to be shipped overseas . . .

Not just opium, they were shipping out prisoners as well, that was the other great trade. Calcutta was the port for shipping out, as it used to be said in those days, drugs and thugs . . .

Many of the characters speak a variety of tongues in *Sea of Poppies*—linguistically it is fascinating for the range of patois it employs. For instance, there's a veritable mining of Anglo-Indian dictionaries like the *Hobson Jobson* for the Anglo-Indian speech of the British in nineteenth-century India . . .

Let me put it like this: if you read nineteenth-century English books they tell you that the British *nabobs* who come back from India spoke incomprehensibly. They spoke a kind of patois—so many were brought up by Indian servants and they grew up learning Hindi or Bengali. So I thought to myself, why does no one ever actually recreate that patois? Because when Thackeray writes about these people they end up speaking standard English but I am sure they were not speaking standard English. They created a complete language of their own, interestingly linked to Hindustani, Tamil and Bengali.

One of the things that has happened to twentieth-century English is that it has undergone a sort of 'whitening' process. People today think that English is a global language so it is accepting many different influences. But actually the opposite is true. I think in the nineteenth century English was a much more open, more permeable language and it took in a great variety of influences. In the twentieth century, through some sort of anxiety, many of these words came to be excised from English. The Hobson-Jobson is one major dictionary of Anglo-Indian words and phrases but it's by no means the only one; there are three or four of them. One of the interesting ways that Indian languages entered English was through gypsy slang which was a very major part of English slang in those days. Take a term like 'Ray Sahib' or 'Rai Sahib' and the famous nineteenth-century novel *Romany Rye* by George Borrow—the Rye in it is actually the same as Ray in 'Ray Sahib'; it means gentleman but it enters through gypsy slang.

Other than exploring the Anglo-Indian hybrid you also use the lilting cadence of Bhojpuri music and songs and the all-but-forgotten nautical lexicon *Laskari*, another patois developed by laskars, Asian and Arab sailors and pirates . . .

That was one of the most exciting things about writing this book. I have always been interested in ships and sailors and I suddenly started looking at actual crew-lists, not only of ships sailing out of India, but of crew lists of ships taking immigrants from England to Australia in the nineteenth century—you will often find that there will be four English officers and sixty laskars. And the laskars came from all over the Indian Ocean—there were Tamils, Malays, Chinese, Filipinos, Arabs and Africans who created their own lingo. I had the great good fortune to actually find a dictionary of that language. It was a dictionary written in 1812 in Calcutta by an Englishman, and was a very popular dictionary for more than a hundred years. Every sailor who sailed in the Indian Ocean had to have this *Laskari* dictionary.

Many streams come together in *Sea of Poppies*—the migration of girmitiyas, the opium trade, the rise of Calcutta as a prosperous entrepôt and the exploration of vanished tongues—but it is also about another important thing: the evocation and exploration of the Ganges, the river of north Indian plains and its vast estuary in Bengal. It's a geography that many Indians regard as sacred but in the nineteenth century it was a strategic and economic waterway, and the main seafaring route to other parts of the world. Were you conscious of this when writing the novel?

A large part of it has to do with my being Bengali because we are a riverside people; rivers mean a lot to us and we think of rivers all the time. But, yes, I really do believe that one of our great national tragedies since Independence is that our indigenous shipping industry on the great waterways has completely dried up. Rivers were the trading heart of India. The Ganges had so much traffic for centuries and today you can barely sail a hundred miles on it. It's also an incredible tragedy because if you think of the technology of sailing it is such an environmentally friendly technology; it's a technology to which we will have to return even though we have wilfully allowed ourselves to forget it.

But, ultimately, it's the cast of characters that drives the narrative of *Sea of Poppies*, which is the first part of your planned trilogy. How did you conceive this huge canvas and its large cast?

The geography, the history and all that is incidental in a novel. A novel is about characters, and if the characters don't work, nothing else will. Until you have the characters, and if the characters aren't compelling for you as a writer, then they won't be compelling for the reader. In the end, it is the characters that carry a book.

Where does the *Ibis* go from here? Do you know how the ship's voyage and the future of its cargo will develop in the coming parts of the trilogy?

No I don't and, even if I did, I wouldn't say.

After years of living in America you have now found yourself a new home in Goa and spend part of the year there. What prompted the move?

It is true that I spent a lot of time in America but, actually, I was spending a lot of time in India too and I never thought of myself as living in America permanently. Now I intend to spend most of my time in a small village in Goa where I have a house.

January 2007 and June 2008

Nadine Gordimer

In the winter of 2008, Nadine Gordimer, the South African novelist, political activist and Nobel laureate was travelling in India as a guest of the Indian government and I made considerable efforts to reach her through official sources. But such are the misjudged notions of government hospitality, her escort was neither a literary-minded civil servant nor someone especially knowledgeable about India; he was an officer of the armed forces who successfully stonewalled contact at every stage. Finally, it was through the good offices of her hotel in Delhi—who ferried a personal written request—and the novelist and career diplomat Vikas Swarup, then India's deputy high commissioner to South Africa, that she agreed to the interview.

Nadine Gordimer (b. 1923) grew up in a mining town near Johannesburg, the daughter of Jewish immigrants. Her education was scanty but she was writing from an early age, first children's stories and later stories for the *New Yorker*. Since her first published novel *The Lying Days* (1953), she has published more than a dozen novels apart from plays, collections of short stories and essays.

She was an early champion of the anti-apartheid crusade, joining the African National Congress when it was illegal and befriending Nelson Mandela's defence lawyers. Several of her novels, *A World of Strangers* (1958), *The Late Bourgeois World* (1966), *Burger's Daughter* (1979) and *July's People* (1981) were either banned for long periods or censored. Many dealt with intense political and sexual relations between black and white people when such connections were considered criminal. When Mandela was released in 1990, Gordimer was one of the first people he wished to meet.

Her post-apartheid fiction, such as *My Son's Story* (1990) and *The House Gun* (1998), deal with rising crime, political violence, racial hatred and personal grief. Nadine Gordimer has been crowned by many literary laurels in her long career, culminating with the Nobel Prize for literature in 1991. 'Writing is making sense of life,' she famously said. 'You work your whole life and perhaps you've made sense of one small area.'

In person she is a small-built, white-haired woman, the image of a cosy grandmother. But her grave, reflective manner can become animated and charged as when she described how she was attacked in her home by robbers in 2006. I carried twin burdens to the Gordimer interview—the nervous anticipation of meeting a great writer but also a heavy bag weighted with her books, from friends and colleagues, to be inscribed. With infinite patience and good humour she finished the pile as I passed her chits with the correct spellings of their names.

You are on Indian soil at a pretty historic moment. America has just elected its first black president. What does Barack Obama's arrival on the world stage mean for you?

It means a great deal because he is black and white. He brings the two together in his own blood and DNA. He has a white parent and a black parent. So it is symbolic but, at the same time it goes further, because I'm sure that it influences him in his values. One can see that this will then pass into the government and administration and, I hope, to the American people. When I was much younger, the Americans said, 'You can never have a Catholic president in Protestant America.' And then we had Kennedy, and now, all these years later, a black. But, as I say, he is not black. He is black–white—which is even better.

Black and white—that has been the subject of your life's gaze both in your writing and in your social and political activism. Yet the abolition of apartheid in South Africa has not ended tensions of race, and it remains, like India in many ways, a divisive, often violent and difficult society. Do you think it's still a matter of two racial communities, black and white, coming to terms in democratic South Africa?

It's not a matter of the two communities. The progress is amazing there. The Congress alliance, which was the African National Congress, was completely black which then became an alliance of white members, the Indian Congress comprising of South African Indians and the small communist party. The strong links forged in the freedom movement brought about the change led by a man like Nelson Mandela who has no racial feelings. Throughout the anti-apartheid movement, there was already a meeting of the so-called irreconcilables of an earlier time. What we have now is something we had never thought of because our eyes were on getting rid of the enemy of apartheid rule. We did, and that too without a terrible civil war. People say it's a miracle. It's not a miracle because a miracle comes from somewhere else—this was brought about by the people of South Africa. But now we have class differences. We have a small but growing black middle class which is a very good thing. But we also have a black upper class along with the white upper class. So class differences have risen.

And when social and political structures rapidly change other problems arise, like corruption . . .

Yes, and the corruption that comes with change. As you well know from your own country's example, corruption goes all the way from the traffic cop who takes a bribe right up to the cabinet. It's the same there.

In one of your recent novels, *The House Gun*, you dwell dramatically on tensions of class when a white couple, whose son is accused of murder, hires a black lawyer . . .

Actually, if you look at that book, it's got nothing to do with colour or even class, for that matter. The white couple happen to choose the black lawyer but not because he is black or white; it's just because he is a good lawyer. What is troubling, therefore, is another question—equitable economic opportunities and employment policies for blacks. Just look into our past, these are necessary, because blacks were discriminated against for so long.

People think discrimination began with apartheid in the 1940s when racial segregation was institutionalized but it actually began in the seventeenth century—and we have had exactly fourteen years to put it right. The world expects us to provide a perfect democracy without any overhang of racial feeling, with houses for everybody, with level education for everybody—in other words, equality where there was none before—after all these centuries of discrimination. It was not all that long ago that the civil service or the post office was not only completely white but completely Afrikaner. Now the post officers are 80 per cent black and the other 20 per cent are Indian and coloured. In the banks there were all white employees; now they are 90 per cent black or Indians and a few coloured.

Despite equitable representation and job opportunities, why are cities like your hometown Johannesburg and others racked with street crime, social tensions and violence?

This is because of poverty. The poverty exists because we have this tremendous burden of refugees. We have over three million from Zimbabwe alone. We have refugees from Somalia and from the Congo. They arrive and they have no way to live because they have no work. If I arrive from somewhere and I have smuggled some of my family in, and my children are hungry, and I walk past you, with your camera, cell phone and wallet, I am afraid that I, too, will become a thief. So we cannot be moral about the motives of the crime that exists.

I was attacked in my home, over a year ago, in the middle of the day. Somebody climbed over from the neighbour's garden, the dog barked at the man, I came out of my little room where I write, but someone was already in the house and I was clasped from behind. There were three very young men. I can't tell you much about their faces because my head was pushed between the shoulder and the neck but an arm was around me. It was a very young, smooth black arm with a beautiful hand. These were young people who shouldn't have been robbing an old woman and her housekeeper. They were not experienced criminals. They did not have a gun and they didn't threaten with a knife. But they treated my black housekeeper terribly. She cried and screamed, so they knocked her down on the floor and, at one point, I just lost my cool. I wrenched my head up and said, 'What is the bravery in all this? She could be your grandmother, leave her.' And I'm afraid, since they were so young, it worked.

The life of the fictional imagination and a life as political activist come together in you. Do you believe that a writer can change the world through his or her writing?

I think when we look at it very humbly, where has this happened? In recent times great writers like Jean-Paul Sartre, Albert Camus and Simone de Beauvoir didn't have much influence on the French government, on the War or on French colonialism. In my own country, I had three books banned and I fought for the collection I had put together of stories by young black writers. I got it published and it was promptly banned. Those of us writing in English have the advantage that it's a world language and the books can be published elsewhere. Where we fiction writers come in is that we go into the lives of the people, into what I call the inner testimony of people—how they lived before the turning point, what brings them to the point of conflict and how they deal with its aftermath. Our work as fiction writers is to give another dimension that you can't get from first information and because you don't know what happened afterwards.

Everybody saw on television and newspapers what happened in the anti-apartheid battles in 1976 when the youth rose up. Some died. But how were their families, their brothers and sisters, affected? You see the moment of conflict on TV and you read the political analysis afterwards in the newspaper—but you do not know what brought the crowd of people to that point, what gave them the guts to face the police.

Did the novelist's imagination, or the search for the inner testimony as you call it, develop in your case because of your interrupted and incomplete education? Because, despite this, you began writing when very young, before you were a teenager, and never stopped. So where did the training to become a writer come from?

Reading, my dear, is the only training for a writer from a young age. You only become a writer by being a compulsive reader. I can thank my mother for making me a member of a children's library when I was six years old. And as she was a friend of the librarian, by the time I was ten or eleven, I was like a pig in clover. I had the freedom of the whole library. I was reading *Lady Chatterley's Lover* by D.H. Lawrence and I first read *A Passage to India* by E.M. Forster then. I also read non-fiction biographies. That was my education. It didn't come from my convent schooling.

Later on, when you became a political activist, was it your encounters in the turbulent politics of South Africa that became the subject matter of some of your most original and insightful fiction?

Yes, because I began to move amongst people whose existential state it was. You could not stay apart from it. You know what Flaubert once said—it's not very polite but true. He said, 'I tried to live in an ivory tower, but the shit kept beating against the walls.' That is what happened. You couldn't just say that I'm going to be a writer and I will write about problems between human beings on the personal side—

love, sexuality, the relationship between children and parents and so on. The outside world presses in upon your most personal life.

So the writer must wade deep into the sea of humanity . . .

Right. The writer is immersed in it. The writer is imbued by what happens in his or her immediate surroundings—at school, at work, in society and, above all, in the laws that enclose us all.

There is a large and old Indian community in South Africa and you are well-acquainted with many of them. Mahatma Gandhi's nationalist revolution also arose out of his life and experiences in South Africa. How has South Africa's freedom changed the lives of Indians in South Africa?

I am proud to say on behalf of the Indian population there that they are unique. There were Indians everywhere, mostly merchants, but the only place where they prominently entered the freedom struggle was in South Africa. They have earned their place to be Africans because they took part in that struggle. Of course we have to thank the Mahatma because he started it off. The African National Congress was influenced by Gandhi's thinking and, indeed, during the 1950s its policy was one of non-violent resistance. But then we came to a stage where the South Africans in power were ill-treating those who took part in non-violent resistance. They were poisoned, they were beaten and they were treated with unbelievable cruelty. There was no white innocent, including myself. If you were born white, you were part of the privileged race.

Nelson Mandela has been canonized in his own lifetime but in neighbouring Zimbabwe, Robert Mugabe has proved to be far from saintly. What's your opinion of Mugabe?

I have been appalled by Robert Mugabe. It is so sad because he was part of the anti-colonial struggle. He was a brave man; and when he first became president, his reforms of the education system, which had favoured the white community, were remarkable. I don't know what happened to him. He is the perfect illustration of the old saying that when power corrupts, it corrupts absolutely. I don't know how Zimbabwe is going to get rid of him. There is abject poverty there and people are starving. As I said, we have millions of them in our country, adding to our problems. Nothing can be solved there because our former president

Thabo Mbeki has tried for many years to bring the different sides together but Mugabe wouldn't give an inch. If God came down from heaven, Mugabe would say, 'You are a white imperialist in disguise.'

This is your second trip to India. You were here fifteen years ago and I hear your favourite spots in this country are the Ajanta and Ellora caves. What are the most noticeable changes you have observed?

I must be very careful about this. I found that Mumbai is twenty times more crowded than it was fifteen years ago, mainly because of people flooding into the city for work. Kolkata I had never been to before—I found the poverty appalling because I was in a beautiful hotel and it wasn't like Mumbai, where the poor live in other districts. They were on the pavement right outside—stall holders, beggars and people sleeping on the street, while I was in an air-conditioned room. There was a wall between you, that was all. I was also very upset to see the abandoned animals, not only dogs, but horses and cattle that, unable to pull carts, were just abandoned. And I thought, India has had independence from oppression by outsiders since 1947 so why is there is still so much cruelty? But I also realize that India is an enormous country and what a struggle it is to deal with it.

November 2008

Günter Grass

Between August 1987 and January 1988, the German Nobel Prize-winning author, playwright and artist Günter Grass (b. 1927) spent six months in Kolkata, living in middle-class neighbourhoods, meeting poets, artists and writers, and walking the streets. The result was a book called *Show Your Tongue* (1989), part sketchbook and part writer's impressions. The imagery of both is dark, often disturbing, and the title refers to Kali's hanging tongue. The volume was a harsh tribute to his 'unbidden love for . . . a city damned to offer lodgings to every human misery'. As for the drawings: 'Forget the twaddle about art,' declared Grass. 'Do decay with a broad brush, with the edge of the pen, with crumbling charcoal.'

Predictably, the book did not please many in Kolkata, though elsewhere it was hailed as highly original. To his surprise, when he returned to the city eighteen years later, in 2005, he was accorded a warm welcome; this time he was staying at the Oberoi Grand on Chowringhee. The artist Shuvaprasanna offered to take him for a walk in the crowded, colourful lanes of Chitpur—brimming with old shops and artisans' stalls—and invited me to join them. This interview was recorded on the steps of a crumbling colonial-style mansion typical of the area.

Born in the Baltic city of Danzig (now Gdańsk in Poland), Grass fought in the German army during World War II, was wounded and then captured as a prisoner of war. Later he studied art, moving to Paris where he worked as a sculptor and graphic artist (he frequently designs his own book covers). He shot to literary prominence with his first novel *The Tin Drum* (1959), an immediate best-seller set in his hometown of Danzig. It was followed by *Cat and Mouse* (1961) and *Dog Years* (1963). The three novels, known as the Danzig trilogy, are the centerpiece of his writing, spanning German history in the first half of the twentieth century, tracing the rise and fall of Nazism, and the ruin of war. Lyrically evocative and picaresque, his language broke free from the heavy propagandist literary style of the Nazi era.

In the 1960s, Grass became active in politics, joining the Social Democratic party, working with Willy Brandt and writing many of his speeches. Grass has written fiction, plays, essays and political commentary, and regularly produced art.

You are back in Kolkata eighteen years after you first came and lived here for six months. How has it changed?

Parts like this [Chitpur] haven't changed so much. There is the same smell, people are busy and still the old-fashioned professions are prevalent, though I don't see them making the murals any more. I hope this kind of life goes on. Modernization should stop here. In other parts of Kolkata, yes, there are changes—flyovers and so on—but I am afraid that this new kind of architecture disfigures the city. But where we are sitting, the architecture is a mixture of Bengal and the British colonial style. It is unique. And this for me is the face of Kolkata.

After you lived here, you produced a book of your impressions of Kolkata with drawings called *Show Your Tongue*. Some of the things you wrote and the pictures you drew were harsh and controversial. Are you aware that they upset people in Kolkata?

When I lived here in the mid-1980s, I stayed not in the Oberoi hotel, but with ordinary people. I walked the streets every day, seeing beautiful things and also the bad things in the whole city. I spoke to the people in the slum areas. And I also saw that the upper class and the middle class don't even look the poor in the eye. There is a growing distance all round the world between the rich and the poor. I know that there are many people who don't like the things I say. But there are so many other speakers who show wonderful things and create nice facades to hide the dirt. I think it is necessary for writers to speak out and put a finger on the dirt.

What upset you was not so much the poverty and the deprivation of the poor but the apathy and indifference of the middle class. Isn't that universal?

When the result of the [2004] general election in India came out, I was not surprised. Everybody in Europe expected the ruling party to come back to power again. But Indians pushed their rulers out, proving again that it is the greatest democracy in the world. When I thought about it, and analysed the election result, it was clear that the poor people had done it. Not the upper class, not the middle class, but the poor who chased out the powerful. That is a reason to be very proud—that ordinary people can use the possibilities that democracy offers.

Many in the world today speak of India as a strong power with its skill, for example, in the IT industry; they talk of India's role in a globalized world. But they do not point out that the strongest force in India is the voice of the poor. How they live from day to day concerns me because they are this country's future.

Industrialization and even globalization is inevitable, but you have consistently pointed out the inherent dangers of modernization. As a writer in the early twenty-first century, do you foresee modernization creating greater problems of inequality and injustice?

The stock markets may be jumping but why are thousands unemployed? The new economies are insensitive to the lives of ordinary people; they are totally out of sync. We face this acute problem in Europe now. There are more than four million unemployed in a rich country like Germany—and the numbers are growing. This is how shortsighted modernization can be.

The shout of globalization only concerns the marvellous things it can achieve—but just at one economic level. Yet there is a deeper cultural level. Is the journey of globalization going to result in a deeper understanding and integration of cultures? That is the question I ask.

Yesterday, I explained to an audience that one of the main influences in my writing and novels comes from the European tradition of the picaresque novel. The picaresque novel had its origins in Spain and was a result of the mingling of Arabic and Spanish storytelling. Perhaps the most marvellous example of this mixture is Cervantes's *Don Quixote*. Globalization is not new but it can only be meaningful and have a lasting effect when it goes deeper, with cross-cultural roots.

You fought in World War II and had your own ghosts of Nazi Germany to exorcize. These are portrayed in your works like *The Tin Drum, Cat and Mouse* and *Dog Years* which make up the famous Danzig trilogy. The world is beset by other ghosts today—the rise of fundamentalist religion and the war on terror. How does the writer engage with these events?

I know what war is and I learnt to be afraid of it. I am very critical of any fundamentalist ideology, Christian or Muslim, which is growing everywhere. Without tolerance, the world will collapse.

A writer cannot remain disengaged from the problems of the world. Take the nuclear danger: after the Soviet Union collapsed, the nuclear material was stolen and it could be anywhere. We have only one main power now, the United States of America. But if they are unable to control their problems, how can they rule the world? Look at the terrible mistakes of George W. Bush—the kind of crime unleashed on Iraq will have long-term consequences. We need to oppose such crimes. That is why I believe that a country like India, and Indian writers, has a very important voice. I also believe that India must have a more prominent role in the United Nations. The old construction following World War II, of veto powers held by a few countries, has to change. Only China and India can restore the balance of power against the United States. Great injustices continue in our new century. Although we have sent people to the moon, we are still incapable of feeding the hungry. Other problems are of climate change and inadequate resources of air and water for a growing population all over the world. War cannot solve these problems. It is as simple as that; but we spend huge amounts on weapons that we could have used for other things.

Can writers really help avert war or feed the hungry? Can literature alter power structures or reduce nuclear arsenals and military adventurism?

Maybe not. But writers can do one thing: they can give a voice to the millions who have no voice. We can be where the losers are. We don't write for ourselves or for the rich and powerful, people who think they are making history. Writers can be on the side of the victims of the story. This is literature's great possibility—it was so in the past and is true today.

And speaking for yourself, have you helped bring about change through your work?

I am sceptical about that but I go on. Sisyphus always pushed the stone and kept the stone from rolling back. I am happy with my stone. Every day, you must roll the stone. That is my philosophy.

July 2005

Ramachandra Guha

Historian and biographer, Ramachandra Guha (b. 1958) is a many-faceted scholar, popular columnist and compelling public speaker—the perfect early-twenty-first-century archetype of Amartya Sen's 'argumentative Indian'.

Although Guha spends much of his life in mouldering archives and poring over decaying documents, there is nothing remotely stuffy, dusty or distant about him, with his tousled grey hair, well-tailored jacket and cricketer's gait. He speaks as he writes—a gifted natural. His muscular arguments are expressed in prose that is clear and stimulating.

Looking back on an acquaintance with Ramachandra Guha of more than a decade, I do not think of him as a lofty historian, but as someone who is at the heart and soul of the indefinable Indian gathering—intellectual and social but essentially a place for letting off steam—encapsulated in the Bengali word 'adda'.

But he is not, as is frequently assumed, a Bengali. He is Tamil, his forebears having moved from Kumbakonam to settle in Bangalore; the family name 'Guhan' was shortened to 'Guha' because they later moved to north India. If Tamil genealogy had been followed, Ramachandra Guha would have been rightly called G. Ramachandra.

Guha trained as an economist after attending Doon School and St. Stephen's College, but he became a biographer by accident. His doctoral research at the Indian Institute of Management, Kolkata, was in the social history of forestry in Uttarakhand, and his first published works were in environmental history, including *This Fissured Land: An Ecological History of India* (1992).

He broke from the mould to produce a critically acclaimed biography of the anthropologist *Verrier Elwin: Savaging the Civilized* (1999). A love of cricket led him to edit *The Picador Book of Cricket* (2001), an instant best-seller that, in turn, led to his pioneering social history of the game in *A Corner of a Foreign Field: An Indian History of a British Sport* (2001).

Between teaching assignments at international institutions, Guha kept up a prolific output in essays and profiles that include *An Anthropologist among the Marxists* (2000) and *The Last Liberal* (2004), before publishing his magisterial history, *India after Gandhi* (2007), an immediate critical and commercial hit. It was chosen as a book of the year by the *Economist*, the *Washington Post*, the *Wall Street Journal* and a book of the decade by the *Times of India* and the *Hindustan Times*.

His reputation as a writer is bolstered by his passionate, often implacable voice as a debater. An example is his joust with the writer-activist Arundhati Roy whom he famously dubbed as 'the Arun Shourie of the Left'. ('I'm inclined to put as great a distance as possible between the Guhas of the world and myself,' she replied.)

Among his many awards, he was honoured with the Padma Bhushan in 2009 and invited by the London School of Economics to serve as the Philippe Roman Professor of history and international affairs in 2011.

Ramachandra Guha has appeared more than once on *Just Books* but this interview was recorded after the release of his latest book, *Makers of Modern India*.

You choose nineteen figures from modern Indian history in *Makers of Modern India*, many of them obvious choices—Ram Mohan Roy, Gokhale, Tagore, Gandhi, Jinnah, Nehru and Jayaprakash Narayan—but some are virtually unknown. How did you pick these nineteen from such a wide canvas, to present their arguments in their own writings?

I had a few criteria in mind: one was the quality of their prose and the other was whether their ideas or words travel across generations. For example, there are some remarkable Indians, like Subhas Chandra Bose, Vallabhbhai Patel and Indira Gandhi, three people who definitively impacted Indian politics and society but never wrote very much. They weren't writers or thinkers. There were other Indians who are outdated; if you read Sri Aurobindo, he must have been an influential thinker in his time, but to us today, his writings seem obscure. The selection is of people who still speak to us, like Nehru, Ambedkar and Gandhi, and some lesser-known figures like the feminist Tarabai Shinde in the 1880s or Hamid Dalwai, the Muslim reformer who died young in 1977. Their writings were powerful then and are utterly relevant to India's predicament today.

In your lucid introduction to *Makers of Modern India* you expand on the argument that 'India is the most interesting country in the world in the most contentious times'. Why do you think so?

First of all, because of our size and diversity. We are much more diverse than any country in the world, and going through many revolutions simultaneously—a democratic, social and economic revolution. There is a cacophony of voices and an intensity of debate that you don't find in countries like China. The United States has our size but not our linguistic and religious diversity. In many ways, India is the most exasperating country in the world, but always the most interesting because its plurality, disputation and contention is articulated through parliamentary debates, dharnas, street protests and other forms of articulation. In my book I have only tried to display glimpses of this diversity.

Was your choice of posthumous figures deliberate?

A historian needs distance. We can't really tell if a political actor today is going to have a lasting significance in India. We need about twenty to thirty years to understand and appreciate the importance of a historical figure. The second reason, as I argue in my book, is that the tradition of the thinker-activist seems to have died out. There are wonderfully gifted Indian novelists, historians, journalists and columnists, but our politicians are not the original thinkers and writers in the way that figures like Ambedkar or Kamaladevi Chattopadhyay were.

You came to writing about history in a circuitous manner. Originally you were a student of economics and took a master's degree from the Delhi School of Economics. You then moved to the Indian Institute of Management in Kolkata to study anthropology. What made you make that shift?

Quite honestly, I was a second-rate economist and I knew I wouldn't make it. But when I was doing my MA I read a book by Verrier Elwin and I became enchanted with culture and anthropology. I then moved towards the study of society and culture, and, by accident, I discovered the archives and the joys of working amongst forgotten, buried and dusty documents. I made a further transition to becoming a historian because these disciplines are interconnected. In my history, there is a little bit of economics and anthropology; there are residues of my earlier training even in my current work.

Your PhD was on the Chipko movement and social forestry in the hills of the north, an environmental study. How difficult was the transition from academic analysis to focus on a single life in your admired biography of Verrier Elwin, *Savaging the Civilized*, which found a much wider public?

It was a difficult transition because the study of an individual and singular life is disparaged in the academy. Because of the great influence of Marxism we are supposed to deal with aggregates: with classes, peasants and workers, or with the state and the nation as a whole. It was with some diffidence and some recklessness—in challenging the received wisdom that a scholar should not attempt biography—that I came to Elwin. Elwin was an utterly captivating character: an Oxford scholar who joined Gandhi, a Christian who became a Buddhist, a bishop's son who started living with adivasis and married one of them, a theologian who became a novelist, and someone who lived in the central Indian heartland but spent his last years in Arunachal Pradesh. The world he spanned made it important, almost mandatory, for me to document his life in all its tensions, diversity, glory and humiliation.

Would you say a many-faceted figure or polymath makes a subject especially attractive to a biographer?

Elwin is special but we have produced others. It's a pity that we lack a modern biography tradition in this country. Take someone like Shivaram Karanth, the great writer and dancer from my own state Karnataka, or Mahasweta Devi, the Bengali writer and activist, still alive, and a remarkable figure in her own way, or Marathi figures like, for example; P.L. Deshpande, the humorist.

I think India has all kinds of interesting medium-range figures. We have written biographies of the Nehrus, the Ambedkars and the Gandhis, but where are the lives of middle-range figures who mediate between the subaltern and the elite, between the countryside and the city, between east and west? Elwin was one such but there are others, too. For example, Gandhi's disciple Mira Behn, the daughter of an English admiral who became a Gandhian social worker. So India, as the most interesting country in the world, does produce many of the most interesting characters in the world. And it is unfortunate that most of them await their biographers.

India at the beginning of this century is often projected as a confident nation with a predominantly young population. Why is it then that controversy erupts time and again whenever a warts-and-all biography of major public figures such as Gandhi appears?

It is unfortunate that we have this censorious culture. A figure like Gandhi doesn't belong to a particular sect, so it's possible to be open about him. But others have been appropriated by a sect or political party: Ambedkar is the property of the Dalits, Savarkar of the Hindutva class and Nehru of the Congress Party. It becomes difficult to write dispassionate serious biographies and it undermines our claim to be a plural and open democracy. It's partly to do with the weakness of our political class. Look at how Rohinton Mistry's novel was dropped from Mumbai University's syllabus. At the first sign of dissent, the government caves in. We should resist and protest this, for in a vigorous literary culture you need openness and critique. You need no sacred cows at all.

And does this propensity of creating sacred cows arise from sycophancy?

Of course. One of the incidental by-products in *Makers of Modern India* is that you see Gandhi and Ambedkar argue with each other over matters of principle. There's nothing personal or visceral or polemical about their arguments. Both are humanized by their arguments. That's how we should see these different figures: as extraordinary but also flawed. The greatness of someone like Gandhi was that he recognized his flaws. We want today a perfect Gandhi, but Gandhi himself knew he was fallible, possessed all kinds of weaknesses, was willing to recognize and correct them.

One of the difficulties that historians face in India is blocked access to the private papers of leading public figures, long after they have departed, and even restrictions on official documents. How big a handicap is that?

It is a problem, particularly with the Nehru-Gandhi family. Jawaharlal Nehru's and Indira Gandhi's private papers have not been shown to historians, though the papers of many other individuals are available. But often, even if their private papers are not available, you can look at oral histories or at old newspapers. Not long ago I was reading, since I'm now working on Gandhi, a fascinating article by you about the making of Richard Attenborough's *Gandhi*, which gives you a sense of Gandhi's afterlife. Apart from newspapers and oral histories, government records and intelligence reports can also be surrogate sources. History is hard work and, in some ways, the research is more exciting than the writing.

But if the historian is also in search of themes, then your trajectory is wide-ranging—from environmental history to biography, to sports history to the sweep of political history as in your best-selling opus *India after Gandhi*. Is each subject distinctive or do they link up?

They are distinctive in the thematic sense. There are broadly four phases to my career: there was environmental history, biography, sports history and, now, political history. But what is linked is that in different ways they all grapple with India's painful, complicated, unfinished yet utterly absorbing and compelling encounter with the modern world. They tell the story of tensions and conflicts involved in this gigantic historical process that has been unfolding in this extraordinarily interesting country in the last 200 years.

Does one story sometimes lead to another?

Sometimes, indeed, it does. Because I worked on environment, I got to Elwin. Then I started writing books about cricket and I got to the story of the Dalit spin bowler Palwankar Baloo. *India after Gandhi* came by accident. A visionary publisher called Peter Strauss contacted me and said historians of India start and stop in 1947 and what we need is a post-Independence history. 'You clearly enjoy archival research, you write less wooden prose than most academic historians, so why don't you try?' So I owe a debt to him that the last step of my journey, political history, as embodied in *India after Gandhi* and in *Makers of Modern India*, was prompted by him.

The wooden prose of Indian historians is not the only deterrent that puts off a wider reading public from engaging with the past. Often fascinating subjects are made so arid and arcane, it appears that historians are writing for one another?

Absolutely. I think Indian history for a very long time was inward-looking and self-referential; it did not pay attention to literary elegance and style to reach out to a wider public. But that is changing. If you look at the remarkable biography of Vasco da Gama by Sanjay Subramanyam; at younger historians of ancient India such as Nayanjot Lahiri and Upinder Singh; Partha Chatterjee's wonderful biography of the Kumar of Bhawal or at someone like Srinath Raghavan, a top-class strategic historian who can make war appealing and sexy, you have a critical mass of Indian historians who conduct archival research and pay some attention to style, language and accessibility. For one without the other is incomplete. There's no point in researching and writing in stilted sociological prose. And there's no point in just writing fun stories without deep research. In the past a few historians may have created walls between themselves and the public but that wall is being breached by the kind of scholars that are around.

Many of the historians you mention are professional academics but there are other examples, not Indians, who have come to history and biography from other disciplines and won new audiences. William Dalrymple comes from journalism and Patrick French combines biography with travel. What do think of them?

I think they both are good examples of people who do original research, write well and communicate to their audience. They have thrown down a challenge to Indians to respond in a similar way. I would still say that it is not enough to tell a story well. There must be an analytical sharpness and robustness to the questions you ask. History is a window into social conflicts, social diversities, the making and unmaking of nation states. I think one should not disparage academic historians too much because they have the necessary tools to link their stories into a wider analytical narrative. I think that is very important. There is room for the academic and non-academic historian; and also for younger Indian writers to write history, non-fiction, biography and political commentary. For too long gifted young Indian writers were enchanted with the idea of writing a novel. Not everyone can be an Arundhati Roy, an Amitav Ghosh or a Vikram Seth. Now that the economics of publishing are changing, non-fiction works also get decent advances.

History and biography need not be about individuals or political events. The two forms can encompass a contemporary narrative as in Suketu Mehta's account of Bombay in *Maximum City*, which is a portrait of a metropolis through its people and conflicts . . .

London has one remarkable book a year. Bombay is a world city in its diversity and conflicts as much as London is. I am sure people in Mumbai will be working on other books on Mumbai, touching aspects that Suketu Mehta could not. We don't have a really good book on Chennai. The last good book about Kolkata was written by Geoffrey Moorhouse in the 1970s. So there are so many subjects awaiting their historians and biographers. I think we saw an efflorescence of fiction writing in the 1970s to the 1990s. Now is the time for historians, biographers, scholars and travel writers to take over.

You have been working for some time on a major opus, a biography of Gandhi. There are already many biographies and studies devoted to virtually every aspect of his life and times. What will be new about yours?

I have been working on it for some years and it will take some more years for it to see the light of day. The first volume is set in South Africa, where Gandhi spent twenty-one years of his life, a period that is skipped over hastily by biographers. I have made four trips to South Africa and I found lots of interesting material there in the archives that sheds new light on his friendships, on his struggles and torments, and on how the colonial state viewed him. My book on Gandhi is going to be based, I hope, on a more thorough excavation of primary sources about him that lie scattered in archives all round the world. Too many biographers of Gandhi had relied simply on his collected works. Having said that, apart from new research material, I think Gandhi is a protean figure that every generation needs to discover afresh. Rajmohan Gandhi wrote a very good book on Gandhi. Gandhi is that kind of man—given his global importance, his multiple roles as a politician, social reformer and religious pluralist—that there are many aspects to his work that a biographer can explore in many new ways.

If history is like a running river, is it open to new interpretations by applying other disciplines of learning or because new facts come to light as the historian digs deeper?

New sources are very important for a historian, or discovering forgotten sources—like the material in South Africa about Gandhi. No one has used it, partly because they didn't think that period of his life was important and partly because, during the years of apartheid, Indians couldn't go to South Africa.

A historian cannot have a compelling story to tell unless his work is carried along by the depth and density of primary material. For example, I saw a cartoon in South Africa where Gandhi is shown as an elephant and General Smuts is riding a roadroller and stopping the elephant. It gives a different spin to the Indian encounter with the South African racial state.

The freshness of history comes in its writing and its fullness comes from the research. Both are equally important. The historian is a researcher who digs deep in the archives and gets good material, but he is also an artist and a writer who constructs his story in an appealing, interesting, evocative and accessible way. But some popular historians are not scholars and many scholars are not writers.

October 2010

Ed Kashi

Mohsin Hamid

Pakistani novelist Mohsin Hamid (b. 1971) presents an image of the global yuppie. Slim, aquiline-nosed and prematurely bald, his urbane manner suggests the international lawyer or corporate executive. Hamid has been both. Though the protagonists of his two acclaimed novels, *Moth Smoke* (2000) and *The Reluctant Fundamentalist* (2007), may bear similarities to his background, they are both, in his words, 'corrupt idealists' with disintegrating lives. The world of Daru, the upscale Lahore banker in *Moth Smoke*, falls apart with his decline into drugs, an affair with his best friend's wife and a hit-and-run car accident. Changez, the high-flying New York-based management consultant in *The Reluctant Fundamentalist*, is transformed by 9/11. Watching the twin towers being blown up on TV he confesses, 'Despicable as it may sound, my initial reaction was to be remarkably pleased.' He gives up his job, grows a beard and returns home to Lahore. The moral ambiguity of Hamid's characters is accentuated by the external events of sabre-rattling on the India–Pakistan border and the war on terror unleashed by the West. Both of Hamid's novels met with immediate critical and commercial success and *The Reluctant Fundamentalist* was shortlisted for the Man Booker Prize.

Hamid grew up between Pakistan and America. He took degrees from Princeton and Harvard Law School, later working as a management consultant in New York and London before returning to live in Lahore in 2009. 'I never believed in the role Pakistan plays as a villain on news shows. The Pakistan I knew was the out-of-character Pakistan, Pakistan without its makeup and plastic fangs, a working actor with worn-out shoes, a close family, and a hearty laugh,' he said of his decision to move back. Mira Nair is making the film of *The Reluctant Fundamentalist* from a screenplay written jointly with Hamid. These two interviews with Hamid, recorded in New Delhi and at the first Karachi Literature Festival, are conflated because of their overlapping content.

***The Reluctant Fundamentalist* unfolds as a dramatic monologue by its protagonist Changez who sits in a Lahore restaurant and recounts his story to an American visitor. How much of you is really there in Changez? Like you he is a Princeton graduate and also works for a management consultancy in New York when 9/11 happens.**

Changez is not meant to be me and he isn't really me. He is twenty-two years old when the novel's action takes place and 9/11 happens. At that time I was thirty; he has been in America for about four years and I had been there for about fifteen, so I was almost half-American. He also has a number of insecurities and complexities which, hopefully, I don't. Yes, I worked for McKinsey & Co. when 9/11 happened although I had been transferred to the London office that summer. I had spent time in the Philippines, Greece and Chile—so has Changez—and so I write about those places. Like him I worked in the corporate world in New York.

I tend to write about what I know; I am from that school of novelists who does almost no research. Similarly, Daru, the protagonist of my first novel *Moth Smoke* was a heroin addict and I can talk about that with a certain degree of familiarity because I knew someone who was. In that case, too, the protagonist wasn't me. But Changez could easily be my little brother or my best friend's younger brother.

The drama of *The Reluctant Fundamentalist* hinges on what Changez undergoes when he sees the twin towers being blown up. He is on assignment in far-off Manila when it happens and he suddenly confesses to pleasure that America has been brought to its knees. What was your own reaction when you saw the terror strikes?

When I was watching 9/11 my thought was of my ex-roommate who happened to work in the World Trade Centre. Seeing the buildings explode and seeing people who worked within fifty yards of that building, my initial reaction was to pick up the phone and start calling people. But, as I said, I was already much more invested in New York than Changez.

His reaction, that sense of pleasure, is one which I think was quite common around the world though perhaps not much remarked upon, because it's difficult to separate what is obviously a shameful reaction to something so terrible. Changez's reaction reveals to him that he has a certain unknown, unrealized resentment towards America which he suddenly becomes aware of at that moment, even though he recognizes that this is a terrible thing.

Yet his reaction, revealed in that introspective monologue, is to turn his back on his comfortable New York life, grow a beard though he is in no overt way Islamic, threatened or ostracized, and return home to Pakistan . . .

In Changez's case it's important to know that his experience in America is not characterized by racist incidents nor by a denial of opportunities; broadly his colleagues at work and his environment continue to encourage him. His reaction comes from within; it's not driven by a sense of being ostracized but driven by something external that is less a personal experience and more, I think, a feeling of the Muslim world being under threat. It's a Muslim world that Changez would never identify with before the war on terror began because he wouldn't particularly have thought himself as part of that world. He is not particularly religious, for example. But when suddenly the invasion of Afghanistan begins, when India and Pakistan almost go to war, he gets this palpable sense of belonging to his people; he feels his calling is to return and to help those people.

***Moth Smoke*, your first novel, was published ten years ago and is a portrait of moral decay in upper-class Lahore. Its protagonist Daru's life, like that of Changez, spins out of control with an adulterous affair and drug addiction. How did that portrait of Pakistan emerge?**

I grew up mostly in Pakistan and, with the exception of a few years in California when I was a small child, I lived in Lahore till I was eighteen. After the age of eighteen, I spent three or four months a year in Lahore until I was twenty-two and I came back for a year after college. I began writing the book then. When *Moth Smoke* began, very little of my life had been outside of Pakistan. As I wrote, more and more time did pass outside Pakistan, but I kept coming back to Pakistan for months at a time to work on it. The book was born out of a world that I had seen, grown up with and knew intimately, so it felt like a novel about the Lahore I knew but didn't see represented anywhere. *Moth Smoke* was written around the time when I was leaving Lahore, and *The Reluctant Fundamentalist*, which is about New York, was written just as I left New York. So maybe there are a few years to digest an experience before I write about it.

Both of my novels are set in different milieus where I myself have been. As I said, I have had friends who have been drug addicts and I have worked in a corporate New York setting. I didn't live the events that happened to Daru in *Moth Smoke* and I didn't live what happens to Changez in *The Reluctant Fundamentalist* but it was a way to explore a tangent of my life. What if I had lived this way? What would that have been like? In a way both novels are about fantasy-reality that starts with a reality quite close to mine but ends up more removed.

If analysed, wouldn't they be characterized as addictive-obsessive types?

Yes they are both obsessive, they both think a lot, they both passionately delude themselves and they are both corrupt idealists in a way. They are quite different characters but they do have these things in common. As a writer, fantasy and reality are close for me because my reality consists of spending many hours a day imagining things that don't exist. A life of fantasy is a part of my real world.

Even generally, the day-dreams we have, the things we imagine doing but don't do, the person we bump into, the way we smile and walk away but later think of for many hours, all of these tangents make us human; and for me, this idea of fantasy-reality is something that I explore in the heads of my characters.

A characteristic of your two novels is their narrative structure. *Moth Smoke* is told in multiple voices and *The Reluctant Fundamentalist* is a dramatic monologue. How did you arrive at these forms?

I get there by doing it wrong a few times first. The first draft of *Moth Smoke* had only one voice. The voice changed. There were different voices and finally a voice like Daru's voice emerged; still the novel wasn't working and then the idea was to let different points of view come in, to unlock the book's different potentials. That is what happened.

In *The Reluctant Fundamentalist*, my first thing was, I don't want to write *Moth Smoke* again so I am not going to do multiple voices. Again, one voice, third person narrative, first person narrative, American accent, Pakistani accent, an omniscient, sort of god-like third person—nothing really worked, and only at the end, I finally stumbled across the idea of what if he tells the story to someone, and what if he has this particular accent as he speaks? I treat form very seriously; form is important but I don't know what a form is until I know my story. It's a convoluted and really inefficient process for me.

You're a lucky writer to produce two novels in eight years and to have both optioned by film-makers. Mira Nair is making *The Reluctant Fundamentalist*, with you as co-scriptwriter, and Rahul Bose has bought *Moth Smoke*. How are the projects going?

Mira loves Lahore and I have spent time with her in New York. We have a good relationship because she is incredibly easy to get along with and there is a lot of artistic sympathy between us. It is an exciting project but it's not yet a film. Obviously the film of *The Reluctant Fundamentalist* won't be a dramatic monologue. The situation we're playing with is how to capture the tension of the novel and its interpretive ambiguity. As for Rahul Bose and *Moth Smoke* I believe that the project is gathering pace but I haven't had a recent update.

You've been an after-hours novelist with a high-pressure day job and an international corporate career. How tough was it, because it is only now after two acclaimed novels that you have the luxury of being a full-time writer.

I worked three days a week for a brand consulting firm in London, and if you write a novel every few years, you need something like that to put a roof over your head. But I learnt from it. I needed the pay, I had a boss, dealt with clients and did things that a huge proportion of the middle class on planet earth does. For me as a writer it was a wonderful experience because writing a novel is fundamentally about being in a room by yourself. But I like to live life so I can write about it.

June 2007 and April 2010

Suketu Mehta

Writer and journalist Suketu Mehta (b. 1963) grew up in Bombay till his family moved to New York when he was fourteen. Twenty-one years later, he returned to live in the city with his wife and two children but the homecoming soon became an exploratory odyssey because, as he later explained, it was 'to understand this central event in my life . . . this fact of migration . . . (that) I became a writer'. The city had changed immeasurably—it had also undergone an official change of name—and was now an exploding megalopolis of 14 million, in the throes of an organized crime wave and recovering from the savagery of communal riots.

By now a graduate of the well-known Iowa Writers' Workshop, Mehta dived into the megacity's dark, dangerous underbelly to encounter and befriend a large cast of characters that included mafia dons, corrupt policemen and an alluring but damaged bar dancer called Mona Lisa. His capacious 580-page non-fiction epic *Maximum City: Bombay Lost & Found* (2004), when it came out, was hailed as a masterly feat of documentary reporting and an intensely-felt personal testament. 'It's the best book yet written about that great, ruined metropolis,' said Salman Rushdie; and writers from Adam Hochschild to Pico Iyer commented on the original and enduring nature of Mehta's work. *Maximum City*, an instant best-seller around the world, struck a universal chord for several reasons: it broke from nostalgia-fuelled fictional portraits of India's largest city and mirrored the harsh future of the planet's megacities, home to increasingly larger numbers of the world's population. It won the Kiriyama Prize and was shortlisted for the Pulitzer Prize.

In 2007 Mehta was awarded the Guggenheim Fellowship to continue his work-in-progress excavating the other half of his life, in a nonfiction account of contemporary immigrants in New York. In 2008 he joined the journalism faculty of New York University. Of these two interviews, merged as one, the first was recorded by NDTV's Shai Venkataraman in an Irani restaurant in Mumbai and the second by me at the Jaipur Literature Festival.

Your family moved to America when you were fourteen but was your decision to return to Mumbai in your mid-thirties prompted by a desire to reclaim your past?

Exactly. I came back with my own family to see if I could find home again. I had come back in the interim to see relatives during holidays. But I wanted to see if it was possible to live in the territory of my childhood again. I grew up in a city called Bombay and when I returned twenty-one years later the city had grown up to become Mumbai. There was a radical disconnect between Bombay and Mumbai and I wanted to see what this new Mumbai was all about.

Did you expect your first book to receive the kind of international response it has?

I had no idea. I remember the reaction of an editor of a Mumbai newspaper at a party when I was researching the book, who said, 'Why would an American readership possibly be interested in such a book on Bombay?' I said to her that you edit a Bombay newspaper. Don't you know how fascinating your own city is? The expectation was that it was a city book and a few people in the city government might read it. So the response took me completely by surprise.

Equally gratifying must be its critical and commercial success in India. But what sort of book did you originally have in mind?

I knew that Mumbai had taken the book as its own when the chokras at the Haji Ali traffic signal offered me a pirated copy of my own book for anywhere between a hundred to four hundred rupees.

When I came to Bombay in 1998 I thought I would write a quick and dirty book about a quick and dirty city. But when I was writing it, I realized most people on the planet can get up and go about their day, perfectly happy without reading anything about Mumbai. Seven long years later I came out with this enormous manuscript: it was twice the length of the book that we have now and I had become obsessed with the city. It is really a chronicle of an obsessive love affair. When the book came out, I began to receive emails every day from people in Mumbai or people from round the world who had lived here and, beyond that, from people who are interested in the future megacities. The earth is increasingly dominated by enormous cities; the definition of a megacity is a metropolis of more than ten million people. This is where most of the human race lives; we have become an urban species like cockroaches or rats.

What are the memories of Bombay that you carried with you in the years that you lived away?

A restaurant like this, for example, just an ordinary little Irani cafe; there used to be many more when I grew up and they were wonderful. The Cafe Naaz on Malabar Hill where I used to go in my childhood or whenever I came back on visits; I would also go there when I was researching my book. It was an institution where you can get a view from the top of the city. Families would come from the suburbs and spend ten or twenty rupees per person; they could have a cup of chai, maybe a snack, and feel like they had an excursion because the beauty of the city was theirs, too. I remember going to the top of Cafe Naaz with one such family and they said, '*Yahan se toh Bombay Switzerland jaisa lagta hai*' (Bombay looks like Switzerland from here) as they gazed down on the sweep of the bay and the lights. But the city government decided to demolish the cafe now and erect some kind of water-monitoring station. Admittedly the city needs water-monitoring stations but these landmarks need to be preserved as part of the city's heritage. A city that loses its collective memory, loses the landmarks of its past, loses itself; it has no soul.

Your book's subheading is 'Bombay lost and found'. What had you lost when you returned to the city?

I was thoroughly frustrated. The first year I came back I couldn't recognize it as the city I knew because so much of the gracious place I had grown up in was lost. I quickly realized that this was my personal perspective and here was a city that now adds one million new people every year: they still keep coming to the city because for them Bombay remains the *sone ki chidiya* (golden songbird).

It was a much darker Mumbai that you returned to as you set about exploring its dangerous twilight zones. How did you choose the stories?

When I was researching the book between 1998 and 2000 the city was in the grip of an incredible crime wave with gangs such as the

D-company and the Chhota Rajan company dominating. Every day the newspapers were filled with stories of shootouts and extortions. It was not as if you would get mugged on the streets, it was organized crime, and there was a sense of the city imagining itself to be more violent than it actually was. There was no way that I could not make that the centre of the book. It seemed to me to be the focus of everything that was good and bad about the city. The city is now a calmer, quieter place but only for the moment. The riots of 1992–93 also came after a period of relative calm and people thought that the city had regained its cosmopolitan character. But who knows when there will be another riot? If we forget what happened to us in the 1990s, it will happen all over again.

Do you think the communal riots irrevocably changed Bombay's character?

They did, because I find that Muslims and Hindus now live in ghettos much more than they used to when I was growing up here in the 1970s. You go to a place like Madanpura which occupies one of the big sections in my book and it's almost entirely Muslim. That makes me sad. The great thing about Bombay was that religion was seen to be immaterial, it was like a personal eccentricity or a hairstyle. It was important to the people who practised it but there was always respect towards all religions and how you practised them. That changed after the riots and I'm not sure if that change has been reversed. But the next riot doesn't have to be between Hindu and Muslim; it could be between Maharashtrians and north Indians.

In your book you say that Mumbai has a multiple-personality disorder, but isn't that true of every megacity? How is it less true of New York?

It is true except that in a place like New York the multiple personalities are relatively well-hidden. In Mumbai they fall out on the sidewalk. The physical infrastructure of the place is obviously in a state of urban ruin. The city is in a grip of a boom and a civic emergency, simultaneously. It desperately needs an urban plan that will take into account what is realistic and politically achievable, but no such plan exists today. The last plan was floated by a voluntary organization, which the state government accepted, under which the idea was that Mumbai could become a world-class city like Shanghai by the year 2020. But as architect Charles

Correa said, that's not a vision, that's a hallucination. I think we should set our sights more realistically to pool together the visions of the city's various stakeholders. Yes, it can be a financial hub, but that doesn't mean that you give wholesale the only large available plot of land, 800 acres of mill areas, to corporations. Mumbai needs public spaces, it needs schools, parks, and auditoriums; it needs a place where you can take a walk, where lovers can walk hand in hand, where people can come with their children. It needs green spaces and green belts.

How did you approach your relationship with the characters whose lives you explore in the book—gangsters, policemen and bar dancers? You penetrate their intricate worlds and spend weeks with them but was it tough maintaining a distance from your subjects?

I abandoned all pretence of being an objective journalist. I wasn't writing for a newspaper. I was writing a very personal book about going home so I didn't have to keep a distance. I did have a separate apartment where I could speak to people who might pose a danger to my family. But I became their friend. I love all the characters in my book, even the murderers. It's not that I sympathize with them but more that I empathize with them. I saw the world through their eyes and I did not want to make any judgements. I wanted to find out what drove a human being to murder. Someone like you or me who might be a good friend, a husband, a patriot, a good cricketer—but what is it that drives that person to pick up a gun or a knife and kill another human being? This is a question that I kept asking over and over again. What does it mean to take a human life? And the only way that I could find out was by becoming a sort of friend to these people, by letting them know that I wasn't going to judge them. I was going to listen and it was up to my readers to judge or not to judge.

Many of the names of these characters in *Maximum City* are disguised for obvious reasons but your friendships with public figures, such as filmmaker Vidhu Vinod Chopra, are not. Did these friendships suffer because of the way you reported the changing relationship?

Obviously, my friendship with Vinod Chopra, who was a great friend, suffered; he felt slighted which is a mystery to me. I believe he said in an interview that he hasn't read my book but it should be banned, which is a curious position. But I hope at some point the friendship will survive because anybody who reads my book will know that I have presented quite a loving portrait of him.

You don't feel that becoming a part of another person's life and writing about it intimately constitutes a sort of betrayal in the context of a relationship between journalist and subject?

Not if you are open and upfront about it. I remember once when I was editing my book Vinod Chopra said, 'There is a little bit about me in your book.' I said, 'No, there is a lot about you, Vinod,' and he said, 'Good, don't edit that.'

How difficult was it to decide what to keep out and what to include? And was there a lot that could not be included?

Editing the book and deciding which stories to keep in and which to keep out was like choosing amongst my children. I had to have my editors Sonny Mehta and David Davidar help me out. In fact, the first draft was twice the size of the current book and there are entire stories which can be put back in. I think this size is hefty enough but a number of my publishers want me to bring out a companion volume to *Maximum City* which puts back many of the stories, a sort of a collection of stories for those who could not get enough of this book.

Do you think you could return to live in Mumbai now that your book is done?

I can come back tomorrow. I am going to keep coming back to the city. The best thing that I found out for myself when I came to Mumbai to look for home is that I don't have to choose. I can go back and forth between these two cities, between New York and Mumbai, and a third city if I want to. What is the price of exile if your round trip home is 800 dollars? I think of people like myself as lucky and privileged if we have friends and family all over the globe. I am thinking of doing a book about New York, and when I finish researching it, I will probably come to Mumbai to write it. Just to establish the fact that I can come home again, and also go out again once more, with greater confidence, into the world.

Everyone likes to compare Mumbai to New York. Now that you are writing about New York how true is the comparison?

I think it is very true. Both of these are dream cities. They are cities inhabited by dreamers; impossible dreams, in many cases, but it's still a dream that keeps pulling people from all over India to Mumbai, and to New York, from all over the world. They have the same kind of commercial energy. They are both the biggest cities in their respective countries but they are not the political capitals. They look down on capitals; New York looks down on Washington in the same way as Mumbai looks down on Delhi. They are filled with the same kind of energy that I am attracted to in the worlds of media, film and finance—with people out for the big scam and big trade. I certainly see these two cities as more like each other than any other two cities in the world.

So you are now embarked upon exploring the other half of your life through a portrait of New York . . .

New York is the one other city on the planet that is dearest to me. I was educated there and my two children were born there. There is a new New York that is forming around us, which is the city of new immigrants. I don't see why there should be a qualifier in front of 'writer' when it is associated with Indian writers. I am just a writer. I can write about Ingmar Bergman or ice cream. I am doing the same thing in New York as I did in Bombay. I am wandering the streets, meeting people, and recording crazy stories, funny stories and sad stories. For example, I walked into a party in a shabby little house out in darkest Queens and a parade of characters started walking up the stairs, including a gangster named Gandhi. He was a young Gujarati boy who told me how he had joined a gang in Jackson Heights. 'They picked on me because of my last name. They said you are Gandhi so you can't hit back. Then I hit them, saying that was Gandhi over there, this is Gandhi over here.'

April 2006 and January 2007

Ved Mehta

Ved Mehta (b. 1934) grew up in the waning light of the Raj.

The turning point in his early life was losing his eyesight at the age of four due to an attack of cerebrospinal meningitis. His father, a doctor, realizing that his son's future prospects were bleak, took the bold step of sending him 1300 miles away to the Dadar School for the Blind in Bombay.

In 1949 Mehta went to Pomona College in the United States, and later took degrees from Oxford and Harvard universities. From 1961 to 1994 he was a staff writer on the *New Yorker*, his writing nurtured by William Shawn, the magazine's distinguished and long-serving editor.

It was in the pages of the *New Yorker* that many of Mehta's explorations of family history first appeared, to eventually become a twelve-book sequence known as *Continents of Exile*.

Daddyji and *Mamaji*, extended portraits of his remarkable parents, originally came out in the 1970s. By the 1990s, however, as can happen to literary lions, Ved Mehta seemed to have gone out of fashion He had lived away from India for too long and his stories carried the tint of fading sepia photographs.

But rereading some of them after a long time, I found myself deeply affected. Mehta's story, and those of his parents, of migration and exile, were the stories of millions of Indians hoping for a better life for their children.

What does it feel like to be back in Delhi after a long gap, a city where your family relocated after Partition? Your old neighbourhood of Nizamuddin, where your father Dr Amolak Ram Mehta built a house, is very different and your family house has disappeared.

I never really became a part of Delhi. I left India back in 1949. All my memories are those of Lahore but I can see enormous changes in Delhi. It's true my family house has gone. My father loved to go for walks in the morning and evening in the gardens of Humayun's Tomb. I remember that when I was here six years ago they had started charging people to walk in Humayun's Tomb. I found that discouraging. I don't think people should make money out of dead emperors' graves.

Daddyji and _Mamaji_, recently reissued in India, are part of a twelve-part autobiographical narrative, an important part of a lifetime of writing that began with a self-portrait called _Face to Face_, your first book that came out in 1957 . . .

Face to Face was a portrait of a man who is not at all amazing, and who is sitting right across from you just now. It was my adolescent autobiography. I wrote most of it when I was twenty. You can call it a self-portrait, although I was writing about the partition of India. It is called an autobiography but what it actually is trying to do is to capture what I imagined was the spirit of India at the time, and the spirit of America.

Daddyji is a moving account of your father's life, a young Punjabi who rose virtually from nowhere to give himself an education to become a medical civil servant under the Raj. After Partition he moved to India to become the first deputy director general of health services, a remarkable rise in life. How did this portrait come about?

Daddyji was a totally different kind of work. My father would visit me in America and was a great storyteller. I felt I should capture some of his stories before he closed his eyes, as it were. But I never thought it would end up being a book. It was just a kind of family saga that I wanted to store in my mind. Then nine years later I wrote *Mamaji*. This series of books, called *Continents of Exile*, was not written at once or with one intention. It grew by itself and it now comprises twelve independent books.

But many of them appeared as long articles during your long tenure as a staff writer on the _New Yorker_ magazine . . .

That's right. But between writing these twelve books I wrote other books, because writing about one's own family or family history can become obsessive. I never thought to write more than that first one book, then two, then three, and so it went on, until I finally reached the landmark of a dozen. In retrospect, that's how the unconscious works. These books acquire an architecture of their own; they are chronological and they fit each other like a jigsaw puzzle.

This obsessive need to create an architecture of family history, as you call it, became part of your ambition as a writer. At a deeper level, what took you down the path of such an excavation?

I can only retrospectively say that it seemed as if I was trying to explain myself and my existence to others. I went to America when I was fifteen. Nobody there in 1949 knew anything about India. The students in the school I went to didn't even know there was any other language besides English. I constantly had to explain to them, and to myself, what this country where I came from was. I could speak Punjabi, Hindi and Urdu, but there was no one there to speak these languages to. So I think originally the series began as an attempt to explain to myself my own origins—and it grew.

Your father, Dr Amolak Ram Mehta, a specialist in tropical medicine, emerges as a larger-than-life figure whom his family adored. In 1938, when at the age of four you lost your eyesight from an attack of meningitis, he made the difficult decision to send you first to school in distant Bombay and later to America. Do you regard that life-changing step as an act of heroism?

It was an act of courage. The truth about these books is that although they are metaphorically about my family, each of the books can stand for the families of many other Punjabis, your family for instance. The person in my family was called Daddyji but I am sure you had a Daddyji in your family and may have called him Papaji or Pitaji or whatever. There were similar stories among all our neighbours who made good and settled in Lahore. So the point of the books in *Continents of Exile* is that metaphorically they stand for many families of Punjab at that time.

Equally *Mamaji*, which came out as a sequel to *Daddyji*, is about another remarkable figure, your mother and family matriarch. But it is also a frank portrait of a marriage, the enduring partnership between your parents. Is that why it is a distinctive book?

Mamaji didn't want the light passed on her at all. Her education had stopped at the fourth standard. I came round to interviewing her because my sister said, 'Well, you have written a book about our father, but what about our mother?' So I had to balance the book. My mother simply didn't want to talk. Then I hit upon the ruse of bringing her to London where I rented a house and she came for a week. I would send my father off to the British Medical Association's library because, when he was around, she would say, 'What is there to tell about my story?' The minute my father had gone out of the door she would make a cup of tea for us and she would tell me endless stories. And that, too, so fast that I could have filled several books called *Mamaji*.

You know that good books are not made because there's so much material but by selection and taking artistic decisions. So I cut a lot from that wonderful portrait of her. Whether she was as happy with that book as my father was, I don't know because she could not read it the same way. My father could read English and respond to what I said but she would have to read it in Hindi to have that same kind of effect.

You once said that you come from five cultures: from the cultures of India, America, Britain, blindness and the *New Yorker*. How would you apportion this amalgam into the creation of Ved Mehta the writer and literary explorer?

There is one more aspect that you left out: psychoanalysis. I think to separate these different portions would be like separating the salt and lemon from the nimbu-soda I had this morning. It's impossible; they are all mixed together and they all have had their profound influences in my development and also on my unconscious self. I can't separate them. The *New Yorker* represents my writing, psychoanalysis perhaps my romantic life, India is the Ulysses aspect of my life, which I left and came back to, and England because I was intellectually very influenced by my three years there and later as a visiting fellow.

And losing your eyesight?

Blindness has been a continuing thing. Perhaps that is why I wrote these books at all, because blindness has traditionally been associated with profound loneliness and solitude, and one way of dealing with it, if not overcoming it, is to reach out and explore the world that you can't see and that you can't accept. So the books, in a way, are my attempt to reach out, to explore and to accept.

Looking back after more than half a century of writing—journalism and a variety of non-fiction books—what has a writer's life been like?

A writer's life is very internal but externals also have profound effect because everything is registered. It is basically a life of reflection, perhaps, even more a life of dreaming. I think the best writing comes out of dreams and discipline comes out of reflection.

It is also a life of hardship. You once said that one of your two young daughters has decided to become a writer and that you would not wish such a fortune on even your own worst enemy.

Well, it is a difficult life. I think I am unemployable so I couldn't have done anything else but become a writer. My father used to think that I would become a musician but I really wasn't cut out for that. I certainly toyed with becoming a professor and that would have been easier, because when you are teaching you are in contact with young students who have new concepts and ideas. Whereas as a writer you are left alone to create your own destiny as best you can.

November 2009

Daniyal Mueenuddin

Because they are racing to meet a publication deadline, publishers occasionally send round unbound manuscripts to critics. And so it was that, leaving to cover the Jaipur Literature Festival one morning in January 2009, I grabbed the manuscript of Pakistani writer Daniyal Mueenuddin's (b. 1963) first book, *In Other Rooms, Other Wonders*, to read on the way. The title was clunky but the advance praise was unanimous.

From the moment my eyes fell on the frontispiece inscription in Urdu calligraphy ('*Three things for which we kill—land, women and gold—* Punjabi proverb') I was hooked. The vehicle rattled unbearably, the manuscript's loose sheets kept spilling and we had to stop for a shoot on the way. On entering the hotel room in Jaipur I flopped down on the bed to finish the last of its 247 pages.

Mueenuddin's debut of eight interconnected stories are forceful both in content and form: they evoke, with unerring precision, life on a feudal agricultural estate in contemporary Pakistan; with cool detachment they examine the bitter predatory relationships between servants and masters, often younger women and older men; and threaded together by the presence of an absentee landlord—a sort of elderly Gatsby-in-decline—they are told in spare but lucid prose.

Mueenuddin and his blonde Scandinavian wife were at the Jaipur litfest that year and with their movie star looks they made a handsome couple. The facts of Mueeddunin's life are unusual: his father, an ICS officer, was posted to Washington after Independence where he married an American. When Daniyal was thirteen his parents separated; he was mostly raised in America, with return visits to Pakistan, and went to Dartmouth College, Yale Law School and later worked in a corporate law firm in New York. But eventually he returned to live and manage the family landholding in a remote backwater of Punjab.

Mueenuddin is not a talkative man; his answers are pointed (and to the point) and he speaks in staccato bursts. This interview took place when his book was shortlisted for the Commonwealth Writers' Prize 2010 in the best first book category but lost out to the Australian novelist Glenda Guest.

It's been nearly two years since your first book, *In Other Rooms, Other Wonders*, came out to widespread appreciation. Do you feel gratified?

I do, but that book is far behind me now. I have been working on other things, so I now feel as if it was a different person who wrote it.

One difficulty a first success can create is high, possibly unfair, expectations from readers and critics for the second book. Writers may feel the pressure of being a one-trick pony. Do you?

I guess there is more pressure on me but surprisingly little change. Writing is a solitary craft, and so at the end of the day, I return to my study and face the computer.

Being half-Pakistani and half-American you've always led a double life between the two countries. But it's also been a life of contrasts—from practising law in New York to becoming a farmer in southern Punjab. How do you handle that?

I have been an acrobat, you see, but I also consider myself lucky to have a number of careers. Obviously, the change from working in a law firm in New York to running a farm in Pakistan was the difference between night and day. It required tremendously different sets of skills. Although, I might say, that the acuity of the lawyer is very much required to run a farm in Punjab.

To me what is exciting about *In Other Rooms, Other Wonders* is not just that the stories are beautifully crafted and cleverly interconnected but they are a close observation of rural life—of farm hands, farm managers, domestic servants and their relationships with employers. So much contemporary fiction coming out of the subcontinent is urban that you would think the countryside doesn't exist any more. Do you agree?

It's not that writers from the subcontinent don't have the time to go to the countryside; they don't have the access. Out of all my literate friends I am the only one who does not live in a city, so I have had access to these lives and these stories and I feel fortunate about that.

But you go deeper into the emotional landscapes of the characters. The relationship between men and women is both symbiotic and predatory—the men are often much older, preying on

younger, vulnerable women who, in the end, will be humiliated and discarded . . .

This is true. Generally in Pakistan women are powerless. There are exceptions, of course, but they have to use whatever means are available to them to achieve their purposes and, obviously, sex is one of the strongest cards they hold. And by definition, if you are looking for powerful men then, generally, they are older men. That's a dynamic I see very much in Pakistan.

Do you perceive these women as victims?

Yes, they are victims who are trying to empower themselves, though often in misguided ways.

And often failing miserably?

Yes. This is the thing about being powerless: when you are powerless, often you do fail. Men generally have power themselves, but women having power through men know that when the affection of the man is withdrawn they'll lose everything that they have gained.

These are stories of heart-rending rejection and failure—Saleema, the servant in a grand house, works her way up trading sexual favours but ends up destitute. Genteel and shabby Husna becomes companion, then mistress, to the fading feudal landlord and is driven out after his death. No relationship is remotely equitable, even among people of the same class. Why?

Yes, these are inequitable relationships because in Pakistan, I think, there is great inequity, not just between older men and younger women, but between all sorts of people. It is a country where there is a great deal of unfairness. The old feudal class is dying and, instead, you see even more cruel versions of the same inequity because, more and more, money rules. When you are a feudal person there is, at least, a connection which is larger than simply that of master and servant. What we are seeing now is that it is becoming colder and harsher. The one thing you could say about the old feudal class is that, generally, they were civilized but that is less and less true of the powers that are coming up or coming in.

There is one story in the collection that is distinct from the rest. It is about a pleasure-seeking, volatile girl who has the chance to redeem

her decadent life but also fails. It is an unforgiving portrait of Pakistani upper-class life but its hedonist frenzy reminded me of Jazz Age writers like F. Scott Fitzgerald. Do you agree?

That is a wonderful thought and you are absolutely right. I think when I was writing 'Lily' I did hark back a little to Fitzgerald. I love the idea of we're dancing as fast as we can while the ship sinks, that things are going so bad we must make the most of it. And so that was part of my story.

Since the appearance of *In Other Rooms, Other Wonders* you have been working on a new novel. What is it about?

It is set in Pakistan and it is a love story. People love 'love', so I hope it will be successful. It is set in an earlier time, in the 1970s, which for us is the golden age; also maybe because I was younger then. It is the early Bhutto era when there was a moment when Pakistan was full of hope and, politically, Bhutto represented hope for millions of people. It was just a gentler time. So I am indulging myself by basking in that for a while.

There has been much comment about the spurt of original fiction in English coming out of Pakistan, with the arrival of writers such as Mohammed Hanif, Mohsin Hamid, Kamila Shamsie and yourself. Why do you think so?

It could be that it is a very complicated time in Pakistan, and therefore there are rich subjects and also rich lives of men like myself, who have grown up in this tremendously complex, conflicted place. We are trying really hard to make sense of it but this also leads to the production of new kinds of literature.

April 2010

Orhan Pamuk

Nobel laureate Orhan Pamuk's *My Name Is Red* (2000) had left a deep impression on me. More than a disquisition on the meaning of art, it was a reflection on orthodoxy and innovation, authenticity and falsification. His quest to evoke the past, using the melancholy-drenched Arabic word *huzun* as metaphor, in *Istanbul: Memories of a City* (2005), made it a unique homage to the great metropolis on the cusp of Europe and Asia. Over seven million of his books have sold in more than fifty languages.

I was also aware of the criminal charges brought against Pamuk (b. 1952) by the Turkish government for condemning the Armenian genocide under Ottoman rule and the killing of 30,000 Kurds by modern Turkish forces. Support from intellectuals worldwide prevented Pamuk from being imprisoned; but his friend, journalist Hrant Dink, of Armenian descent, was jailed and later shot dead. For his free-thinking opinions, Pamuk has been targeted in Turkey by pro-Europe secularists, diehard nationalists and Islamic fundamentalists.

In Mumbai, where our interview took place, I encountered a man of patrician good looks and a reserved, observant manner. Later on, at dinner in a restaurant, he became warm and expansive, discoursing knowledgably on Mughal painters learning perspective from the Portuguese in Goa, and how, when the demand for miniatures dried up in Turkey, Turkish artists migrated to the court of Akbar where the tradition flourished.

So much of your work is about tradition and modernity and this may not be a coincidence because you come from Istanbul, the city that straddles Asia and Europe, and from a country which has been through so many convulsions—centuries of Ottoman rule followed by Kemal Ataturk's discarding of traditions and language. Once again, given Turkey's shifting politics of secularists versus nationalists and the rise of Islamic fundamentalism, the conflicts have deepened. How do they affect you as a writer?

I sometimes think that to be torn between tradition and modernity is the definition of Turkish identity. Westernization was not started by Kemal Ataturk, it was introduced more than 200 years ago by the ruling Ottoman elite. For me, the meaning of human life, why are we on this earth, what do we do here, what makes us happy, philosophically what is happiness, what is the aim of life—these are the more important issues. But, yes, the general political frame of my books is east and west, the impact of modernity, morality, the urge to embrace personal identities and traditions. And then, of course, the attractions of modernity, with its values, its freedom of speech, respect for human rights, women's rights, and so forth. These are all contradictory things. I don't make strong statements about these issues but try to create lively, convincing characters who face them.

Not many people may know that you actually began your career training to be an architect. Then you dropped out and decided that you really wanted to devote all your time to writing. For eight years, between the age of twenty-two and thirty, you sought refuge in your mother's house, struggling very hard to write your first novel and then trying even harder to have it published.

I come from a family where my grandfather was a civil engineer and my uncle and father were civil engineers. It was the family tradition—not to run after money but to become engineers which they considered more respectable. They thought that I should go to Istanbul Technical University where all my family went. But then they also saw me as a little bit of an artsy person. I was twenty-two and everyone thought that I would become a painter. So they said that, as he's also interested in painting, why not architecture which combines civil engineering and painting. I believed them and got through the entrance examination to enrol at Istanbul Technical University's architectural school.

Three years later I realized that I actually wanted to lead a private life and I was not the sort of person who gives orders or takes orders from others. I wanted to continue to live the life of an inventive and a creative person as I have narrated in my book *Istanbul*. Of course, my mother warned me that it would not be an easy life.

Your early books were generational and historical stories but it wasn't till the early 1990s, with the publication of *The White Castle* and *The Black Book*, books that were published abroad and gave you a much

wider audience, that you found your true voice—the Orhan Pamuk style that delved into questions of identity, history and memory. Would you say the themes of crossed identities, unfolding mysteries, memory and loss are characteristics of the Orhan Pamuk style that emerged?

If someone else defines it like that I would agree. But I cannot say that this is my style. It is true for all artists that when you're doing something that you don't know about, not sure about the quality, you feel like a musician pushing keys. Some music is coming out but you are not aware of what it means. It is when a book is published, when people read it and tell you, as you told me now, what it is, then you begin to imitate what you have found. But while you're finding it you don't know what you will find.

Your foray into history came with the book that many consider your masterpiece *My Name Is Red*, about the death of a miniature painter at the court of Sultan Murad in the sixteenth century. The book is told in multiple voices, inanimate and animate voices telling stories. The book is also about the connection between art and history—the falsification of art, its authentication, and interpreting art in temporal and religious terms. What aroused your interest in art history, particularly the art of miniature painting?

As I already told you, I wanted to be a painter between the ages of seven and twenty-two but, suddenly and abruptly, I stopped painting and declared I will be a writer. Then, between thirty to thirty-five, when I had finally managed to establish myself as a novelist, at least in Turkey, making some money and gaining a readership, I said to myself, 'Now I will write the novel about painters.' So I put in all these ideas into how miniatures were made not only in the sixteenth century but also between the twelfth and the sixteenth centuries in the Islamic world. Also, miniatures are not only an Islamic thing. Before the Renaissance they were made the same way in Europe. They imply a medieval way of seeing things. Most philosophical discussion about how Europe perceives Islam is actually medieval. So in order to explore these issues I invented a story and the work became rhetorical: it is about character, style, the uniqueness of human beings, which is a western ideological standpoint. They say we [the west] invented the Renaissance, we developed portrait painting which the non-western world did not have, implying that human significance and uniqueness is the base of western civilization.

Some of these notions I believe, some are ideological and false and some I disagree with. But these opinions are not in my novels. I never say I disagree. I try to identify with all points of view. In my novel *Snow*, which is a political novel about Islamic fundamentalism, I don't openly say I disagree. As a political citizen I say so but as a novelist I have to understand. So I draw a whole picture with a lot of personal energy, as I would when I wanted to be a painter. A painter makes a picture with his hands and his mind follows later.

I now teach a semester on comparative literature at Columbia University and sometimes teach my books too. I always say that when I write the novel I don't know what I am doing. Two years pass, three years pass, it's translated into many languages; then I'm told by people and I understand what I did in that book. And then I teach them at Columbia!

A life of the imagination and teaching hasn't disconnected you from the realities of a writer's role. You have frequently come under attack in your own country for your political views—in particular for the shame of history, for condemning the killing of a million Armenians during the last decade of Ottoman rule and 30,000 Kurds by Turkish forces. It made the government of Turkey press charges against you. Did you see that as an issue of repression of free speech or as an example of the nationalist–secularist conflict that dominates Turkey's public life?

These two are closely related but, for me, it's more of a freedom-of-speech issue. It is not as hot as it was two or four years ago, at least not for me. But for us Turks it is essentially an issue of freedom of speech. Also when I compare myself to other Turkish authors, so many of them in past years, my case is really different. I never ended up in jail. I am now here happily talking about my books. In so many countries of the non-western world, there are all these issues of free speech and respect for human rights. Optimistically, you may even say naively, I believe that if there is freedom of speech in such countries then all the issues that you referred to, such as the sway of history, of coping with tradition and modernity, would be resolved. Once everyone can easily speak out his or her mind, then facing history, tradition and modernity can be resolved in a nice way

In the Islamic world the conflict is often perceived as being violent, inflammatory and regressive. In the context of Islamic extremism, indeed any form of militant fundamentalism, let's not forget that we are sitting in Mumbai, a city that a few months ago was under siege, in one of the worst terrorist attacks that happened on 26/11 in several locations in this very neighbourhood. Do you see the rising tide of extremism as irreversible?

When you say extremism there is Islamic extremism and Islamic fundamentalism, and in political Islam there are many shades that we should pay attention to. In Turkey and other countries, extremism is centred not necessarily on radical religion but forms of radical nationalism. I agree that radical nationalism and radical religion sometimes go hand in hand in directing the anger of youth towards western civilization. But xenophobia or anti-westernism is not exclusive to the non-western world. I strongly think that we should not derive forms of representation of Islam, or India or whatever, from the language of America. I think non-western countries should develop new languages, new concepts to look at themselves. We blame political Islam. But it is not so different than, say, the German Christian conservatives. There are Christian fundamentalists too.

But because I am a novelist, my persona is always first of a writer, I try to understand these questions through the suffering of the human heart, from the suffering of people who fall into these situations. I understand the suffering of the girl who wears a headscarf. I understand the suffering of the girl who wears a miniskirt even though she is not allowed to wear a miniskirt. My job is to address these issues, to see them in totality. I don't justify my novels. I don't write my novels to be ethically correct. Identifying with a girl with so many cultural pressures and honestly writing about people like her, without being scared that I would be called politically correct or incorrect—I think putting it in a form is the job of the novelist and I try to do that.

You call yourself a novelist but one of your most-loved books is, in fact, a work of non-fiction: your ode to *Istanbul: Memories of a City*, rare in its shades of sadness, tragicomedy and *huzun*, its pervasive melancholia. It began as an autobiography, then digressed and diverged into so many areas, that it is a magical portrait of a city. Will you continue with that kind of memoir?

Yes, in *Istanbul* I wrote about my town and my autobiography. I combined these two different things and tried to put them together in my own way to make a form. But at the heart of it lies my desire to be a painter and to see this city through the eyes of a boy who wants to be a painter and then associate this city with its inner essence, its meaning. It was Baudelaire who said in his criticism of painting that the feeling that we should get from a landscape should be associated with the painting. An urban landscape should convey an essential feeling about the town. *Huzun*, which is not a big word and is used in the Quran, comes from this Turkish melancholy I felt there. The fact that we are living at the edge of Europe and were so poor; it felt as if we will be eternally poor in the 1950s, '60s or '70s; and also this pathetic feeling that we will never recover, we will never be like the Europeans, we will never be as rich—that is the defining point of that culture. [That] poverty will never leave us was the dominant feeling in the book, although I myself am from an upper-class family.

Tell us about your new novel *The Museum of Innocence*.

It is a long book, a love story that takes place in Istanbul between 1975 and the end of the century. It covers twenty-five years of a love story but it is essentially about human attachment and, of course, rampant romantic attachment too. We fall in love with a person—some people get out of it easily after two years and some people never get out of it. [This book] is about the person who can never get out of it. It is also an exploration of the nature of attachment and about attachment not only to girls, women, men or objects. It's about collecting, and it's also about museums. I sometimes look up the Net to see what people are writing on all sorts of websites and someone wrote a good summary of the book, saying that it's the story of a guy who falls so much in love with a girl that he makes a museum about their love.

March 2009

Salman Rushdie

Salman Rushdie (b. 1947) is all things to all people: a dazzling literary figure who changed the course of Indian writing in English, a detested infidel who blasphemed a religious text, a fugitive on the run for nine years from a fatwa by Ayatollah Khomeini and a social celebrity hunted by New York paparazzi for his liaisons with beautiful women. His hooded eyes, goatee beard, compelling conversation and acid wit make him a widely recognized enfant terrible of the late twentieth century, although as a writer he is as responsible for cultural assimilation as for cultural misunderstanding.

Rushdie, who once told an interviewer that he wanted to 'write globe-swallowing, capacious books', was born in Mumbai, the son of a wealthy businessman. After his family migrated to Pakistan, he completed his education at Rugby School and King's College, Cambridge, where he was a member of *Footlights*, the amateur drama club. (A desire for performance never left him since, and he has had walk-on parts in films such as *Bridget Jones's Diary*.) He worked in advertising in London before his second novel *Midnight's Children* (1981)—a large, energetic work of magic realism that deals with the split identities of a fractured subcontinent—won the Booker Prize and became an instant cult classic. In 1993 it was awarded the Booker of Bookers, by public vote, for the best novel in twenty-five years of the Booker Prize.

Rushdie's success was bolstered with *Shame* (1983), his novel on the political turmoil in Pakistan but hell broke loose with the appearance of *The Satanic Verses* (1988) for its perceived unholy depiction of the Prophet. Protests erupted in many parts of the world and the book was banned in eleven countries including India. In early 1989 Iran's Ayatollah Khomeini issued a fatwa, offering a bounty for Rushdie's head. Britain broke diplomatic relations with Iran and a heavily guarded Rushdie went into hiding, changing as many as thirty safe houses, as world opinion became sharply polarized over the controversy.

The fatwa was officially rescinded in September 1998. In the spring of 2000, Rushdie paid a quiet visit to India after twelve years. He spoke to me at length about his years of exile and how his life and thinking had changed. The first interview here predates the advent of *Just Books* and was recorded for a series called *Talking Heads*. The second interview was recorded by NDTV's US correspondent Sarah Jacob in New York after the publication of his last novel, *The Enchantress of Florence* (2008).

Rushdie's subjects and landscapes have shifted. He enlarged his literary oeuvre with the appearance of an allegorical children's book, *Haroun and the Sea of Stories* (1990), essays and criticism in *Imaginary Homelands* (1992) and two major novels, *The Moor's Last Sigh* (1995), a family chronicle that spans a century of India's history, and *The Ground Beneath Her Feet* (1999), an alternative account of rock-n-roll, rooted in his adolescent passion for rockers such as Elvis Presley.

Rushdie's move from London to New York led to his fourth marriage to the glamorous model and *Top Chef* host Padma Lakshmi, twenty-three years his junior; it put him firmly in the league of the jet-set club. 'Celebrity,' sniffed the British commentator Hugo Young, 'is a justifiable reward for exile.' The marriage ended in 2007, leaving him emotionally wounded, and his last novel *The Enchantress of Florence* drew mixed reviews. Khushwant Singh's pithy comment was: 'Salman Rushdie's inkwell has dried up; it is time he bought a new ballpoint pen.'

Rushdie was knighted in 2007 for 'services to literature'. The same year he became a distinguished writer in residence at Emory University. His latest book *Luka and the Fire of Life* (2010) is another children's fable offered as a gift for his younger son on his twelfth birthday.

~

What does it feel like to be back in India after twelve years?

It is an enormous feeling and I knew it would be. When I knew I was coming I thought to myself that I don't know what it is going to be like, good or bad, but I knew it was going to be a very large experience and so it has proved. It has been terrific, particularly because I was able to bring my older son with me, Zafar, who is about to be twenty-one. He was very keen to come so, in the end, I arranged the whole trip around him. It started out as just a trip for the Commonwealth Prize dinner but ended up as a kind of father-and-son road movie.

You managed to slip in pretty much unnoticed. Does that have to do with your experience of learning to become an invisible man?

I am certainly not going to reveal the tricks—you know a conjurer never reveals his tricks. But I must say that the security forces here have been fantastically helpful and very flexible at helping us to have this private time. We spent a couple of days in Delhi; then my son and I went to Jaipur, Fatehpur Sikri and Agra, and then to my old family cottage in Solan, which for me, was a very moving time because my father is no longer alive, but he had gifted this cottage to me on my twenty-first birthday, and I was taking my son to it just as he was approaching his twenty-first birthday. It felt like I was completing some promise to my father. In the meanwhile this cottage had been pinched by the Himachal Pradesh authorities and I had to fight a long legal battle to get it back. To have it back into the family and to be able to go and spend some nights there was deeply moving for me.

Many people regard this as India's defining decade of change. What are the biggest changes you have perceived during your travels?

There are the obvious things such as the big technological changes and, alongside that, the enormous expansion of the urban middle class, India's much greater wealth and prosperity. There is evidence of much more money around than there used to be. Then, of course, there is the political change; a shift of relative party strengths, the emergence of new governments, and the decay of the old establishment. That is something I am trying to keep my ears and eyes open to and absorb as much as I can. But I also find that beneath that there is a lot of India that is the same as it ever was; people are the same as they ever were, and if you like mess, the mess is the same as well.

I do sometimes wish that while everybody is patting themselves on the back for having turned themselves into a third-millennium nation, they would remember how much remains undone. One of the things about travelling in the countryside is that you immediately see how change really hasn't trickled down to the mass of the people. The same old things need doing—still no drinking water that you can drink, and basic amenities like health and education are strongly lacking. To me, these simple welfare issues seem to be much more important than the nuclear bomb. If you really want to be a country that competes with the United States as one of the world's great democracies, then it can't only be limited to the success of the middle class. You have to provide a better country for the whole nation, particularly the poorest and the most disadvantaged, and there is no evidence if that's changed.

One of the things, if you come from Bombay particularly, is that you are always aware of what is called the 'hovel-and-high-rise-culture' where there is this incredible contrast between the lives that are lived in the sky and the lives that are lived in the gutter. The physical shape of Bombay dramatizes that but, I think, it is really true everywhere that the extremes between the great wealth and the great poverty of India are wider than I remember them being. That can't be good. That is a recipe for resentments and unrest.

Your period of exile started in February 1989 when Ayatollah Khomeini issued that fatwa against you. Looking back now do you remember what your immediate reaction was?

I locked the front door and shut the shutters. No, of course not, but clearly the power of Khomeini was very great. I was under no illusion—it meant there was a serious physical danger. The book had been published six months earlier, and although there had been dispute and controversy and discussion, there had never been any physical danger. In many ways, I thought that it was quite valuable, because one of the things that literature does for a society is to say the unsayable, to ask difficult questions rather than easy ones, to propose that things might be thus rather than thus, and how would the world be if we thought of it like this. Those are the kind of questions that art asks of us and of course, sometimes those questions elicit strong responses.

If a book generates argument, if it is called 'controversial', that can be a very good thing. Out of that controversy we understand each other a bit better; we air our differences and then move on. That seems to me one of the important functions that works of art can perform in a society and, actually, that was what was happening until the fatwa. Oddly, the fatwa silenced that conversation because from then on it became another conversation which was about life and death, terrorism and security, which are much less interesting.

Apart from the fact that a fatwa is an attempt to murder somebody, it's a completely banal event. What does it say? All it says is 'Shut up!' And if you don't shut up, we will kill you or actually we will kill you anyway. That was a dull conversation, but before that there had been a very rich conversation. The kind of debate *The Satanic Verses* may have stimulated might have just run its natural course. But it was interrupted by the Iranian fatwa. That is one of the many disservices that the political act did.

How would you say it changed you as a person or, indeed, as a writer?

As a writer, it is easier to say. If you are any kind of writer then you look at an experience like that very seriously and try and learn from it. I also think that if you are somebody who, by nature, is a comic or satirical writer then, in many cases, writers like that find it easy to know what they are against. Much satire is about identifying your targets. Yet what I saw very early was that I needed to understand what I stood for. If somebody is trying to send out terrorists after you, it is rather easy to know what you are against but you also have to know what you are upholding, what you are fighting for, and that was something that I thought a great deal about in these years. It did give me a much better understanding of the kind of values on which the art of literature is based, on which my own life and values are based and, I hope, values of imagination, of truth-telling, of artistic fearlessness and of dedication. If you had asked me twelve years ago if there was anything that I would have been willing to die for, I would have looked at you as if you were mad because why would anyone want to. And yet here were people trying to kill me. I discovered that I cared enough about the things that were endangered to want to fight for them, even though it placed my life in danger. And that was a very interesting thing to discover about yourself, that you feel that strongly about something.

The fatwa also polarized opinion. It divided the world into two—a free world and an intolerant, almost totalitarian, world of religious fanaticism, fundamentalism. How did you face up to that conflict?

It was very strange; it was like a very bright light shining with no grey areas suddenly. There was this way and that way, for or against, black or white, right or wrong. Suddenly these incredibly polarized conversations were happening and, yet, actually the business of literature is the business of grey areas. One of the great things about the novel as a form is that you can contradict yourself and, indeed, you must contradict yourself. If all the characters think the same way, then you are writing a polemic, you are not writing a novel. In a novel you must allow people to have world views and opinions and feelings which are unlike your own. The nature of being a novelist is to be pluralistic in that way but then, suddenly, to be pushed into a situation where in order to defend my work, in order to fight for principles, one had to speak in a politicized way. That was, for me, one of the strangest aspects because it was like using a false language. The politician's language is really devised to obscure truth whereas the writer's language is devised to reveal the truth. There is a very beautiful passage in a novel of Saul Bellow's that I have always taken as a kind of text. It is in *The Dean's December.* The central character is an American dean who has a Romanian wife and they are in eastern Europe. It is winter and he's looking out at this park and he hears, in the distance, a dog barking. Bellow wonderfully has his character imagine that what the dog is doing is protesting about the limits of dog experience; he imagines that the dog is saying, 'For God's sake, open the universe a little more.' A beautiful phrase. I have always thought that it is the artist's job to open the universe a little more and that is what I tried to do.

Were you hurt when *The Satanic Verses* was banned by the Indian government and do you think enough time has now passed for them to lift the ban?

I was hurt. It was a different government and Rajiv Gandhi is not around any more so it's a little pointless, but one of the reasons I was upset is that India's own due process in these matters had not been followed. The book had not entered the country, it had not been judged by the panel that was supposed to judge these things, whether it was a book that deemed banning or not, there were no attempts to answer the case and no fair hearing. It was simply a fiat; the book was banned before it had ever come into the country, and as a result, the conversation about it was very largely uninformed because nobody could lay their hands on a copy for a long time.

That was very disappointing. I know the censorship argument about hurting sensitivities and so on, but I do, in general, think that people need to start being a little less sensitive. I don't mean that just for India, I mean that as a global problem. There is a culture of complaint as the Australian critic Robert Hughes calls it, that you somehow carry your 'offendedness' almost as a badge of identity: if you don't have anything to be offended about then you don't have any self. People take offence very easily—and this is true in America, Europe and it is true here. I do think it is a cultural problem worldwide that people have become so thin-skinned.

A culture of political correctness taken to extremes?

Yes, it is political correctness on the one hand and communalism on the other hand. It has many an impetus but the effect is this desire of people to find something to be offended about. In my view, a democracy and a free society is a much more robust thing. It is not a place where everybody is careful not to step on each other's toes. It is a place where everybody says everything. It's a noisy bazaar; it is not a quiet library with a sign up saying 'Silence please'.

A democratic society is one where people yell at each other or disagree strongly or don't even agree to differ. I think, in order to do that, we have to stop being such shrinking violets, we have to allow people to exist who do not think as we think. It doesn't mean we don't argue with them but we cannot say that they mustn't speak, because then we will end up with something that is not a free society and which none of us would enjoy living in. When you start restricting the speech of one, you end up by restricting the speech of all, and in the end, nobody can say what they think; and if you live in a country where nobody can say what they think, that is a definition of insanity.

Whereas your earlier books like *Midnight's Children* and *Shame* were set solely in the subcontinent, you have been moving ground in recent works like *The Moor's Last Sigh* and *The Ground Beneath Her Feet* . . .

The first book in which I really tried to write about somewhere else was *The Satanic Verses*, much of which happens in England. But, yes, a lot of *The Moor's Last Sigh* is in Bombay and the last bit is in Europe. In *The Ground Beneath Her Feet*, the weight is slightly different. Some of it is in Bombay and most of it is abroad. That is just because my life experience has been in many countries and so I have more than one route to draw on. I had always felt, until *The Ground Beneath Her Feet*, that the other experience was something I had left underexplored and so I feel pleased to have done that. Characters in my novels keep saying goodbye to India forever. The characters keep doing it but the author never succeeds in doing it. I have long ago understood that I mustn't ever say that I will or won't write about India again because I literally don't know. I have always thought that my greatest good fortune as a writer was to have these many routes and I intend to use them more.

You have drawn flak for an anthology of Indian writing that you edited recently because you included just one writer from a regional language, Saadat Hasan Manto, and said that writing in Indian languages wasn't really of the same standard as English. Do you stand by that or did you put that in as a tease?

It is always good to have something in an anthology that gets a little attention. What happens with anthologies is that they annoy people. People always attack an anthology for what is *not* in it. All I can say is that it wasn't a conclusion I had expected to reach; I read a lot of stuff and made a selection and that was the selection I made. I said that in a slightly polemical way. The answer to an anthology is more anthologies.

There's been a lot of press lately about your personal life, your association with the model Padma Lakshmi and your move to New York from London. Do you resent the intrusion?

It is bizarre for me because it never happened before.

Falling in love?

No, the media hubbub about my private life. Falling in love happens to me too often I think. I quite like my private life to be private and my public life to be public, but I guess the world is not like that these days.

April 2000

***The Enchantress of Florence* travels between Akbar's Fatehpur Sikri and Renaissance Florence, a swashbuckling Italian adventurer and a beautiful princess who is probably a witch. But would you say that at its heart your new novel, more than any other, is a love story?**

At the heart of it, yes, the plot couldn't happen except with two people falling in love. It brings from the east to the west this beautiful lost princess Qara Koz, and from the west to the east this pale, handsome, slightly effeminate Italian warrior called Nino Argalia. The moment at which Argalia and the princess meet on the field of battle in Persia, where the Ottomans defeat the Persians and he liberates her from the possession of the Iranian Shah, she falls in love with him. That moment is the moment where the worlds join. The moment where they first look at each other is where I am able to do the thing I said I could do—to just go click—and in the story is the story of that love.

There is also humour in the book and some parts are irreverent and hilarious. Your readers expect satire from you but they don't expect steamy sex which *The Enchantress of Florence* has . . .

It is certainly the sexiest book I ever wrote. I think there is more sex in this book than I have ever written before. At the beginning of my writing life I was very shy about sex. There is almost no sex scene in *Midnight's Children*, just a brief description of the protagonist's parents in bed together but it's very indirect. I almost felt ashamed to write openly about sex. I think that is a very Indian reluctance. Gradually over the years, I have become braver. It is also present here because it was a very sensual time. There was a lot of similarity between Akbar's court and Medici Florence. The figure of the courtesan, a kind of a high-class whore, is very powerful. And these are worlds in which people are drinking a lot, smoking opium and taking drugs. We think of them as high cultural, poetic and artistic worlds but actually they were full of debauchery.

***The Enchantress of Florence* comes out at a time when intolerance against creative expression is on the rise in India. Artist M.F. Husain is in exile abroad, the author Taslima Nasrin has been hounded out, even a recent film like *Jodhaa Akbar* could not be released in Rajasthan. As someone who lived as a fugitive because of a fatwa, how worrying is the trend?**

I think it's greatly to India's shame that these things are happening. The idea that Deepa Mehta can't make a film without having the set attacked, that Husain is driven into exile in Dubai and London, and even his work is driven into exile so he is having to build a museum in the Gulf for his work—what a loss to India that is. It doesn't matter how good or bad a writer Taslima Nasrin is or how important intellectually. None of that is important. It is dreadful that she is hounded in this way; and that India has become a country where a library in Pune with rare manuscripts can be attacked because somebody does not like what somebody said about Shivaji. It is shameful at this moment when India is trying very hard to give the impression of emerging as a serious, modern superpower. If India looks like China where nothing can be said without people being beaten up and jailed, it will damage the world's view of India; anyway, it damages my view of India because this is not the India that I know about, this is not the India that I admire and care about. Yes, I think Akbar at the end of the book sees a darker time ahead, and maybe he is not looking any further than Aurangzeb because the darker time is not that far away. Readers reading it now can certainly make a connection to our own time.

As a Muslim how difficult is it to write in a polarized post-9/11 world?

First of all, I am not a Muslim, but let's say a post-Muslim. I am definitely post-something. I think it's a difficult world to live in whoever you are right now. It is a disturbed, divided and contentious world and if you are a writer looking at that world, it is hard to be optimistic about it.

One of the things I found, going back 400 years, is the way it helped because it showed me that there is nothing new about this. This is the kind of species we are—if this is a brutal age, that was a brutal age, and if that was an age out of which great beauty came, so is this; and so whether you look at the good in us or the bad in us, it's always been there. We are not doing anything now that we did not do 400 years ago; we are just doing it differently. In a way that comforts you because it shows you that the human race has gone through this before.

Exile and identity are running themes in your fiction. If you are 'post-something' as you say, where are you from?

I am from Bombay—that is where I am from. I have always been a Bombay guy and I have always thought of myself as that. I see Bombay in other places. One of the reasons why I like it here in New York is because I see Bombay in it; I see all kinds of echoes and similarities. Wherever I bounce around in the world that's what I am, wherever I go in India I am happy to be there, but the place where you were a child and grew up has a kind of power over you that nowhere else does.

You have been bouncing around in New York for almost nine years. How has it affected your identity and your writing? Are you a New Yorker?

I do feel pretty much at home here. I like it a lot because it's a city which lets people in very easily. Most people who live here didn't come from New York, so it is a great city for immigrants; it is a city invented by migrant cultures, whether Jewish, Italian or now south Asian. But then I also feel at home in London and at home in Bombay. From the age of fourteen, I started travelling and so my idea of home has been pluralistic ever since then. I don't find that very problematic. One interesting thing about going back in time is that, in a way, it excuses me from the endless and tedious debate about who is an Indian writer. Does it make any difference whether you live in India or abroad? Writers from all countries have lived all over the place. Graham Greene lived in Monte Carlo but that didn't stop him from being an English novelist.

Many regard you as one of the most admired writers in English but at the same time some of your recent fiction may not have received the kind of critical acclaim that *Midnight's Children* or *The Moor's Last Sigh* did. Does that bother you and do you care about reviews?

I am getting better at not caring. Anybody who says that they don't care is probably lying, unless they're Doris Lessing—she is the only person I know who really does not care. I have got better at it and I think, truthfully, one of the great liberations for me was when *Fury* came out. It was the worst review of my work that was ever published and it completely set me free because I still think it is pretty good and I think it will be vindicated among the good books that stick around. In colleges in America it is the book that young people read and also *The Ground Beneath Her Feet* which, according to the gods of criticism, is not as good as the others. In a way you have to let your books go. They have to go out in the world and make their own way. There are books that will be fashionable at some point, and not at another, and other books that will be more interesting later.

Shame is a book which seems to have come into its own, given all that is happening in Pakistan these days. It seems almost more relevant now then when I wrote it in 1983. People's interest in particular books comes and goes. What I try to do is—what I think any serious writer tries to do—that you have an ongoing conversation with yourself, and you also have this ongoing engagement with the world in which you live, and you try and find books which you write at the place where those two conversations intersect, your view about the world and your internal dialogue. The books become reports from your consciousness as you go through your life. Of course, I would prefer that people like my books. I am always happy when people like my books and less happy when they don't.

But there is a point when you realize that no matter what people say about your books, this is still the direction you want to go in. It is one of the benefits of growing older: that you begin to see that the amount of time left is not so great and if you are a slow writer then how many books are you going to write in that time? So you have to seriously think about the books to which you will give your time. Once you have gone through that process of thought and you know why you are doing it, that is what matters.

I don't regret a word or a thing that I have written. Some of the writing of mine that I like the best is actually the India part of *The Ground Beneath Her Feet*; the first half of the book contains some of the best stuff I have done. *Shalimar the Clown* wasn't so badly received, so I have no complaints about that. It actually got me my first ever Indian literary prize, which took me all these years to get.

April 2008

Amartya Sen

Nobel laureate, economist and philosopher, Amartya Sen (b. 1933) is one of the great thinkers of our age. To spend an hour in his company is to come away illuminated, for amongst his prodigious intellectual gifts is an ability to communicate—putting across complex ideas, theoretical concepts and philosophical debates clearly and uncompromisingly. This he often does, in both his writing and in conversation, by drawing upon a wealth of quotations from a variety of literary, historical and religious sources, as well as examples from everyday life and the world around us.

That is one reason his books such as *The Argumentative Indian* (2005) and *The Idea of Justice* (2009) have been able to reach audiences far wider than books by academics usually do. 'Prolixity is not alien to us in India. We are able to talk at some length,' are the opening words of his collection of essays in the former book, before entering the byways of India's age-old tradition of heterodoxy and rational debate; the latter volume starts with a quote on perceived injustice by the young hero of Charles Dickens's *Great Expectations*. Sen also has a remarkable talent for putting his interlocutors at ease, so that after a few minutes it seems that this small-built, soft-spoken, attentive listener is gradually drawing the interviewer out rather than the other way round. A conversation with this argumentative Indian may not be ground-breaking but it covers a lot of ground.

Amartya Sen was born in Santiniketan but schooled in Dhaka where his father was professor of chemistry at the university; his maternal grandfather was a close associate of Tagore and the second vice-chancellor of Visva Bharati University. After Partition his family moved to Kolkata where he joined Presidency College, topping the university's undergraduate economics examination in 1953; that same year he moved to Trinity College, Cambridge, an institution with which he developed a lifelong connection, obtaining a starred first in his second BA. His outstanding academic record led him, at the age of twenty-three, to be appointed as founder and head of the department of economics at Jadavpur University. He returned to Trinity College to complete his PhD in 1959 and, winning a prize fellowship for four years, chose to study philosophy. He later explained the connection between economics and philosophy, saying that 'Social choice theory makes intense use of mathematical logic and also draws on moral philosophy, and so does the study of inequality and deprivation.'

He taught at several leading American universities but completed his major work, *Collective Choice and Social Welfare*, in 1970 at the Delhi School of Economics, where he was professor for more than a decade. His seminal works include *On Economic Inequality* (1973), *Poverty and Famines: An Essay on Entitlements and Deprivation* (1982) and *Hunger and Public Action* (with Jean Dreze; 1989). From 1977 to 1986 he was professor of economics at Nuffield College, Oxford, and later Drummond Professor of Political Economy at All Souls College at the same university. In 1986 he joined Harvard University as Thomas W. Lamont University Professor of Economics. In 1998 he was appointed as Master of Trinity College, Cambridge, but returned to Harvard in 2004. His pioneering studies on poverty, hunger and famine relate to human freedom and capability and are regarded as revolutionary in the field of development economics. His writings have influenced the UNDP's 'World Development Report', and articles such as 'More Than 100 Million Women Are Missing' in the *New York Review of Books* have provoked controversial debate.

He was awarded the Nobel Prize in Economic Sciences in 1998 and the Bharat Ratna, India's highest civilian honour, the following year. His works have been translated into more than thirty languages, and he holds honorary degrees from eighty universities around the world. He is based in Cambridge, Massachusetts, travels widely, but returns to his home in Santiniketan each winter.

The *Idea of Justice* is an illuminating and wide-ranging book. One of the first theoretical arguments that you bring up is of the political philosopher John Rawls's work, *A Theory of Justice*, which hinged on the notion that just institutions are key to conveying justice. But you argue that justice is also about human emotions and feelings, or as you put it in your introduction, 'Justice is ultimately connected with the way people's lives go, and not merely with the nature of the institutions surrounding them.'

John Rawls is the great political philosopher of our time, and so even when one disagrees with him, one draws on his ideas. This book is actually dedicated to John Rawls even though it disagrees with him throughout. My main focus is on human freedom rather than, specifically, happiness. It is an attempt to depart from Rawls at the very foundational level, arguing that justice is, primarily, not about perfect justice: it's about removing injustice or an enhancement of justice. Secondly, institutions never alone determine how our lives should go. So you can't have a pure institutional theory of justice. There are other ingredients to our lives.

As in your previous book, *The Argumentative Indian*, you take forward connections in history between east and west, comparisons between the tenets of Gautam Buddha and the eighteenth-century Age of Enlightenment in Europe, or the question of moral choice as argued in the conversation between Arjuna and Krishna in the *Bhagavad Gita*. How are these linked to notions of justice down the ages? What are the similarities and points of divergence?

Mine is a very reason-based view of justice. Reasoning is central to the idea of justice. That's the common ground between John Rawls and indeed the big western tradition going back to Immanuel Kant in particular, and also to John Locke and Jean-Jacques Rousseau. Reason-based understanding of justice is part of many non-western civilizations; it is not so much that eastern thoughts are quintessentially different from the western, but, in fact, it may be just the opposite.

The Age of Enlightenment gives the word 'enlightenment' a certain standing. The Enlightened One, Gautam Buddha, was born more than two thousand years before the Age of Enlightenment—it's the same word, but it's not a coincidence that it's the same word because they are both emphasizing the path of knowledge, understanding, analysis and criticism. My point is not that here are eastern ideas which have been neglected, but that here are some arguments that are not quintessentially eastern. It happens that they have been discussed in the context of Indian civilization—or Chinese, Japanese, African and other civilizations that I give small examples of—and that these arguments are quite relevant to aspects of western theories of justice.

In the *Gita*, the contrast between Krishna and Arjuna brings out a sharp difference between two ways of looking at what continuity is. Similarly, one of the distinctions that I draw throughout the book is between the two basic words used for justice in Sanskrit, namely, *niti* and *nyaya*.

What is the difference between *niti* and *nyaya*—the two words remain in common usage and both underscore reasoning . . .

The underlying reliance on reasoning is not the distinction between the two. It's just that *niti* is concerned with rules, institutions and arrangements. Krishna's argument is that you, as a warrior, face a just war and must fight. It's based on what your duties are, not so much on what consequences will follow; because they are the right rules, you must do your duty irrespective of the results. Arjuna is talking about *nyaya* to basically say, 'Look, you may say that this is what I ought to do, given my duties, but that people will die; indeed, I will be killing people myself. How can I say that it would be right for me to do that because it is my "duty" since I will be causing such terrible consequences?' That's what the argument of the *Gita* engages in and, of course, it ends with a victory for Krishna.

But that is not the entire story of the *Mahabharata*. Arjuna's arguments get a greater airing and, in the end, when the just war is over, the unjust kings are overthrown and the just kings gain the right to the throne, there is great grief in the Indo-Gangetic plain where the battle was fought, with women weeping over the loss of their men and funeral pyres burning everywhere. It is a very difficult thing that the *Mahabharata* is trying to tell you—don't worry about *nyaya*, just do your duty. This is a huge and an epic battle between two perspectives.

John Rawls's is a very *niti*-based theory because, in his discussions, institutions are central like the rules of behaviour that Krishna enunciates, the rules of institutions that enshrine 'principles of justice' as he calls them.

Your philosophical disquisitions quote not only from examples in history and epic, east and west, but also contemporary notions of justice as, for instance, in the United States' invasion of Iraq in 2003 that led to untold human misery and death. Does this lead you to believe that there should be some form of global justice or, indeed, global government?

Yes to your first question and no to the second. I don't think that we can get a global government because I think the idea of global government being necessary for global justice has been an albatross around the neck of the theory of justice. I don't think we need that. The basic key to the teaching of Rawls, his theory of justice, is why the right way of proceeding is public reasoning and that we can't have public reasoning without global government. Admittedly, if you ask for perfect public reasoning, you will need a global democratic state, but even then you won't get perfect public reasoning.

How then would there be any certainty that world leaders and governments will act justly to avoid conflicts, wars, devastation and death, say, on the scale that the US action caused in Iraq?

That's a very good question because it illustrates the point that I am trying to make: that if the way ahead is public reasoning, and in the context of global issues where one country invades another, it is global public reasoning that you are looking for, then the last thing you want is to stifle debate. That's exactly what happened in Iraq. In the case of the Iraq attack, the decision to move in, by the US and the Coalition of the Willing, was basically an attempt to shut down the views of those who were on the other side, not just within world forums like the UN, but generally there was a kind of unilateral view on the part of the United States.

I was then Master of Trinity College and I happened to be in England, but I did go back to the US often, and both my wife and I were horrified to see how limited the public discussion was. Anyone taking the view that the Iraq war might be a mistake immediately agreed with the notion that they hadn't understood the horrors of 9/11, overlooking the fact that Saddam Husain had nothing to do with 9/11, nothing to do with Al Qaeda, and the idea of weapons of mass destruction also proved to be wrong.

But it was difficult to make that point. I have seen the debate on TV channels where people who were trying to make the alternate point were immediately snubbed by others who said that when Europe had lived in the terror of Nazi attacks, America had stood by it, and 'now that we are in terror, why are Europeans saying it's none of our business?' But that's not what Europeans were saying; they were saying that this was a stupid war, it would kill a lot of people and, as a result of that, it would be a very nasty war.

You devote chapters to concepts of justice within institutional democratic or judicial frameworks but why is it that after more than sixty years of independence, widespread injustices in India persist at the most basic level in the lives of people, there are more malnourished children here than in sub-Saharan Africa, food insecurity despite public distribution systems and uncertainties of primary healthcare, education and essential welfare?

Thank you for that question. Indeed, in my earlier works, which are not generally books on philosophy but on Indian economy, development and freedom of thought, I had tried to argue how central these concerns were. And in some ways what I am trying to do as far as the application of ideas of justice is concerned is to integrate those earlier works because, unfortunately, they still remain contemporary. I wish I could say that I wrote a book fifteen years ago dealing with famine and undernourishment and that, happily, those have gone. Unfortunately, that's not the case, and that's the sadness of the situation.

The course of your question is that while we may have a democratic system, we may have a good judiciary and a system of good public media, these problems still remain. I think there has been a lack of engagement on these issues; there is some conceptual confusion which has to be removed. When we were talking earlier about *niti* and *nyaya*, [we must understand] quite a lot of public debates in India tend to take place over what one political party or another takes to be the wrong *niti*—it could be acquisition of land or the Indo-US nuclear deal or caste-based reservations. These are important questions, important because they affect the lives of people. So we have to see to what extent they will impact the lives of human beings who make up our society, and that's a *nyaya*-based question. And from the perspective of *nyaya* the things that you point out—the massive incidence of undernourishment in India or continued illiteracy, lack of medical care, right to primary education—you are quite right to ask why it has taken such a long time. Institutions are part of *niti*-based reasoning that are satisfied with answers like, 'look, we have democracy' or 'look, we have general elections', but *nyaya* is where the institutions combine with human behaviour to translate into action. I think there has been a shocking lack of engagement with many of these issues in Indian democratic politics. The voice of the underdog has been so low in India that the massive deprivation of people either because of caste, class or income—or if you happen to be a woman from a low-caste, low-income family—is a situation that hasn't received any attention.

I see myself politically on the Left and sometimes people worry if I am critical of the Left. And that is because I am disappointed that the Left has not done enough to concentrate on the issue of *nyaya*, the massive deprivation of the people; rather [it has] dwelt on issues of national sovereignty and what would happen if India were to drop the nuclear bomb. I would have thought there is a real reason for redirecting our political attention towards *nyaya*—removal of the injustices like the ones we are speaking of.

In the public discourse at home and abroad there is talk of India's emergence as an economic powerhouse, the creation of an affluent, educated middle class and other achievements. Yet even in your own state, West Bengal, where you spend part of the year, tensions prevail—over industrialization versus the interests of small farmers—and threaten the future of the Left government. How do you view these contradictions?

Let me make two points—a general point and a specific one. The general point is that it would be a mistake to think that only the educated-class-group's point of view is represented. I think there is a great deal of sympathy among different classes in India. Let us not forget that the 'anti-untouchability' movements have been led quite often by 'touchables', Mahatma Gandhi being a good example, as indeed a whole lot of others.

On the other hand, have these served the interests of the underdog and has the underdog had adequate recourse or recompense? The answer is no. So it's inadequacy rather than absence we are talking about. In West Bengal it is much the same story though the communist government did come up with some major achievements. It did implement land reforms in a way that no other state has successfully done and it handled the panchayat movement very well, and yet, at some level, other issues did not receive the attention they should have had.

I think the present debacle in West Bengal has a complexity that politically boggles the mind of the Bengali. I had the privilege to start the Pratichi Trust after I got the Nobel Prize and we have been working with the primary teachers' union to increase accountability in schools, to make sure that the teachers are punctual and, so far, we have got a very positive response. I think what we need are more public organizations and movements to bring about change when political parties are bureaucratized. There is a case for regarding the unions as not a very good thing because what do unions do and whose interests do they reflect? But talking to leaders of the primary teachers' union, I found they were not that resistant and immediately accepted that their job was not only to pursue their own interest but also the national interest. We have done it on a tiny scale but we need to do it on a much wider one. But in the end I am an optimist and I think these changes can be made. And I hope that Indian democracy, given time, can deliver a lot more than it has so far.

August 2009

Aradhana Seth

Vikram Seth

Vikram Seth (b. 1952), arguably the most gifted of his generation of Indians writing in English, nurtured no early ambition to become a writer. He loathed his boarding school because he was 'extremely introverted . . . incapable of looking people in the eye'. But he was academically outstanding and won a scholarship to a British public school, and later to Oxford where, left to his own devices, he began to write poetry. 'I was incredibly unskilful,' he said of his first attempts. In 1975 he moved to Stanford University and spent the next eleven years 'not getting an economics PhD'.

In 1980–82, while researching his unwritten doctorate in Chinese demography at Nanjing University, he undertook a journey that unexpectedly led him home to Delhi across the overland route. *From Heaven Lake: Travels Through Sinkiang and Tibet* (1983), an original and diverting travelogue, won a prize, got him noticed and was a promising start.

It was California, however, that liberated his personality and unleashed his creative powers. Chancing upon an old copy of Pushkin's verse novel *Eugene Onegin* inspired him to write *The Golden Gate* (1986), set among West Coast yuppies, and composed of nearly 600 sonnets in iambic tetrameter. It brought him instant fame; Americans, it was reported, threw flowers at him at poetry readings.

Vikram Seth's story is well-known from then on: of how he retreated for six years to his parents' home in Delhi to write his epic-length novel *A Suitable Boy* (1993); of his shrewd negotiations to sell it for £250,000 ('a very large novel written by a very small Indian,' he quipped), and how his next novel, *An Equal Music* (1999), about a group of western classical musicians was inspired by, and dedicated to, his French violinist friend Philippe Honore. Seth has also produced several collections of poetry, including translations from Chinese and Urdu. The best known are *All You Who Sleep Tonight* (1990) and *Beastly Tales* (1991). His last book, *Two Lives* (2005), was a biography of his great-uncle and his German wife. In 2009 he announced that his next work would be *A Suitable Girl*, a sequel in which Lata, the would-be bride of *A Suitable Boy*, goes in search of a match for her grandson.

A polyglot (he is fluent in Mandarin, German and French) and music lover (he plays the Indian flute, the cello and sings Schubert), Vikram Seth is a man of changeable moods: he can be reflective, even remote, or warm and quizzically loquacious. There is no accounting for where the creative impulse will take him next. The last time I saw him at the Abu Dhabi Book Fair in 2009 he was armed with paintbox and sketchbook, and off to paint in the desert.

This interview, recorded after the Indian release of *Two Lives*, nearly didn't happen. I had carefully planned it as a walkabout on a winter afternoon along the outer wall of Humayun's Tomb, but just before we were due to start, the camera's batteries failed. Replacements were sent for but daylight began to fade, and Seth grew restive. Luckily, a mutual friend, passing by on a stroll, distracted him for a few minutes, and his mood improved. We got going in the nick of time and he was soon his insightful, witty and engaging self.

~

More than one of your books are inspired, or based on, family life. Your early travel book *From Heaven Lake* culminates in returning to the family fold in Delhi after your journey across China. Your fictional opus *A Suitable Boy* is inspired by incidents and characters of family history. But *Two Lives* is pure family history . . .

Yes it is. It is based on the story of my great-uncle who was Indian and my great-aunt who was German. I stayed with them as a young student when I was about seventeen years old when I was sent to England. They were, in effect, my local parents there. Of course, I knew my uncle but my aunt looked very strange. He was quite short and didn't have a right arm and he practised as a dentist with his left arm. My great-aunt was taller than him, very German, very particular, meticulous and rather brusque. He, on the other hand, was very welcoming and warm. They were both born in 1908 and they lived very long lives. My aunt died at the age of eighty and, in the last decade of his life, my uncle was very lonely. He didn't really know what to do with himself. And I, for my part, having written *A Suitable Boy*, was at a bit of a loose end. My mother suggested, 'Why don't you interview Shanti Uncle? Why don't you talk to him about his life? He has lived in very interesting times and he has had a rather heroic life.'

Although a biography, *Two Lives* is also a fragment of autobiography, with you arriving at Shanti and Henny's doorstep in London. What was it like to recapture your life at that moment, about to enter an English school and later compete for Oxford?

I was painfully shy in those days. The idea of staying with people whom I didn't really know very well didn't please me. And they were unknown quantities, in more ways than one. For instance, Aunty Henny and Uncle Shanti would start talking in German suddenly at the breakfast table when they wanted to say something in private or if they were bickering. It wasn't as if they would go into another room, they would just talk in German. So I didn't really understand what they were on about. It was only after I discovered, owing to an obscure regulation in the university statutes that I had to learn a European language in order to go to university in England, that I decided I had better learn German, since they also spoke it.

A close bond developed between you and your German aunt, almost as close as with your uncle? You almost became the child they never had?

I think that is true. For instance, my aunt was very particular in referring to me as her husband's nephew. But once I started speaking German, then she quite often introduced me as 'my nephew'. And for my uncle, who used to call me 'my nephew', I became, '*mein kleiner Sohn*' which means 'my little son'.

You knew very little of their early lives because Aunty Henny was secretive about her tragic past . . .

Not only was she secretive with strangers, or with people like me, but even with regard to Uncle, who had lived with her family when he wanted to take a room in Germany, where he was studying dentistry—she wouldn't talk to him about the past. I should backtrack a little: Shanti was sent by his family to Germany in the early 1930s when he was a young man of about twenty-three to study dentistry. His family had an accountant, a lawyer, a judge and an engineer, so why not a dentist? He didn't know a word of German. He had to take courses in perhaps the most advanced dental institute in the world. One thing he decided to do was not to stay with any family that didn't speak in German, so that he could get a bit of practice. Aunty Henny's family took him in. He had to convince them to charge a slightly higher rent than they would have done because this was the first time they were letting a room out in their rather palatial flat in a fashionable part of Berlin. Eventually he became accepted as a part of the family. But Henny's first reaction, when she heard from her mother and her sister that they were taking in an Indian lodger was, '*Nehmen Sie den schwarzen Mann nicht*' which means 'Don't take the black man'.

Both were caught in the whirlwind of history. She has to flee from the horrors of Nazi Germany and he goes to the battlefront. They meet in Berlin, are separated by World War II, and meet again in England later. Both have lost their homelands. Are some lives stranger than fiction?

Yes. In the case of Henny, it was the loss of her family and the loss of her homeland. In the case of Shanti, he was sent abroad and eventually chose not to return. He didn't get a job in Germany because of the various laws in effect there under the Third Reich. He requalified in Edinburgh and started practising in someone else's surgery in London. Then war broke out, he signed up, and was taken to various places in Africa and the Palestinian front. His right arm was blown off by a piece of German shrapnel during the famous battle of Monte Cassino in the Italian campaign.

In the course of telling their individual stories, the microcosms of their life led me to meditate on the macrocosms of history. After all, both their lives began in 1908 and were almost co-terminus with the twentieth century. Whether it was the Indian freedom struggle, or the Italian campaign of World War II, Nazi Germany or Israel and Palestine. These matters come in ineluctably into the story.

You call *Two Lives* 'history writ little' as opposed to history writ large. What is it about ordinary lives that make them dramatic, almost heroic?

It isn't necessarily that heroism is foisted upon them. It could just as well have been the opposite. In the case of these two people, I feel that, yes, a great deal of endurance and heroism became their portion in life.

Obviously it isn't something they would have necessarily chosen. But it was their reaction to circumstances that made their story dramatic.

There is heroism, too, in the fact of a dentist practising with one arm . . .

I was very intrigued by my uncle's story and ability to pursue a profession with just his left arm. It was an act of courage to re-establish his confidence. I was treated by him and he was a wonderful dentist. Competent, kind, thorough, and explaining everything that needed to be done. He believed in preserving teeth at all cost. He didn't believe in the British idea of 'if in doubt, take it out'.

***Two Lives* is also a portrait of a thirty-eight-year-old marriage. It's a subject you've dwelt on at length in your fiction. What is it about the alchemy of marriage that interests you?**

If I could put my finger on it, there would be almost no need to write a book of this complexity and length. The fact is that it is very difficult to say, there is no such thing as an ideal happy marriage. Happy marriages in themselves are every bit as various, just as unhappy marriages are.

In this particular case, their marriage was a mixture of reticence, of having great confidence in each other without necessarily sharing great confidences. For instance, Shanti knew Henny's family and grieved for them. But when he tried to talk to Henny about the great disaster that happened, the fact that they had been killed in Nazi concentration camps in Herzfeld and Theresienstadt she told him, 'Shanti, I don't want to enter the graveyard.' Whether this was to spare him the hurt, or whether to close off a certain area of her life, so that he wouldn't bring up the subject, is difficult to say.

There is a key difference between writing fiction and biography. In fiction, you can reconstruct and imagine life even if it is inspired by real incidents or people as in *A Suitable Boy* but in biography you can't . . .

The facts are the facts. It is certainly true that you can select certain facts, you can give a certain kind of interpretation, you have to analyse them and so on, but you can't set up three or four different scenarios, as in fiction, and then say, I wonder which is going to be the most exciting or the most interesting or the most true to character, and follow that particular construct. In biography you need to take these hard nuggets and make what sense of them you can.

For *Two Lives* I had to find the material wherever I could. There were these very moving letters sent to Aunty Henny by her friends when she is trying to find out what has happened to her mother and her sister. Also Aunty Henny, being so German, sometimes kept carbon copies of her own letters. So these were primary source material. But then I tried to find out exactly on which train her mother and sister were sent out of Berlin to the concentration camps, quite late in 1943. And that took me—when I happened to be in Israel because of a translation of a book of mine—to the Holocaust memorial, Yad Vashem, in Jerusalem. There I saw the actual Geheime Staatspolizei, the secret state police, documents—with the lists of all these people and the incredible comment that their property had not been destroyed and would be sent to the financial administration to be dealt with.

But in the end, a book is a book, whether biographical or a novel. However, when research comes into it, it's not a dissertation. You're not supposed to yawn when you read it, you are supposed to be gripped. I felt that some of the aspects that I learned from fiction have carried over into non-fiction as well, in that, character is very important and the grip of the story is crucial, and the worlds in which these characters move have to be made as tangible—smellable, feelable and tasteable—as possible.

In fictional narrative, there can be a single or multiple narrators. But in biography—which in this case is also a piece of autobiography—how did you arrive at the decision of where to put yourself in or keep yourself out?

This is, of course, the problem of writing the kind of book I have written. There was no definite rule—how much do I introduce myself into the book or how much do I withdraw to keep a correct authorial distance? This is one of my chief fascinations in writing this book. And I don't know if I have got the balance right, even for myself, let alone anyone else.

You live in Britain but come to India more than once a year. That combination of distance and proximity must make you observe changes in India. Which are the ones that strike you the most?

The considerable change is political and economic. On the whole, I feel pleased with the change. What particularly pleases me is the fact that two generations have been brought up with a form of reasonably functioning democracy. It's a huge achievement. Secondly, the worst of poverty could, to a certain extent, be said to have been reduced. There are also two particular areas of anxiety—the fact that rural India should not be left behind, and second, India shouldn't lose its sense of tolerance, its sense of being a country for all its people and not just people of one particular religion. These are two things I am most concerned about. Yet, there is a great sense of calm confidence—at least that's what I noticed.

But, for me, the main draw is my family. First and last, I am a family person: it isn't just that I feel that there is a haven in the family; my family, in a sense, has also been my patron. When I had two degrees in economics from rather high-powered universities, my parents still allowed me to live at the top of the house and write this interminable novel, *A Suitable Boy*. In effect, I sponged off them for years. They acted as my patrons, or patron and matron, you could say.

Does India remain, and will it continue to remain, a central motif of your writing?

I would say it does but I can't predict from one book to another or what I will next be writing about. With *A Suitable Boy* I was taken to task, usually by foreign publishers, for not having enough foreign characters. But there weren't any in that particular world as I imagined it. On the other hand, in *The Golden Gate* or in *An Equal Music* there are no Indian characters, and again, many people ask why there aren't any Indian characters. The fact is that you cannot compel your muse in providing you with a certain quota of Indian and foreign characters in any particular book. Nor should one try to.

And how does the muse come and go, especially for a poet?

I have always, at heart, been a poet. In fact, one of the things that has recently given me a great kick is that my Indian publisher has issued all my poetry in such a beautiful edition that, even if it were blank pages, I would probably go out and get them for myself. Poetry is so dear to me that, even in every prose book that I write, I somehow manage to inveigle a poem at the beginning by way of a dedication or something like that.

A verse novel set in California, a big fictional opus set in India, a novel set in London and a biography. Your writing not only moves from continent to continent but across a gamut of genres. What makes you want to try out different forms?

There is no particular desire to experiment. If the inspiration comes to me in a particular form, then it's a desire not to shy away from that form.

And what will you try next?

Ah, now if I knew that, and I was at this particular moment inspired by some other form or some other idea, then we wouldn't be having this conversation at all. I would be hard at work.

January 2006

Bapsi Sidhwa

Pakistani author Bapsi Sidhwa (b. 1938) describes herself as a 'Parsi–Punjabi–Indian–Pakistani'. She could add Texan, as she has been based in Houston for many years though she returns to Pakistan regularly. Sidhwa's early life is a profile in courage in the face of personal adversity. Stricken by polio at the age of two, her schooling was interrupted, though she later went on to take a degree from Kinnaird College, Lahore. Married early into a Parsi family in Mumbai, it was an unhappy union. 'My first husband said, "You can't walk; you can't talk. What you can do?"' she told an interviewer many years later. When the marriage broke up, she returned to Lahore; her two children were separated as she was compelled to leave her son behind. 'I know the difficulties of the India–Pakistan relationship only too well,' she told me without a trace of rancour in Karachi in 2010. 'I had to battle for months to move between the two countries.'

It was only after her second marriage that she began to write. Words became her salve, a form of inner liberation. Her first novel, *The Bride* (1982), started as a short story and, based on a real incident, took four years to complete. It is about a young girl married into a tribal community in the mountainous Karakoram region who runs away but is later pursued and murdered in an honour killing.

Sidhwa's second novel, *The Crow Eaters* (1982), pokes gentle fun at the Parsi community; it found no takers initially and she had to publish it herself. 'It was very frustrating to peddle your own books as I did in Lahore. I would go from bookstore to bookstore saying, "Please read *The Crow Eaters*."' It only reached a wider audience when a copy reached the distinguished editor Liz Calder at Jonathan Cape in London who immediately accepted it. *Ice Candy Man* (1988), her best-known novel, is a partly autobiographical account of a city convulsed by communal riots, as observed by a nine-year-old girl. It was made into the successful film *Earth* (1998) by the Canadian–Indian film-maker Deepa Mehta with whom Sidhwa established a longer association. In 1991 she was decorated with the Sitara-i-Imtiaz, Pakistan's highest national honour in the arts. More recently, she has edited the anthology *City of Sin and Splendour: Writings on Lahore* (2006).

Her difficult life has not dimmed Bapsi Sidhwa's resilient good humour and zest for travel. Though she has appeared more than once on *Just Books*, this interview was recorded at the Abu Dhabi Book Fair in 2010. I saw her again some weeks later in Karachi; she had recently sold her family home in Lahore and was busy promoting a collection of writings by her brother Minoo Bhandara, the eminent Pakistani politician, columnist and owner of the famous Murree brewery who died tragically in 2008 after a car accident in China.

~

When film-maker Deepa Mehta picked up a copy of your novel *Ice Candy Man* in America, which she later made into the movie *Earth*, it didn't have that title. It was called *Cracking India*. Why was the title changed?

Because my publisher in America said 'ice candy man' is slang for a drug peddler and that would give a wrong impression of the book. It has nothing to do with drugs. There are too many books written about drugs in America in any case.

You have had an interesting collaboration with Deepa Mehta. When she made the final part of her trilogy called *Water*, she asked you to write a novel of the film, whereas it is usually films that are based on books. How did the reverse collaboration between film-maker and novelist work?

Deepa insisted that I 'novelize' the film and she is very difficult to refuse. I thought, 'Can I do that in three or four months?' She wanted it in time for the release of the film. But when I saw the film I realized that the child in it was very like the child Lenny in *Ice Candy Man* and through her I could capture the character of the book. And then, don't forget, the plot and characters were already there. I found it much easier to describe them and to unravel the plot. Of course I ad-libbed a lot, especially to add to the humour of the eunuch Gulabo. I put more fun into it.

One reason why *Ice Candy Man* is such a memorable novel about the subcontinent's partition is that the tumult of the city and the world outside is presented from a sheltered child's viewpoint. Its show-don't-

tell technique heightens the drama and denouement. Was it conceived like that?

In a way it was drawn from life. I was afflicted with polio at an early age and was not sent to school. I had a very lonely, withdrawn childhood, until I discovered books, started reading, and the characters in the books became my friends, my role models. I literally began to inhabit those pages. But up until then my world was very dry. In fact, I wrote out of the silences in my life. So it wasn't a happy childhood, yet my work is very happy. My work can be serious too, but it is always infected by humour.

Which is true of *The Crow Eaters*, your novel about the Parsi community. Its comedy is contagious. Long before writers like Firdaus Kanga, Rohinton Mistry and Farrukh Dhondy wrote about the Parsis, you were really the first one to draw a wry and affectionate portrait of your community . . .

Firdaus Kanga met me after he had written *Learning to Grow*. He said that he had never thought Parsis were worth writing about till he read *The Crow Eaters*. Boman Desai said the same. A lot of writers felt that. Ours is a small community, only about 1,00,000 left in the world, and although the numbers are shrinking I don't think that they are going to just disappear. That would be a sad thing because, in its own way, it's a nice, charming and sweet community.

You once told an interviewer that you became a writer because you went through periods of despair in your life, not only your restricted childhood because of your ailment, but even later. In fact, you said, that if you had had a happy life you probably wouldn't have become a writer. Is that true?

Had I lived in a milieu where I could have had boyfriends, gone to dances and had fun, I don't think I would have written. Because at certain times in my life I was going through periods of great despair, as you rightly put it, anguish in a way, it eased me into writing. For example, writing took me out of a very severe debilitating twitch I used to have. Just the act of writing removed much unhappiness. Now that I am pretty reconciled to my life and am happy, I don't feel the urge to write. But at those moments I was driven to write. Of course it also had a lot to do with being youthful.

***City of Sin and Splendour*, your most recent book, is a tribute to Lahore, the city of your birth and coming of age. It is a varied anthology of memoirs, essays and profiles. What makes it special that its contributors, many of them famous, are from both sides of the border. How did the book come about?**

It took three years of my life to compile, sitting in Houston, because I had to translate many of the essays and stories myself. I visited Pakistan and India two or three times to get the stories. There are an equal amount of Indian and Pakistani writers in it; it was a labour of love because Lahore is a city I love, the heart of Punjab and very much a part of my ethos. It was actually an Indian publisher [Penguin] that asked me do it and I jumped at the chance. But in a way it deprived me of writing another novel because three years is a long time out of a productive phase of one's life. At the same time I feel that I owed it to the city in which I grew up.

What are you working on now?

I am working on a collection of short stories which is almost near completion.

March 2010

Khushwant Singh

'So you've come to write my obituary?' That was the salty sardarji greeting me when, some years ago, I went up to his summer home in the hill station of Kasauli to record an interview. Khushwant Singh's preoccupation with death, sex and much of the daily business of life betwixt and between makes him one of India's most widely read columnists, a hugely successful editor in his heyday and a notable fiction writer. In a long life crammed with controversy and a phenomenal output, there is scarcely a genre of writing that he has not attempted: as biographer and memoirist, historian and chronicler of people and places, and retailer of dirty jokes, his is the contrarian's take on everything from the body politic to bodily functions.

Khushwant Singh (b. 1915) is a life-enhancer, and spending an evening in his company is an unmatched pleasure. Erudite and exhibitionist in equal measure, he is the bon vivant par excellence. Pouring Patiala pegs of single malt that evening in Kasauli, savouring every sip himself, he urged more libations on my crew and me. 'Keep me company. Have another, there's lots to go.'

Born in present-day Pakistan, Khushwant Singh, the son of a wealthy builder, was educated at Government College, Lahore, St Stephen's College in Delhi and King's College, London, before reading for the Bar at the Inner Temple. But he practised law, and later served as a diplomat in Britain, Canada and France, only briefly. His true calling was writing and his first novel, *Train to Pakistan* (1956), on Partition-torn Punjab, was an instant critical and commercial success. More fiction followed, and a landmark two-volume *A History of the Sikhs* (1963) established his credentials in scholarship. But his rise to national prominence came during his editorship of the *Illustrated Weekly of India* (1969–78), a dowdy journal that he turned into a sparky, controversial magazine that pumped up circulation and set the course for *With Malice Towards One and All*, his immensely popular and ongoing column.

Khushwant Singh had a tangled relationship with the Gandhi family and the Congress party. He supported Indira Gandhi's Emergency rule in 1975 and was a champion of her son Sanjay Gandhi's ill-starred politics. Nominated to the Rajya Sabha as MP (1980–86), he kept his seat but returned the Padma Bhushan after the Indian army's siege of the Golden Temple in 1984. Later he fought a long and costly legal battle against Sanjay's widow, Maneka Gandhi, to lift the restraining order on his autobiography, *Truth, Love and a Little Malice* (2002).

I recorded more than one interview with Khushwant Singh for NDTV but the most complete took place at his home in New Delhi after the publication of his anthology *Why I Supported the Emergency: Essays and Profiles* (2009). Subsequently he turned down all my requests for TV interviews.

'Please do not ring the bell unless expected' reads a neatly printed notice outside his flat. However, some days before the publication of his novel *The Sunset Club* in November 2010, I rang it, courtesy of his daughter Mala Dayal and our mutual friend Nandini Mehta. *The Sunset Club* is about three friends in their eighties—a Hindu, a Muslim and a Sikh—who meet on a Lodi Gardens bench each evening through a single year, 2009–10, to pick over their lives and the events of the day: politics, scandal, sexual fantasy and their past. It is a valedictory rumination on friendship, old age, infirmity and changing India.

The author was in fine form. 'Pour yourself a stiff one,' he said cheerfully, motioning towards the whisky. Conversation, punctuated with laughter, was stimulating, as he talked about Philip Roth's obsession with constipation ('a trait that Jews and Indians share'), poetry (quoting Ghalib and Hilaire Belloc), crossword puzzles ('I finish three to four every morning), daydreams and nightmares ('I have a fear of having no money, of being unable to pay a restaurant bill'). A few questions from that evening are incorporated in this interview.

A new novel at ninety-five is pretty good going. How did you find the time and stamina to write it?

I can't garden or do other work; the only thing I can do is scribble. Writing two columns a week plus book reviews is killing, but I also keep a daily diary recording what I did that day, the weather and changing seasons. While going through a year's diary I came across incidents like the Haryana politician Chander Mohan Bishnoi who became Chand Mohammed to marry his Hindu girlfriend who became Fiza. He then left her and reconverted to becoming a Hindu. I thought why not put in stories like that, mix public and personal events, as seen through the eyes of three octogenarians.

Is Sardar Boota Singh in *The Sunset Club* a version of yourself?

My characters are a combination of fact and fantasy. I start with a character but then it begins to dominate. It won't do things I want it to do and starts doing things on its own. *The Sunset Club* is mostly from my imagination. I have been going to the Lodi Gardens for years; I used to know every tree there. So I thought why not set it in a place I know so well?

You are one of Delhi's great chroniclers. The city features again and again in your writing and you've even written a novel about it. Your father, Sir Sobha Singh, was also one of the builders of modern Delhi. How has the city changed in your lifetime?

This was essentially a city of refined Muslim culture. Then it was suddenly invaded by Punjabis, Hindus and Sikhs, and that completely changed its character. When my father built this block of flats [Sujan Singh Park] it was beyond the cemetery, that is, beyond what were then the city's limits. He built the Ambassador Hotel and rented it for Rs 10,000 a month. Today I am told a ground floor flat in this block rents for two and a half lakh rupees.

I used to love Delhi but now I find it uninhabitable. I can't find my way around. You can no longer see the moon and the stars—even the joy of darkness has been robbed. The frogs, sparrows and owls have all gone. The corruption and extravagance are unbelievable. Diwali is just over and I am amazed at the gifts people send. I shouldn't complain too much, though. I had a lovely haul of whisky, fourteen or fifteen bottles I think. But I find living here a pain in the arse.

You started out as a lawyer and then became a diplomat. You took to writing later in life. Would you say you became a writer accidentally?

Completely. I flopped at everything I did in my early years. I threw up job after job. I became a writer because my generous and remarkable father stood by me. I lived off his bounty for years.

Many regard *Train to Pakistan* as your best novel. But looking back on all these years of writing–fiction, histories of the Sikhs and many other books–is there one work you are especially proud of?

Train to Pakistan was the most popular and was later made into a film. But I think my novel *Delhi* is quite good. Also some of my other fiction, for example, *I Shall Not Hear the Nightingale*, is probably better and more filmable than *Train to Pakistan*. But you can't really tell with books—it's not always the best books that sell best. As for my histories, I seem to have become some sort of a guru for the Sikhs. But they don't realize that I am an agnostic.

Your first moment of success in journalism came when you became editor of the *Illustrated Weekly of India* in the 1960s, staying on for nine years. Did you have a formula in mind to turn it around?

I was fortunate that I had no boss at the magazine, because the company that owned it had been taken over by the government. I was free to do what I liked. The *Weekly* was full of silly stuff like pictures of newly-weds and Aunty Wendy's column for children. I had a three-pronged formula: inform, amuse and provoke. It worked, and a stagnating circulation of 80,000 rose to 4,00,000. Also, there was no competition those days.

But in the end, the Jains who owned the company managed to retrieve it from the government. They fired me. I wrote a small tribute to the *Weekly*'s readers, wishing the magazine well. They wouldn't allow it to be published and wanted me to leave before my contract was up. I thought that was very discourteous; I just picked up my umbrella and left. My letter was published in other papers afterwards. The owners lacked breeding.

Do you have another book in mind?

I don't know. According to the Hindu sages I have reached the fourth stage of my life—vanaprastha, the final retreat to the forest or wilderness. I plan to see no one and I must learn how to do nothing. The English poet Hilaire Belloc's lines keep turning in my head: 'When I am dead / I hope it will be said / His sins were scarlet / But his books were read.'

You supported the Emergency though you say you were a reluctant supporter. You told Indira Gandhi that you opposed press censorship but you were quite partial to her son Sanjay Gandhi.

Yes, that's quite correct but let me explain why I supported the Emergency when it was imposed. In every democracy there are rules for the government and there are rules for the Opposition which they must not break. The government was under severe criticism for what Sanjay Gandhi was doing but the Opposition was just enjoying seeing the whole law and order system collapse—no trains or planes running on time, schools closed, colleges closed, huge processions smashing private and public property and no action being taken. The last straw was when Jayaprakash Narayan himself endorsed stopping elected members of the legislature from performing their functions.

He called for a total revolution . . .

Yes. In Gujarat students gheraoed the Vidhan Sabha and then threatened Parliament here. Narayan then called for almost a revolt—exhorting people to not pay taxes, and the army and police to revolt. No democratic government in the world can really support that kind of breaking of rules by the Opposition. I wrote to Jayaprakash Narayan protesting. I said you can go so far but you can't stop people who have been elected from doing their jobs. He wrote back to me, a very lengthy letter that I published in full in the *Illustrated Weekly of India*.

I remember the day on which the Emergency was imposed—hundreds of our leaders were put in jail but there was not a squeak of protest. In fact there was a sense of relief that law and order had been restored; apart from people like George Fernandes who went underground there was no protest and it was generally welcomed.

What went wrong was the misuse of power. Mrs Gandhi set a bad example by settling personal scores to get two women, who were organizing farm labour, to be arrested and put in jail; then the Rajmata of Gwalior and Gayatri Devi of Jaipur were put in jail. Then other members of her family followed suit—Maneka Gandhi and her mother were settling their scores, anyone who said anything against them was promptly locked up.

Many of the Emergency's excesses were allegedly committed at the behest of Sanjay Gandhi whom you were fond of. You called him a

'loveable *goonda*' [ruffian]. You were quite infatuated by him, weren't you?

Well, I admired him because he got things done, though he made a mess of the Maruti car project no doubt. I liked him because he was a man of action who said *kaam zyada baat kam* [work more, talk less]. You owe a lot to him, for instance, clearing up slums and planting trees . . .

But he also promoted the forced sterilization campaign which made the Congress party lose the 1977 election . . .

I think that was a vastly exaggerated story. What he had in mind was right. This country needs compulsory family planning. It won't respond to these advertisements of *hum do, hamare do* [We Two, Our Two]. They don't cut ice. The population problem is a priority problem in this country and Sanjay had it right. The stories of compulsory sterilizations, of picking up people from bus stands and cinemas, are not true. There were some excesses but there were no numbered targets of vasectomies. It was totally exaggerated but it paid the political opposition a dividend.

You were also very fond of Sanjay's wife. Maneka Gandhi. After all, you helped her with her magazine, *Surya*, during those days . . .

Yes I did. I was not particularly fond of them, but they came to me and later Maneka's mother came to see me in Bombay . . . She asked me if I could help them because they had no experience. So I got permission from my employers who dared not say no because of the Emergency. I used to come almost once a week to Delhi and spend the weekend here, and the first few issues of *Surya* were entirely organized by me.

And what was your friendship with Maneka like?

It was a working relationship and nothing more. I saw a lot of them in their home, also members of their family and others whom I perforce got to know. And they were in and out of my house all the time.

Maneka Gandhi and you had a bad falling out later when she took out an injunction against your memoirs and hauled you over the coals for writing about the way she quit Mrs Gandhi's house after Sanjay Gandhi's death.

Yes, she did. A judge of the high court gave them the injunction. It took me ten years in an appeal to get the injunction removed and that hurt me in more ways than one. We were not on talking terms. But now the injunction is over, my autobiography is in the market, and I have forgotten all of that.

What do you think of her son Varun's speeches of hate against Muslims [during the 2009 general election]? Do you believe it was right to jail him under the National Security Act?

I think the National Security Act should not have been used in this case but Varun Gandhi should have been taken to task. The Election Commission censured him for what he said. I censured him personally because I can't take any words of hatred against Muslims. He went further and slurred the entire Sikh community saying, *Inke bara baja dunga* (I'll settle them). You may say those things in your home but you don't speak them on election platforms. He did that and I think it was unpardonable.

But you also said that Varun Gandhi was a very personable young man when he brought his book of poetry to you . . .

His anti-Muslim speeches came as a very unpleasant surprise to me. I thought the man was into poetry and it was generally good poetry. I thought, thank God, at least one member of the family is out of the dirty business of politics. When I heard what he said in his mother's constituency, and the words he used, I was very deeply disappointed.

You've had a complex, often contradictory, relationship with the Gandhi family and the Congress party. You returned the Padma Bhushan after Operation Blue Star but you stayed on as a member of Rajya Sabha. And you never really came out in strong condemnation of Rajiv Gandhi's statements about the killing of Sikhs when he said, 'When a great tree falls, the earth shakes.'

I did. I protested. I thought that what he said was unfortunate. I mentioned it several times in my articles that he should not have used those words. I am glad that, after all these years, the Congress party itself felt that it did badly because it was the principal mover in the massacre of Sikhs. Manmohan Singh gave a public apology in Parliament. I think to some extent that softened the hard feelings of Sikhs.

Three thousand Sikhs were killed in those terrible weeks following Indira Gandhi's assassination in 1984. You yourself had to leave your

home and seek sanctuary with friends. Yet it was only when a Sikh journalist hurled a shoe at the home minister that Congress party candidates for Parliament like Jagdish Tytler and Sajjan Kumar were made to withdraw. Don't you consider that too little, too late?

I go along with all that you say. This should have happened much earlier. It's been too late and the people who were the criminals, including those in the Delhi government and in the police, should have been punished long ago. So far, to the best of my knowledge, only thirteen people have been convicted. But there is also a positive side that people tend to forget—the number of Hindus who came to help the Sikhs during that period. I remember that seventy-two gurdwaras were destroyed in a few days but it was a Hindu industrialist family which undertook to rebuild them all.

You have written at length about the working of the Justice Nanavati commission which investigated the targeting and killing of the Sikhs in 1984 but do you believe that the government inquiry or the many other informal inquiries conducted ever really gave the Sikh community justice?

That's a very large question. At least the Nanavati Commission indicated that Sajjan Kumar and Jagdish Tytler had much to answer for and so did some of the others. There was an independent report published, titled *Who Are the Guilty?*, that listed their names. Tytler came to see me once soon after and gave me his *safai* [justification]. I said, 'Jagdish, if you allow me to cross-examine you and you prove to me that you had nothing to do with it I will write in your support.' He never came back. So there it is. He should have withdrawn his candidature himself. That would have been a more gentlemanly thing to do rather than embarrass the Congress party.

Nearly seventy years or more of writing that includes a vast and varied output of fiction, history, memoir, journalism, biography and a weekly column brimming with malice. What makes you so prolific?

Somebody asked me how I was so prolific and out came my answer without a second thought: 'Because no one has yet created a condom for the pen.'

Also you have never missed a single deadline or column in sixty years . . .

Never. Even if I am sick, or I have to keep up all night, I meet my undertaking. If I have given my word it will be there at this time, then it will always be there.

Does it come from a strong sense of discipline and commitment—of waking at four o'clock every morning and getting down to work?

Yes I get up at 4 a.m. I lead a very disciplined life. It's regulated by the stopwatch, not the ordinary watch. I have also learned how to be ill-mannered. People don't drop in. I don't see them without an appointment and when I invite them it's strictly between 7 and 8 p.m. I can be very rude to anyone who stays even a minute after eight.

And at seven o'clock the good Scotch comes out . . .

That's the one luxury I have never denied myself. I don't have any other bad habits.

One of the reasons for your wide readership is your sense of humour. Among all your serious writing is a best-selling pile of Khushwant Singh joke books and your columns are peppered with corny jokes, ribald jokes and bad jokes. What is it that keeps you laughing at your own community and at fellow Indians? Is it your belief that by and large Indians lack a sense of humour?

I'm a born joker. I don't take myself seriously and I don't take anyone else very seriously either. Everyone has a laughable side, including oneself, and I look for that. I meet a lot of politicians and, when they start bragging, that's good material for me. It's an Indian habit to talk about oneself. A favourite topic is what they did and how important they are. Well, that's excellent material for a malicious man like me.

You are also malicious about yourself. One funny piece in your recent collection is called *On Being Buggered*, about a doctor examining you for piles.

Yes, that thing was ticking inside my bottom and I was in pain. When the doctor asked me to fart to bring some relief, I thought it was too funny to be forgotten so I immediately thought of writing about it.

At a more elevated level, one of your abiding passions has been your love of Urdu poetry. Before I end this special interview, will you recite

a verse by Ghalib, another denizen of Delhi, who too lived in turbulent times?

Ghalib is my favourite, and my favourite lines are about himself, Asadullah Khan, ageing and the joy of life ebbing from him. I find these lines apply to me very much:

Woh badah-e-shabana ki sarmastiyan kahan
Uthiye, ke bas ab ki lazzat-e-khwab-e-sehar gayi
Maara zamaane ne Asadullah Khan tumhe
Woh walwale kahan, woh jawani kidhar gayi?

(What happened to those nights of intoxicated ecstasy?
Arise, for the sweet dream of morning has gone.
Time and age have beaten you, Asadullah Khan,
Where has the effervescence of youth gone?)

One of your recent collections was called *Death at My Doorstep*, a collection of obituaries you have written. Are you tempted to write one of your own?

I have already done so. I have written my obituary two or three times. In *Death at My Doorstep* I have put them all in.

How would you liked to be remembered?

As somebody who brought a smile to people's lips.

April 2009 and November 2010

Alexander McCall Smith

Alexander McCall Smith (b. 1948) was staying at Tikli Bottom; this is not Fawlty Towers but a gracious house, an elegant replica of a Lutyens bungalow, built by an eccentric English couple in the rural depths of Haryana. It is situated behind a village called Tikli from which it acquires its delicious name. On an intensely muggy day in July I went down to interview the famous Scottish novelist and found—to my satisfaction—that McCall Smith was exactly as I had imagined him.

McCall Smith—creator of the blockbusting *The No. 1 Ladies' Detective Agency* series, of unforgettable female sleuths like Precious Ramotswe of Botswana and Isabel Dalhousie of Edinburgh; newspaper serials such as *44 Scotland Street*; and with a parallel career as emeritus professor of medical law at Edinburgh University—is tall and slightly stooped; his white thatch of hair and crumpled cotton suits convey the air of a distracted don. But this impression is quickly dispelled by twinkling blue eyes, merry chuckles and wry observations to fit the picture of a jolly Scotsman 'of traditional build'.

By his own admission he is 'one of the biggest literary enterprises in the world': more than forty million copies sold in forty-six languages (and a brand that involves fifty publishers round the world). He writes four to five novels a year, children's books, radio plays, short stories and serialized weekly fiction for the *Scotsman* and the *Daily Telegraph*. These later materialize into books with names such as *The Unbearable Lightness of Scones* and *The Dog Who Came in from the Cold*.

Born in Bulawayo, Southern Rhodesia (now Zimbabwe), the son of a public prosecutor, McCall Smith took his PhD in law from Edinburgh University, went on to become a professor of medical ethics, serve on international commissions and produce a host of specialist legal volumes. These bear titles like the *Forensic Aspects of Sleep* and *Errors, Medicine and the Law*. He lives in the same Edinburgh neighbourhood as J.K. Rowling and Ian Rankin, plays the bassoon as part of The Really Terrible Orchestra and advocates the raising of pigs. His packed international schedule often includes halts in India, a country he likes to write in, partly because of his admiration for the novelist R.K. Narayan.

On better acquaintance he prefers to be addressed by his nickname 'Sandy'. But as you may expect from the co-author of *Forensic Aspects of Sleep*, nothing escapes him. Five years after our first encounter at 'Tikli Bottom' I interviewed him again at the Jaipur Literature Festival in 2010. I had barely introduced him formally on *Just Books* when he cut in, 'I would prefer it if you called me Sandy. If you don't, Isabel Dalhousie will soon be at your doorstep. She is planning a trip to India and would like to know what's going on in Delhi.'

Opening a new Alexander McCall Smith I am often reminded of Evelyn Waugh's tribute to P.G. Wodehouse: 'Mr Wodehouse's idyllic world can never stale. He will continue to release future generations from captivity that may be more irksome than our own. He has made a world for us to live in and delight in.'

Did it tickle you to arrive at a house called Tikli Bottom to begin your tour of India?

How could one resist a house called that? I had to come here and stay. What a beautiful house, though it deserves a more dignified name. I thought it would be really nice to find somewhere where I can sit in peace and write the last pages or the last chapters of my latest book in the series of *The No. 1 Ladies' Detective Agency*. I like India and therefore I thought that this was the place to write it.

Where and how did Precious Ramotswe of *The No. 1 Ladies' Detective Agency* in Botswana, one of the great female sleuths of our time, emerge from?

She happened by accident really. I started her as a short story and she was just going to be about three or four pages of a woman who starts a little detective agency. But I found that I liked her so much; and we are now on volume seven. I was in a village in Botswana and was taken by my hostess to visit this lady who was giving us a chicken for next day's lunch; and we went to see her at her house. There was a chicken walking about the yard in blissful ignorance of what lay ahead for it; and this wonderful lady, who was a traditionally built lady in a red dress, chased the chicken. The odds were distinctly against her but she caught the chicken and wrung its neck and gave it to us. I thought what a remarkable woman and how interesting it would be to write about a woman in Botswana who leads a good life, and who has probably done a lot of good in difficult circumstances—maybe brought up children on very little money—and made a success of her life. Out of that came the character of Precious Ramotswe.

Your phrase to describe a woman of sturdy proportions, 'of traditional build', has almost entered the English lexicon. Is it your affectionate view of the world that makes your characters and books so universally loved?

Precious Ramotswe describes herself as being of traditional build which I think is quite a useful description. When I tour the United States, ladies of traditional build themselves come up to me and say, 'Thank you for that term.'

Would you agree that *The No. 1 Ladies' Detective Agency* series delight millions not only because of characters like Precious Ramotswe and her simmering love for Mr Matekoni, but also for their gentle, ironic prose which releases readers from the anxieties of the world and from the complicated forms of writing that surround us?

I think that one should be able convey a great deal in a very simple way. I don't think writing should be too complicated, too mannered. I think you should try and make it as simple and direct as possible. You can say everything that really needs to be said about humanity in a very straightforward fashion.

I also think that people want to believe in the possibility of good. They want to believe that there is a part of the world that is just. They want to believe that there are people who are not selfish but who are out to help other people. And Precious Ramotswe is a person like that—she is not preachy, she doesn't wear her heart on her sleeve and she is not prudish but she is, nonetheless, really a very good woman and that, I think, is an important factor in her success.

You have sometimes been compared to the great Indian writer R.K. Narayan with his imagined map of a place, his quirky humour and classic characters like Raju the guide who are perennial favourites. Do you owe a debt to R.K. Narayan?

I owe him an immense debt and I am flattered by the comparison. I think he was one of the greatest writers of the twentieth century and I think it's a great pity that R.K. Narayan did not get the Nobel Prize for literature because I believe he rightfully deserved it. I am currently writing introductions to new editions of a number of the Narayan novels which are going to be published in New York. I am just delighted because I think that he managed to get across so much within a small compass by creating a smallish place with a set of characters who say everything about the world.

You also seem to have caught the India bug. Do you love coming here?

People fall in love with India for many reasons but I enjoy the conversations I have here. I think people here still take pleasure in conversations and I like that very much. It's a country that's so complex and there's so much to learn about. There are some countries that one goes to and one gets the picture very quickly. With India it's a lifelong learning process. I started rather late but nonetheless am now trying to make up.

Were you very surprised in 1998 when the first *The No. 1 Ladies' Detective Agency* novel became an international hit?

I was astonished. I had no idea that that would happen. The print run of the first novel was 1500 copies, a very small print run from a Scottish publisher. It was only a couple of years later that things started to take off in a dramatic way. I remember the exact day. I went to see my publishers in New York, expecting that I would have a brief cup of coffee with them, but I discovered that I was being introduced to a whole range of people and being taken out to lunch, which in New York is virtually illegal now—you know, to have lunch. Lunch has been abolished in New York because everyone is working so hard. But we went out to lunch and I thought that maybe they have something planned. And indeed they did.

You created one African woman detective who became a worldwide hit and another entirely different one, the amusing, cerebral Isabel Dalhousie in your native Edinburgh. How did she appear?

She appeared because I wanted to write more about Scotland and Edinburgh. I thought that I would create a woman who is typical of a certain sort of lady that we meet in Edinburgh: an intellectual lady with an interest in philosophy and with a rather dry wit. Many people remember Jean Brodie, who was Muriel Spark's creation of an Edinburgh lady in *The Prime of Miss Jean Brodie*, beautifully played by Maggie Smith in the film version. I've tried to create somebody who is a bit reminiscent of Jean Brodie while at the same time not being Jean Brodie herself.

You have had a long and distinguished career as a professor of medical law and ethics. How has that academic life, together with your childhood in Zimbabwe, influenced your writing? Because some of your fiction can be very dark and disturbing, such as your short-story collection titled *Heavenly Date*.

I had this rather unusual childhood in what was southern Rhodesia, now Zimbabwe; it gave me a feeling for Africa and the African landscape and eventually inspired the Precious Ramotswe books. But from a professional point of view I was concerned with issues of a moral and ethical nature in my work; issues of responsibility and what we might describe as aberrant or disturbed behaviour. Looking at those as I do, for example, in the context of criminal law and the context of the relation between law and psychiatry, one sees a side of humanity which is not very edifying.

But I think that creates great drama. The issue of people behaving badly is quite a dramatic one and offers quite a lot of possibilities. You don't actually have to be very graphic about describing behaviour. I think the best way of describing bad behaviour is suggesting it; I think that's probably better than being very explicit.

You are one-man literary industry, selling millions of copies in dozens of languages—including Swedish, Estonian and Thai—and a huge brand. You produce four to five novels a year, are said to knock off 1500 words before lunch, of your 44 Scotland Street stories, in the manner of Charles Dickens; and you travel almost ceaselessly. How do you do it?

Oh dear. I remember when I first went to my London publisher, my editor pointed his finger at me and said, 'Remember, one book a year,' but now he himself is editing four to five of mine every year. It's a bit of a surprise for me as I didn't anticipate that this would happen. If you sat down and said to yourself that I am going to write thirteen best-sellers, you would fail. Some people may have done it but I think that there is luck and a great deal of serendipity. I don't think one can count on it. I think what one should do is write the type of books one wants to write, write what your heart tells you to write, and if it works that's a bonus.

Take *44 Scotland Street* which continues as a newspaper serial. I am only four days ahead of the newspaper so I have to write a chapter a day to keep up with things. I like serial novels because readers can get involved and they can write to me. People ask me where the new characters in *44 Scotland Street* keep coming from. I don't know; I suppose they knock on the door and ask to be admitted. I've been thinking about them obviously and they come into existence but then they do things that I haven't planned for them. And that's the other curious thing. They take on this life of their own and they start behaving as if they are independent actors—which can lead to problems for the author. Although some of my characters are actually based on real people and appear with their permission.

And you do one more thing in your busy life. You are a bassoonist in an orchestra called The Really Terrible Orchestra.

It's a really terrible orchestra. My wife and I started it about seven years ago for people who can't play instruments very well, people who wanted to be in an orchestra but would never get near one. It is unashamedly for musically challenged musicians.

And are you truly terrible?

Oh, we certainly are. Occasionally we play reasonably but that's very rare. I don't go beyond the high D on the bassoon because the fingering becomes rather complicated. So I don't play the whole bassoon, only that part of the bassoon which is more accessible. But we have great fun, give concerts and get hundreds of people coming. They come hoping that something will go wrong. And that's the best part—we never disappoint our audience.

September 2005

Paul Theroux

When I heard that the American novelist and travel writer Paul Theroux (b. 1941) was in Kolkata, planning his visit to the Indian North-East, and happy to give an interview, I leapt at the opportunity because Theroux's *The Great Railway Bazaar* (1975), his trailblazing train-hopping account from Britain to Japan and back, was regarded as a classic of travel literature from the moment it came out. More recently, his disquieting memoir, *Sir Vidia's Shadow* (1998), of the rupture of his thirty-year-old friendship with V.S. Naipaul, had created a frisson in literary circles. (This was before Patrick French's fascinating, and often disturbing, authorized biography of Naipaul, *The World Is What It Is*, appeared.)

Theroux was born and educated in Massachusetts, but left home early to work in Africa and Singapore. After his first marriage to a BBC producer he settled in London to raise his family. His early novels, *Waldo* (1967), *Fong and the Indians* (1968) and *Saint Jack* (1973) drew upon his experiences in Africa and Asia and were moderately successful. They were, as he says in this interview, 'in the tradition of Americans making a hash of things abroad'. It is a theme that runs through Theroux's fiction, from the dysfunctional family in Central America in the prize-winning *The Mosquito Coast* (1981) to Americans opening 'wrong doors' in *The Elephanta Suite* (2007) and *The Dead Hand: A Crime in Calcutta* (2009), which are both set in India.

The success of *The Great Railway Bazaar* prompted Theroux to undertake a series of other journeys, notably to South America, China and Africa—and described in *The Old Patagonian Express* (1979), *Riding the Iron Rooster* (1988) and *Dark Star Safari* (2002)—that burnished his reputation as a travel writer. His prolific output in fiction and non-fiction has, on occasion, led to a blurring of the two genres and aroused controversy.

This interview took place in the severe, fortress-like American Centre building on Chowringhee. Theroux is a distinguished-looking man, with the bearing of a retired professor or banker rather than a footloose agent provocateur. He lives with his second wife in idyllic

Hawaii and Cape Cod, where his chief occupation, when not travelling or producing fiction, is bee-keeping and raising geese.

Is it true you don't remember how many books you have written?

Not exactly; when James Joyce's father was asked how many children he had, he said sixteen or seventeen. So if Joyce's father can't remember how many children he had, I certainly can't remember the number of books, but about fortyish.

And they are set in far-flung corners of the world, in Asia, Africa, Europe and the Americas . . .

Places that I lived in because I was more of a resident than a traveller. I was a resident in Africa, a resident in Singapore and a resident in England. But I have been at this for forty years. I published my first book in 1967 so it's now my forty-first year. If you spend that much time working, inevitably you publish a lot of work.

One great quote I remember from an interview you gave was about your advice to young aspiring writers. Should they read classics of literature or should they take creative writing courses? Neither, you said. You summed it up in two words and said 'Leave home'.

Go away. Yes. Leave home, leave your parents and leave all the comforting things that hold you back. Also leave home, because if you stay at home, people will always ask you what you are doing—what you are writing, what you are publishing. When you are home you are always being asked questions to which you don't have the answer, but if you leave you find your own answers and, actually, no one is pressing you.

You left home pretty early, didn't you?

Yes, probably when I was in my teens. From about the age of eighteen I have been away.

You were a Peace Corps volunteer first and taught in a school Malawi . . .

I objected to the war in Vietnam. I was a noisy radical but I wanted to do something positive. So I became a teacher in Africa rather than a soldier in Vietnam. And I still think it was a good decision. I discovered Africa, a continent that I enjoyed travelling and living in.

But then you got involved in African politics and were actually expelled from the country . . .

I was deported from Malawi for giving aid and comfort to the political opposition. It's very easy to get deported in Africa. You don't really have to do much wrong. It's interesting that my first acquaintance with India was in Africa. In Malawi there is a Gujarati community and in Uganda there are Bengalis, Sikhs and Gujaratis. My best friend in Kampala was a Bengali who edited a magazine.

And there you began to write for a well-known literary magazine?

It was a great magazine. But in Kenya even the Indian community, who were at the forefront of the independence movement, were sidelined after independence and that actually told me a lot about what might be my future in Africa; that no matter how much I did, it wouldn't be remembered. The Indian contribution to independence was not remembered and it still isn't. I made many Indian friends in Africa whom I subsequently visited when I came to India.

When you went to teach at Kampala University in Uganda you met a man of Indian origin who helped change your life and influenced your literary career. It was V.S. Naipaul and he became your mentor. You wrote a very flattering portrait of his work. Then, a few years ago after a friendship of thirty years, you wrote your controversial memoir of him, *Sir Vidia's Shadow,* a rather sarcastic exposure of a friendship gone sour. What happened?

It wasn't an exposure but a description of a friendship. Friendship is a very funny thing: when you write about a friend you can write about him in a flattering way. People write about love affairs but the actual beginning, middle and end of a friendship, as opposed to a love affair, is very seldom written about. But it is also a book about how I became a writer, how a person becomes a writer, how you make money and how you lose money. Naipaul's fortunes when I met him were very low. I remember in the 1980s—probably 1983 or 1984—he was complaining; 'Life's been cruel to me, what am I doing here, Paul?'

V.S. Naipaul was more than a mentor to you, he was your friend, philosopher and guide at a certain stage and you almost hero-worshipped him . . .

I liked him. But you've got to watch about sitting at someone's feet because they can turn out to be feet of clay. In Naipaul's case, his fortunes were very low and then very high. He is an interesting monster as a person. As writer, of course, he is wonderful but some of his books I think are very feeble. His best books are as good as books can possibly be. I would not have become the writer that I subsequently became without his belief in me, but also because he is an amazing personality. I owed him a lot. He told me why writers become so eccentric. He said, 'No wonder we become so cranky, we spend so much time alone.' History will absolve me. People criticize me and say that my book was sarcastic, but it wasn't sarcastic. I think it's a book which describes the trajectory of a friendship. I was lucky to have met him and very lucky that the friendship ended, because when the friendship ended, I saw him much more clearly.

Were you hurt when he turned his back on you?

Well, my pride was hurt. But ultimately I thought that it's good. Experience is good fortune, you know, because whatever happens to you is wonderful in the end and you look back and can smile on it. Naipaul is a very odd man. If you have interviewed him, I don't have to tell you how he will rebuff you, or jump down your throat, or bite your nose off, if you ask him the wrong question.

To return to your long association with India, the first journey of your many memorable journeys was your best-seller *The Great Railway Bazaar* that came out in 1975. It took you on trains from Europe to Japan and back again, and Indian train travel featured. What was India like in 1975, and now that your new novel *The Elephanta Suite* is set in India, what is it like now?

India is the same, except prouder. It's the same except there were, and are, certain hot spots in India. India is eternal; it's attached to its past. It loves its history as opposed to China. China's history has been cruel to it. India's history has something great, golden, noble, something to look back upon and smile. The Chinese never look back because what they see is the Cultural Revolution, starvation, famine, cruel emperors, the Japanese, something awful . . .

India has dark shadings, too, in its recent and past history . . .

Yes, of course, shadings, but they are just shadings. You have a lot of compensating glories. You were asking what the difference is and I will tell you. One interesting thing is that last year I took the same *The Great Railway Bazaar* trip again. I left London and took the Orient Express and went to Turkey and came to India. So I went to exactly the same places, and in some places, I met the same people that I had met thirty-three years ago. India was one of the places I was looking forward to seeing. Although I have been here since, I haven't done it in a methodical way; and some of the great things about India haven't changed at all. Other aspects of India, Bangalore is an example—a small town, now turned into a gigantic, uncontrollable electronics marvel. But progress isn't always to be admired, you know, because the machine can destroy you. So I loved coming back but I noticed these differences. Not the same differences that you notice in China. China has obliterated its history. India has preserved it.

Your novel *The Elephanta Suite*, set in various parts of India, contains explosive, often sexual, misadventures between contemporary Americans and Indians. Strange, subversive, dangerous things happen when American executives or tourists encounter India and Indians. Is it a comment on persisting cultural misunderstandings?

The Elephanta Suite is three novellas. I understand Americans but I don't necessarily understand what is going on in the mind of an Indian. It would be presumptuous of me. But I think I understand an American coming to an Indian spa or a girl backpacker looking for enlightenment or a lawyer looking for a sex partner. I think I can figure that one out. It's in the tradition of Americans making a hash of things abroad and thinking, 'Why don't they love us?' Do you know Paul Bowles' work?

Yes. Do you mean *The Sheltering Sky*?

Yes. [*The Elephanta Suite*] is a book that I would have loved to send to Paul Bowles: 'See, even I can do it?' But that's the inspiration of a foreigner opening the wrong door, then going through that doorway, and anyone knowing what this person wants to say will suggest, 'Don't go through that door, this is India, stay in your hotels.' It's about Americans going through the wrong door.

What is it about the world of the imagination that writing about the real world won't allow? You draw the distinction between fiction and non-fiction, say your travel writing, by saying that fiction allows you to do more than arriving at emotional truths which the reality of travel writing can never do. What is the difference between the two genres which you have explored at length for more than forty years?

I say it's simple. Do you know Yeats's concept of the anti-self? With the anti-self it is basically a skinny man who writes about Rambo, a hero, or a conqueror. That's his anti-self he is writing about, someone he wishes to be; it's a fantasy. With travel, in my view—and not every travel writer would agree with this—you have to be factual. It's not about the anti-self inventing dialogue or inventing people, it's an autobiography, it's the pathetic little person that you are; you describe your progress through the world but it's who you are. It's not fantasizing, it's living, and it's as close to autobiography as I will ever get. And it's best and interesting with all the delays and nuisance left out. You don't want to hear about how you deleted the file from your computer or how you couldn't call your wife. Whereas in fiction you know the history of a fiction writer, his or her fantasy, what that person wanted to do, what they wanted to be and what their intense, intimate personal life actually was. So that's the big difference, though not stylistically.

Some of your fiction, though, leans on biographical fact. You have written short stories clearly based on your late father and short stories which deal with your ex-wife. She once protested to the *New Yorker* about, she said, an imagined encounter with the writer Anthony Burgess in her presence. Such a melding of memoir and fiction has got you into trouble. Is it a form of faction?

First, let me say, that I am very impressed by your background reading. You have really done your homework and I am impressed because you know these things. Actually, the fact that my ex-wife objected to the story that I was fictionalizing was theoretically a story about Anthony Burgess. But it really wasn't.

It was about a woman called Anne and Anne Theroux is your ex-wife . . .

Yes, that's true, and she objected that I put her in the story and I should have changed her name. Ultimately I did change her name. I think fiction is in the realm of the imagination. I might say: So what if I use my own name? But I think fiction implies a lot of latitude and you can't mistake fiction for autobiography. Although with a lot of fiction the distinction is not clear. For example, James Joyce—*Ulysses* is a fabulous work of the imagination, but it is also a very autobiographical book with a lot of imagination in it. The line that I would draw between fiction and travel is that, I think, travel places you under an obligation to be factual, to be scrupulous, that you tell the truth.

It's a Naipaul concept, actually, to tell the truth and if the truth is prophetic, if you describe a place as it actually is, you will see the seeds of what it will become. If you start inventing and making up a place you want to see, what will it become? If you are in London will you be looking for Dickens's London? Or if you are in India will you be looking for E.M. Forster's India? I am not interested in E.M. Forster's India, I am interested in your India, or my India, or the India that I actually see.

You undertake long journeys, sometimes several times a year, and are in the habit of constantly leaving home. And in more than forty years of an itinerant life you have regularly produced travel books, novels, short stories apart from a wide range of journalism. How have you kept up the great pace and output?

How have I? By not having another job. And also by showing up. You know, most of life is about showing up and getting to work. I think that many of us wait for inspiration, writers and painters wait for inspiration, but the rest of us have got to work every day. It's also about taking the job seriously. I had a large family to support and children to educate; I was trying to make a living. I did not want to be a starving artist and I realized that since I am never going to win a Nobel Prize, or have a fabulous best-seller, I have to work. I have to keep at it. So when someone asks me to write an article about Costa Rica I say, 'Yes, I will do that. I can do that.' They say they want an essay on the future American and I can do that.

You can't rest on your laurels. You can't assume that all the experiences you are going to have are going to be written about. You have to keep living. Do you know what Ernest Hemingway was doing when he was my age? Nothing; he was dead. Henry David Thoreau was dead, they were all dead. I have outlived them.

You need to feed the imagination and you have to keep on living. If you keep living and if you are still interested in the world, you won't say: 'I don't want to meet any new people, I am through, and I am going to just live on my farm and raise geese.' I do raise geese, actually, and I am also a bee-keeper, and I raise bamboo, and I do a lot of things like that, but that's not all I do. I am also interested in the world, and if you are interested in the world, you refresh the imagination, you revitalize the mind, and you are still interested.

I am very curious about how things change and how the world has changed in my lifetime. India is a great example of it. The world is not a static thing, it is changing and it has changed, and decayed everywhere, in India and in America. The population of the United States has doubled in my lifetime and that is a profound change. All of these changes mean that you are looking for a way of portraying them, either in fiction or non-fiction, gathering the pulses from the air and turning it into writing.

February 2008

Mark Tully

To his public, the broadcaster and author Mark Tully (b. 1936) was for decades the most familiar voice reporting and interpreting events in India—great and small—as an engaged, reasoned, ubiquitous presence. Foreign correspondents say that they are still frequently accosted in far corners of the country with the words, 'BBC? Tully sahib?' In New Delhi, which he has made his home since the mid-1960s, he is among the unofficial but undisputed doyens of the media world, much in demand for his views that are expressed in a benign, even-handed manner. In face-offs between journalists and media managements, he supports the rights of the former, himself having resigned in 1994, after thirty years, in protest against the BBC's turning into 'a secretive monolith with poor ratings and a demoralized staff'.

Tully has distilled his experience of India into a series of successful books, among them *Amritsar: Mrs Gandhi's Last Battle* (1985), *No Full Stops in India* (1991) and *The Heart of India* (1997). His most recent book, *India's Unending Journey* (2007), offers deeper, metaphysical insights into India's spiritual truths that coincide with his own lifelong quest.

Born in Kolkata, the son of a successful British executive, his family had old connections with India. He was mainly educated at a public school in England, and later Trinity Hall, Cambridge, where he studied theology, before abandoning his early ambition of becoming a priest. He returned to India in 1965 to join the BBC's Delhi office in a junior position and rose to become bureau chief, covering major events including the Bangladesh War, the Bhopal Gas Tragedy, Operation Blue Star, the assassinations of Indira and Rajiv Gandhi, and the demolition of the Babri Masjid.

In private, he can present a persona quite distinct from his public image of the confident, worldly and authoritative journalist: his tall frame, creased brow and smiling face become ruminative and gentle, his voice soft and hesitant, as he describes his inner search for 'a sense of the transcendental' in the absorbing religious pluralism of India.

For more than a decade he has presented BBC Radio 4's weekly programme *Something Understood*. Mark Tully was knighted in 2002 and awarded the Padma Bhushan in 2005.

After more than forty years in India as a broadcaster you have, in recent years, established a reputation as an author. In fact the two careers now happily go together. But your new book, *India's Unending Journey*, is mainly a spiritual quest, something many people may not expect from you . . .

I suppose you could call it that. It is a book I was very nervous about and, honestly, I didn't know how it would be received. There is a strange contrast in it because a theme I take up strongly in the book is humility, and yet I am writing about myself which doesn't seem to be a very humble thing to do. But, on the other hand, it seemed to me that if you want to make points you have to authenticate them through your own experience. One of the things I have learnt in India is that experience is an essential part of religion. If you have not had religious experiences, if you didn't feel God, if I may put it that way, then you haven't got to the heart of religion.

The book is also autobiographical. Although born in India you went away to Britain at the age of nine to an upper-class public school, later to Cambridge, but you wanted to become a priest at the start of your journey . . .

That is very true. I did originally want to become a priest and in those days when I was at Marlborough which, as you said, is a posh school, then Cambridge, and later in the British army, there were actually times when I was highly confused. I probably still am confused. I wouldn't like to give the impression that this is the end of my journey because one of the things I try to say in this book is that it is very important in life to keep a sense of balance. The other thing about this journey is that I think it goes on until we die and, of course, we don't know what happens after we die. It is interesting reaching old age, being over seventy now, how you again see things so differently and you realize you're at a different stage of your journey.

You disliked your public school although your father, a well-off boxwallah, could afford to send his six children to the best schools. Was it a difficult time?

That's the funny thing. I didn't really dislike the public school. I was quite happy there; I made good friends, but I had made myself a place there by being a rebel. I was rebelling against a lot of things, but, in a strange way, I didn't want to be a rebel. In some ways I became a rebel because I didn't think I was very bright; I couldn't cut the mustard, so I thought if I can't be bright I might as well be rebellious. The one thing I did get out of Marlborough, which I still have, was that I loved going to chapel, loved the liturgy and the music of the Anglican Church. That love has remained with me ever since. I wanted to go for ordination and was committed to reading theology for one year. At the same time I absolutely loved some really wild friends of mine. We used to drink a lot and go to pubs.

Were you were a bad boy at Cambridge?

Yes I was. But internally there was a conflict between being a bad boy and developing the spiritual side of my life. I had this idea that spirituality was all about morality, so each time I had too much to drink, or each time I thought that, 'Gosh! She's a lovely girl and I'd like to kiss her,' I felt that this was bad and unspiritual.

That was the start of the change because, having failed to become a priest, I did various things, but I didn't feel settled in any location and, in particular, I didn't like living in London. When I came to Delhi to work for the BBC in 1965, that first day, I smelled marigolds and other winter flowers; I smelled the malis cooking their food. A sense of smell is one of the most nostalgia-inducing senses we have. Somehow my childhood went rushing through my mind. From that moment on, I think there was something special about India for me. I didn't know what it was.

One of the first books you picked up in Delhi was a small ninety-two-page volume, *The Hindu View of Life*, by the Indian philosopher Dr Sarvepalli Radhakrishnan, later President of India, and it affected you greatly. What did you learn from it?

I picked it up because when I first went to the Christmas communion service in the Cathedral of the Redemption in Delhi, I noticed that there were Christians, Sikhs and Hindus in the congregation, and I couldn't understand this. When I was at Cambridge, my Roman Catholic friends wouldn't even come to an Anglican church.

I started asking and was told about India's religious pluralism; someone suggested that, for a start, you should read Dr Radhakrishnan's book. It is very direct, simple and extremely thought-provoking. It is from that time that I started thinking of the idea of religious pluralism and how it might affect other aspects of your life. In a sense that is what this book is about. It was from Dr Radhakrishan that I understood 'neti neti neti' in the *Upanishads*, which means that you can never say anything complete and final about the Supreme Being, whether Rama or God, or whatever you may call it.

What was that early baptism of becoming a full-fledged radio correspondent in the early 1970s like? Because it was a difficult decade in India with the Bangladesh War, the Emergency and the BBC having to close down its Delhi bureau for a while . . .

The BBC was chucked out in 1969 because of Louis Malle's documentaries *Phantom India*. The Indian government thought they demeaned India and the BBC insisted on showing them. My good fortune was being out of India at that time, and so, when the BBC decided to come back again they decided to send me because I had experience.

I really began to cover India extensively after I returned from Britain; I had gone back for a couple of years and became the chief commentator at Bush House for the BBC World Service during the Bangladesh War. I went to Bangladesh twice during that war and I came to India as well. That was where it all really started. If I can be a little immodest, I had a certain talent for it, and I felt that I had really found what I wanted to do. But it took a long time. I was thirty-five years old by the time I came back. But often we had tricky times in those days because the BBC was very influential. Doordarshan was in its infancy and All India Radio was very much the voice of the government, so many people turned to the BBC. Sometimes we were accused by the government of being the voice of the Opposition.

Your earlier books of essays and stories like *No Full Stops in India* and *The Heart of India* are accounts of places and people caught in the

conflict of tradition and change—social, political and economic. After decades of reporting and writing on India, in what way have these changed?

Fundamentally, I have a strong belief that most Indians are balanced people and they understand plurality in every sense. I am absolutely convinced of that. If I may add two important things: one is that religion often gets blamed for social tensions, but you have to search for the political motive when there are, for example, religious riots. And, two, if politicians hadn't messed around with caste reservations, you wouldn't have the tensions that keep erupting. Politicians must often bear a lot of the blame; if they were to concentrate on delivery rather than on winning votes on spurious religious and caste grounds, it would make a major difference. At the same time, you have to have a system of checks and balances in this country.

You quit the BBC after thirty years in protest against some of its policies. Yet for the last ten years you've gone on to present a weekly show on BBC radio called *Something Understood*, a contemplative programme that is a compound of music, poetry and reflections. How did you return?

Fate again. When I left the BBC it was after making a speech that criticized the management for becoming too business-oriented, too inclined to swallow everything management consultants told them. And I thought, 'That's it, I will never broadcast on BBC again.' But out of the blue I was asked to do these programmes and I said okay. As a result, I get asked to speak quite often in England and in India. I have been putting these ideas across so I thought it would be worth trying to put them down in a book form. It sounds presumptuous but I just believe these ideas are worth discussing.

India has taught me that there are many ways to God, but it is more than that. It has taught me that we are always on a journey, not a pilgrimage, because a pilgrimage comes to a stop when you reach the destination. It is a sense of the transcendental, occasionally glimpsed in your search. I come back to what I said at the start about humility—such a sense makes us humble.

I think one of the greatest dangers to mankind is arrogance. We think that we have done everything for ourselves as a species; we arrogantly command nature and believe it is for us to do with as we want. Consider the debate on climate change. So much energy is being put into claiming that we can solve it through technology, but nowhere are people saying that what we really need to do is to balance our relationship with nature and have the humility to say that we are part of nature.

You call yourself a person who belongs to two cultures, a citizen of two countries. Do you see yourself as a bridge between India and the western world?

I see myself as someone who is inevitably going to be British because I was brought up to be British in every way. But if we go back to karma, I have been deeply influenced by India. I have had the huge privilege of being made so welcome in this country that sometimes I do have a different understanding than people who don't have these cross-cultures within them. As I said before, I see myself as a confused man. That is all I can say.

June 2007

Acknowledgements

My first thanks are to the author Namita Gokhale for originally floating the idea for this book and passing it on to Ravi Singh, publisher and editor-in-chief of Penguin Books India, who responded with enthusiasm. He requested Nandini Mehta, an old colleague and friend, to act as editor; her discriminating eye, deft hand and attention to detail were of inestimable value. I thank them both sincerely.

My special debt of gratitude is to Radhika and Prannoy Roy of NDTV for their continual encouragement, friendship and support. I am also grateful to K.V.L. Narayan Rao and Sanjay Nigam at NDTV for their help in making this book possible.

The way the spoken word is recorded, especially in conversation, with its ellipses, pauses and repetitions, is not the way it falls on the printed page. Careful and sensitive editing is necessary for greater clarity and fluency while adhering, at all times, to the integrity of a writer's thoughts and cadence of speech. The transcripts of these interviews went through several painstaking drafts. I thank Yamini Joshi and Pooja Roy for preparing the initial transcripts. But my special thanks are reserved for Saiyam Khosla for rechecking each transcript with the recording before sending it on to me. Saiyam joined as a young assistant in the early days of *Just Books* and has gone on to become the show's accomplished producer. Our weekly association is a little like that between architect and builder: by turns argumentative, accommodating and conciliatory. Only now and then, when things go completely right, do we stand back to consider our work with shared satisfaction.

My special thanks to Suparna Singh and Arun Thapar for reading parts of the manuscript and offering insightful suggestions.

A number of other colleagues and friends at NDTV over the years have either contributed to or keenly supported *Just Books*. These include Aneesha Baig, Barkha Dutt, Sarah Jacob, Swati Maheshwari, Ankita Mukherji, Sonia Singh, Vishnu Som, Puja Talwar and Shai Venkataraman—I thank them all. I am also grateful to all cameraperson colleagues and editors, too numerous to mention individually, for their creative excellence.

I also thank Ira Pande of *IIC Quarterly* for permission to reproduce my interview with the novelist Nadeem Aslam, recorded in the India International Centre lawns and later published in *The Great Divide: India and Pakistan*; Saeed Naqvi and Mahmood Farooqui for their help in an accurate rendering and translation of Ghalib's verse in the Khushwant Singh interview; R.P. Jain, retired professor of German, Jawaharlal Nehru University, for correcting the German references in the Vikram Seth interview; and Sonal Joshi for checking the invocation to Lord Krishna that Javed Akhtar recited in his interview.

My greatest debt is to my wife, Shalini, and daughter, Jayati, whose unfailing support and love are a source of inspiration and strength.